Ms. Cleckler,

Thank you for your mentorship and guid[ance] over the last few years. [You] have helped me for not only to be a better leader but also have more balance in my life.

Sincerely,
MSgt Bert

In *The Greats on Leadership*, Jocelyn Davis distills the most important learnings from some of the greatest leaders and authors in history into one manageable book for anyone who wants to be a great leader.
Marshall Goldsmith, #1 *New York Times* bestselling author of *Triggers*, MOJO, and *What Got You Here Won't Get You There*

The Greats on Leadership brings to life the writings of many of our most-loved authors and applies their thinking to present-day business. It's a pleasure to read and the tools are supported by practical examples. This is a book you will return to, time and time again.
Karen Blal, CIPD Regional Director Asia

To find a single book that captures the essence of the leadership wisdom of the past 25 centuries is simply priceless. A most enlightening read.
Catherine Alphonso, Director, Forum India Learning Solutions

A rare blend of old and new. Davis draws together leadership lessons from the Bible, Shakespeare, Mary Shelley, and James Joyce, combines them with the best of modern business writers like Marshall Goldsmith and Peter Drucker, and finishes them with her own observations.
Robert Mass, Partner, Head of International Compliance, Goldman Sachs

Jocelyn Davis has done it again. Her wisdom is evident as she uses the greats to outline a practical roadmap and accessible insights for aspiring or ambitious leaders. For anyone who wants to be inspired to take their game to the next level.
Srini Pillay, CEO, NeuroBusiness Group; Assistant Professor, Harvard Medical School; faculty in Executive Education, Harvard Business School

A uniquely insightful take on leadership development—eras come and go, yet great leadership practices remain the same.
Charles Miller, SVP Leadership Development, Citibank

Jocelyn Davis has always pushed for a deeper meaning of what it takes to be a successful leader. In *The Greats on Leadership*, what's old is new again.
Kevin Higgins, CEO, Fusion Learning

This book is a great reminder to think about leadership in terms of the scope of the leader's impact and not rungs on the corporate ladder. I love the concept of the levels of leadership, and I'm looking forward to trying these out.
Carmelita Lubos, Director, Global Talent Management, Burberry

With compelling stories, practical tools, and a crisp, clear writing style, you have a powerful, modern book that offers a path to leadership based on the best ideas of yesterday and today.

Amy Tananbaum, CEO and Principal, Results By Design

Leaders, and we are all leaders at various times, will be inspired by *The Greats on Leadership*. It is one leadership book you will refer to again and again throughout your career. Davis has an uncanny ability to relate great books to the problems of modern management, and by respecting the intelligence of her readers, she uplifts us all.

Robert Bienenfeld, Assistant Vice President, Environment and Energy Strategy, American Honda Motor Co.; Trustee, St. John's College

Jocelyn Davis has spent the better part of two decades observing and writing about the characteristics of high-performing leaders and their teams. Now she combines her insights with the wisdom of great writers of the past two millennia to create a boldly original and eminently practical guide for leaders of all stripes. A must-read for anyone who is serious about continuing their own evolution as a leader.

Ed Boswell, Co-founder and CEO, Conner Academy; retired Partner and former leader of PwC's People & Change Practice

Among the reams of books on leadership emerges one that goes beyond simple prescriptions to uncover a more profound understanding of the art. *The Greats on Leadership* is filled with the voices of the most important leaders and thinkers of their time; their wisdom is even more relevant today as we face unprecedented challenges in business and society. I highly recommend it.

Joe Wheeler, Executive Director, The Service Profit Chain Institute; co-author, *The Ownership Quotient*

History and biography can often provide more leadership wisdom than the latest management idea. Davis has provided a valuable resource which rightly focuses on the cultural and psychological dimensions of leadership, brought to life by a superb range of examples, from Plato to Jung, Herman Melville to Peter Drucker. Her discussion of fourth-level leadership, or subsuming one's own ambitions to look for the common good, raises it above other titles in the field.

Tom Butler-Bowdon, author of 50 *Psychology Classics*, 50 *Self-Help Classics*, 50 *Success Classics*

THE GREATS ON LEADERSHIP

Classic Wisdom for Modern Managers

JOCELYN DAVIS

NICHOLAS BREALEY PUBLISHING

London • Boston

For George and Zara Roberts,
exceptional leaders

First published by
Nicholas Brealey Publishing in 2016
An imprint of John Murray Press

An Hachette company

A CIP catalogue record for this title is available from the British Library.

Hardback ISBN 978-1-85788-639-9
Paperback ISBN 978-1-85788-648-1
eISBN 978-1-85788-992-5

Printed in the UK by Clays Ltd, St Ives plc.

John Murray Press policy is to use papers that are natural, renewable and recyclable products and made from wood grown in sustainable forests. The logging and manufacturing processes are expected to conform to the environmental regulations of the country of origin.

John Murray Press
Carmelite House
50 Victoria Embankment
London EC4Y 0DZ
Tel: 020 7122 6000

Nicholas Brealey Publishing
Hachette Book Group
Market Place Center, 53 State St
Boston, MA 02109, USA
Tel: (617) 523 3801

www.nicholasbrealey.com
JocelynRDavis.com

CONTENTS

preface

WHAT'S IN THIS BOOK AND HOW TO USE IT

The Greats on Leadership is a tour of the best leadership ideas of the past 25 centuries with classic authors as your guides. In it you'll find profound yet practical advice from history's masterminds.

WHY CLASSICS?

I've long believed we can learn more about leadership from the likes of Shakespeare, Machiavelli, and Jane Austen than we can from today's MBA programs and management theorizers. If you want to be convinced, try reading a business journal article on employee motivation, then read the "Saint Crispin's Day" speech from Shakespeare's *Henry V* (there's an excerpt at the start of Chapter 8). Which do you find more enlightening, not to mention motivating? Consider, too, that many of today's most successful leaders are fans of the classics. President Bill Clinton has said his top choice for a leadership book is the *Meditations* of Marcus Aurelius, a second-century Roman emperor and philosopher.[1] Facebook's Mark Zuckerberg names *The Aeneid*, Virgil's epic poem about the founder of a city who "knows no boundaries in time and greatness."[2] And Oprah Winfrey's favorite is *To Kill a Mockingbird*, Harper Lee's book about a small-town lawyer taking a stand against prejudice in 1930s Alabama.[3]

Classic books have three main advantages as reading for leaders. First, unlike most contemporary business case studies, they take seriously the risks we run when we seek to lead. Second, they don't stick to topics found in an MBA course catalog; they explore a much broader subject, one great leaders know a lot about: human nature. ("When you reread a classic," said Clifton Fadiman, host of the 1940s quiz show *Information, Please!*, "you do not see more in the book than you did before; you see more in you than there was before.") Finally, they have stood the test of time. While their settings may speak of eras long past, their concerns are our concerns and their advice is as relevant as ever. The classics are like the Appalachian Trail or the Appian Way, ancient roads that still guide and delight the modern traveler.

But even the best-built old road can benefit from some new signposts, so *The Greats on Leadership* contains much more than a reading list. Setting out to cover most of what a leader needs to know, it addresses 24 leadership topics in as many chapters. Each chapter centers on a classic book, weaving the ideas together with practical insights for business leaders. Most of the classic selections are fewer than 100 pages, and I hope you'll be inspired to read some of them; if time is short, you can simply read the summary at the start of each chapter and get the gist of the author's wisdom. You'll find tools (self-assessments, conversation guides, and the like) and examples to help you put the concepts into action. And each chapter points to a modern leadership guru—from Peter Drucker to Jim Collins to Doris Kearns Goodwin—who descends from and stands on the tall shoulders of the classic thinker.

The Contents Map on pages x–xi shows what's covered in each chapter. If it looks like a lot to absorb, rest assured there'll be no need to commit all of it to memory. As you'll see in the Introduction, learning to lead is a matter not of memorizing lists of strategies and tactics, but rather of immersing yourself in great stories and treatises and applying their wisdom to your work. The outcome of such a process is that you'll be able, like any practiced professional, to exercise knowledge and skill—in this case, leadership knowledge and skill—without needing to stop and refer to the manual.

WHAT'S NEW, WHAT ISN'T

Many of the ideas in this book are well known; you won't be shocked to learn, for example, that leaders must adapt, or communicate well, or have courage. But while they may be common knowledge, they're certainly not common practice, and this is the ill that *The Greats on Leadership* sets out to remedy. It seeks not to invent new precepts, but to illuminate time-tested precepts so they may be appreciated and applied by today's leaders; not to manufacture new treasure, but to provide maps and tools so you can find and unearth your own riches from stashes long buried. I can promise you the journey will be enlightening, entertaining, and above all useful.

And there *is* something completely new at the end. The four leadership levels presented in Part VI offer a different way to think about our aspirations as leaders: a new "corporate ladder" whose rungs correspond to the impact we make rather than to the title on our business card. Though well suited to twenty-first-century organizations with their flatter structures, this new ladder arises from the deep understanding of leadership that can only be acquired from the great teachers of centuries past.

TWO WAYS TO USE THE BOOK

You can read *The Greats on Leadership* on your own or with a group. Here are some tips for each method.

On your own Read the book straight through, paying closest attention to the topics you find most interesting and dipping into a few of the featured classics. Or, create a self-study plan that suits your needs. Table A.2 in the Appendix lists seven common leadership challenges and the chapters that address them. To design your program, pick one or two of those challenges to work on. Read the indicated chapters and their associated classics, and apply the tools to your job. With this approach, you'll build your leadership abilities and make progress on your specific issues.

With a group Gather a group of colleagues or friends and go through the book together. Read and discuss each chapter and each featured classic, try out the tools, and help one another apply the insights. For detailed guidelines and a sample schedule, see the Appendix. This level of investment in learning will earn you stronger leadership skills than most of today's business school graduates possess—not to mention a better understanding of the great ideas of civilization. I hope some day to see universities offering Master of Leadership Arts degrees based on this classic approach to leadership education. For now, perhaps happily, we are on our own.

Contents map

CHAPTER	KEY IDEA	CLASSIC THINKER/BOOK	A DESCENDANT
1. One Myth, Three Truths	Charisma doesn't make a leader; these three behaviors do	Moses/Exodus	Susan Cain
2. Eight Traps	When leaders stumble, it's into one of these pitfalls	William Shakespeare/*King Lear*	Marshall Goldsmith
3. Change	Good leaders know how to navigate the stages of the Change Road	Niccolò Machiavelli/*The Prince*	George Land
4. Justice	Treating everyone equally may get you accused of injustice	Plato/*The Republic*	Marcus Buckingham
5. Power	Are you trapped in the King's Paradox?	Sophocles/*Antigone*	Dale Carnegie
6. Authority	Authority's sources are legal, traditional, or intrinsic	William Shakespeare/*Julius Caesar*	Frank Abagnale
7. Character, Defined	Leadership character is about finding the center	Winston Churchill/ *Great Contemporaries*	Martha Stout
8. Crises	When disaster strikes, stay in the learning zone	William Shakespeare/ *Henry V*	Ronald Heifetz
9. Competition	Military captains show us how to gain and maintain advantage	Theodore Dodge/ *The Great Captains*	W. Chan Kim, Renée Mauborgne
10. Dilemmas	Dilemmas have no solutions, but they're manageable	Alexander Hamilton and James Madison/ *The Federalist*	Barry Johnson
11. Communication	Great communicators make their audience proud	Pericles and Abraham Lincoln/ Speeches	Stephen Denning
12. Character, Developed	Philosophy is the best school for character	Plutarch/*Moralia*	David Brooks

Contents map (cont.)

CHAPTER	KEY IDEA	CLASSIC THINKER/BOOK	A DESCENDANT
13. Motivation	Meaning motivates even when hope is gone	Viktor Frankl/*Man's Search for Meaning*	Frederick Herzberg
14. Personality	Study this field guide to humans of all types	C.G. Jung/*Psychological Types*	David Kiersey
15. Decisions	We can mitigate blind spots by understanding the biggest one	Roald Dahl/"Lamb to the Slaughter" and other stories	Michael Roberto, Gina Carioggia
16. Culture	Anthropology helps us grasp cultural differences	Ruth Benedict/*The Chrysanthemum and the Sword*	Geert Hofstede
17. Character, Anchored	Courage means talking with your monsters	Mary Shelley/*Frankenstein*	M. Night Shyamalan
18. Relationships	Smart leaders know a friend from an ally	Guy de Maupassant/"Boule de Suif"	Doris Kearns Goodwin
19. Accountability	Increase accountability by driving out fear	Herman Melville/*Billy Budd*	W. Edwards Deming
20. Talent	To develop talent, learn to recognize potential and non-potential	Jane Austen/*Emma*	Linda Hill
21. Vision	How to pursue a vision without getting burned	George Bernard Shaw/*Saint Joan*	Malala Yousafzai
22. Character, Revealed	Character is tested in moments of truth	James Joyce/*The Dead*	Susan Scott
23. Three Levels	Are you an initiator, an encourager, or a cultivator?	Greats revisited: Shakespeare, Shaw, Churchill	Jim Collins and John Maxwell
24. The Fourth Level	"By not dominating, the Master leads"	Lao Tzu/*Tao Te Ching*	Peter Drucker

If your actions inspire others to dream more, learn more, do more, and become more, you are a leader.

JOHN QUINCY ADAMS

The farther backward you can look,
the farther forward you are likely to see.

WINSTON CHURCHILL

Be not afraid of greatness. Some are born great,
some achieve greatness, and some have
greatness thrust upon 'em.

WILLIAM SHAKESPEARE

Introduction
THE CLASSIC ART OF LEADERSHIP

Leadership is neither a skill set, nor a theory, nor a collection of strategies. It is nothing so formulaic. Good leadership is a form of *practical wisdom*: an elusive and holistic quality acquired through study and experience and applied with judgment, moment by moment, to an unpredictable flow of challenges. No single workshop or how-to book can teach it. But in this book, you'll find a roadmap for developing it.

"WHEN'S LUNCH?"

Cecil B. DeMille (1881–1959), the famous Hollywood film director and producer, was known for his ability to construct movies on a grand scale: pictures such as *Cleopatra* and *Samson and Delilah*, with colossal sets and crowd scenes involving thousands. And, being the revered director he was, he generally had no trouble getting a throng of actors to listen and obey as he called out instructions for a take.

Once, however, while filming the Exodus scene of *The Ten Commandments* (the 1956 version) on location in Egypt, the 75-year-old DeMille ran into a leadership challenge.[1] As the story goes, he was facing a crowd of several hundred extras dressed as Hebrew slaves while goats, camels, and geese waited with their handlers on the sidelines. It had been a hard morning's shooting, and the noonday sun beat down as DeMille, atop a platform with a megaphone, gave directions for the next take, which would be one of the most challenging in the film. Now and then a goose honked or a camel snorted, but the humans were all silently attentive—except, DeMille noticed with irritation, for one young woman halfway back in the crowd, who kept chattering to the person next to her. After a few minutes of this, DeMille was fed up and shouted to the chatterer, in the time-honored style of a teacher dealing with whispering students: "Young lady! Would you care to share what you have to say with the rest of us?"

"Yes!" she shouted back. "I was wondering when the bald son-of-a-bitch was going to call lunch!"

A horrified hush fell over the crowd. Everyone looked nervously over at the young woman, then up at the imposing, but undeniably balding, director. DeMille lowered his megaphone and looked down at his feet as a few seconds passed.

Then he hoisted the megaphone once again and called "LUNCH!"

GOOD LEADERSHIP IS PRACTICAL WISDOM

What DeMille demonstrated in that moment was the kind of leadership you'll never find in a tactics guide. He showed the ability to take in an entire situation (a tricky one he'd probably never faced before), decide how to respond, and act in a way that keeps things moving forward smoothly, all within seconds. He didn't consult a manual. No training seminar could have told him what to do. But what he did worked: after he called lunch, the crowd burst into laughter and applause and off they went for a break, coming back in the afternoon to shoot the scene.

This ability—to see the big picture, make a decision in context, and choose the most effective action from a nearly infinite list of possible ones, all in the space of a moment—can be described as practical wisdom. It is the quintessential quality of a good leader. In fact, good leadership can be defined as "practical wisdom applied to any situation where you're in charge (or trying to be)."

This isn't to say that leaders don't need skills, theories, and strategies; they do, but more than that they need the ability to integrate those skills, theories, and strategies and use them as a basis for action. A leader's practical wisdom is about seeing and grasping the big picture in every sense: all the people and their needs, talents, hopes, and fears; all the possible paths forward and the obstacles that might obstruct them; and, perhaps most important, all his or her own motivations, strengths, and weaknesses. It's about being able to hover above the fray, choosing just the right action in an instant, even when things go sideways—even when someone in the crowd starts yelling about the bald son-of-a-bitch (or, if you're female, the big-haired bitch) on the platform.

Think of learning to be a medical doctor: there's no way to capture in one textbook, let alone one PowerPoint presentation, the huge range of possibilities for action associated with being a good physician. Yet that doesn't mean medical students can't master those possibilities. They can, and they do. To be sure, they do it by studying theories, practicing skills, and memorizing strategies, but what is most important is putting it together, so that, ultimately, they can take action without needing to refer to the manual. The same is true of becoming a good leader.

But how does one learn these things?

LEADERSHIP AND THE LIBERAL ARTS

The boy who would grow up to be Alexander the Great used to sigh in exasperation whenever his father, Philip of Macedonia, vanquished yet another Greek city. "There won't be anything left for me to conquer when I'm king," he would say to his friends.[2]

Of course, when Philip died (in 336 BCE) there were still plenty of opportunities, and Alexander, now king of Macedonia at 20 years of age, summoned all the Greek leaders to a council in Corinth to make a plan for overthrowing the Persian Empire. He set off with a small army and a large debt. Within four years he had under his belt an unbroken string of victories that placed him on Persia's throne.

Throughout these campaigns he led by example, sharing every toil and danger with his men, who as a consequence were fanatically loyal. His allies, attracted by his reputation for generosity and trustworthiness, were staunch as well. He was both strategist and tactician, with a mind for high-level goals and gritty details. Those who heard him speak called his oratory inspiring. In just a few years he transformed a collection of fierce but unruly mercenaries into a disciplined army, equipped with innovative weapons of his own design and trained to perfection. And by the age of 32 he had completed the conquest of the whole world as the Macedonians knew it, with an army five times larger than his original one and treasure worth several billion dollars in today's money.

What accounts for his extraordinary ability? As a boy he clearly had a big personality, and of course he was the son of a king, but many precocious children from powerful families grow up to be nothing more than full-sized brats. He had wealth, but money doesn't make an effective leader. He must have had plenty of talent, but raw talent won't make someone king of the world.

Alexander's talent, however, had an exceptional cultivator: his tutor, the philosopher Aristotle. Historian E.H. Gombrich describes Aristotle as "the teacher of mankind for 2,000 years" and says:

> ... what he had done was to gather together all the knowledge of his time. He wrote about the natural sciences—the stars, animals, and plants; about history and people living together in a state—what we call politics; about the right way to reason—logic; and the right way to behave—ethics. He wrote about poetry and its beauty ... All this Alexander studied too.[3]

We don't know the details of Alexander's lessons, but we do know that he grew up to be a lover of history, poetry, and literature. As king, he surrounded himself not so much with military captains as with learned men, whose conversation he enjoyed. His favorite book was Homer's *Iliad*, which he kept under his pillow next to his dagger. It's said he tamed his war horse, Bucephalus, not through ordinary training methods but by noticing what none of the professional trainers had: that the horse was afraid of its own shadow. Alexander turned the stallion's head toward the sun, putting the shadow out of sight, until it lost its fear and would tolerate a rider.

The sort of education Alexander the Great had from his tutor Aristotle was in the liberal arts: a curriculum consisting of classical languages, humanities, pure mathematics, and sciences. The ancient Greeks invented the concept of *artes liberales*, or "studies for free men"; the seven subjects were grammar, logic, and rhetoric (later named the Trivium) plus geometry, arithmetic, astronomy, and music (the Quadrivium).

By the early sixteenth century, these subjects, along with Latin and Greek, were seen by Europeans as the correct type of schooling for princes, government administrators, clergy, doctors, and lawyers. The system lasted for several centuries and worked well:

people thus educated not only had been taught how to observe, reason, and communicate, but also had been immersed in great ideas of politics and philosophy and great stories of past leaders, their times and decisions, rises and downfalls. This kind of learning was supposed to transform how people understood the world, not just to load them up with facts and techniques. As the first-century Greek historian and philosopher Plutarch put it, "Education is not the filling of a pail, but the lighting of a fire."

In the nineteenth century, however, there was an industrial revolution and technical knowledge began to be seen as the thing to have if you wanted to get ahead. Among business leaders, so-called scientific management methods gained popularity and were touted by theorists such as Frank Gilbreth, an early advocate of process improvement and familiar today as the efficiency-obsessed father in *Cheaper by the Dozen*. Gradually, as people saw the impressive results achievable with these methods, from assembly lines to anesthesia, they started to view the liberal arts as impractical; certainly not something on which doctors and lawyers, let alone businesspeople, should be spending their time.

HOW DO WE LEARN TO LEAD?

Nearly every organization today with more than a few dozen employees has some kind of leadership development program. But the trouble with all these learning programs is that most don't work. A percentage (perhaps 15 or 20 percent, in my experience as a learning consultant) are well designed and well integrated into the organization, and pay off in the form of better leadership.[4] Many, however, are simply opportunities for people to take a break from work and bond over some fun activities. And plenty of them—the PowerPoint marathons held in windowless meeting rooms with bad coffee—aren't even enjoyable. Leadership training is by and large a disappointment to participants and sponsors alike.[5] And while HR can improve the competency models, hire more dynamic instructors, or design apps and portals to replace the slides and binders, such efforts won't solve the problem, which is the currently prevailing understanding of leadership and how to teach it.

Let's set aside the debate over whether leaders are born or made. Let's assume that leadership can be, to some extent, learned—or at least that nascent leadership ability can be developed. The question then becomes: *How do you learn it*? Is leadership a "skill set" in which people can be trained, as dogs are trained to sit and stay? Is it a theory one can absorb and then apply to certain problems, as one might do in the physical sciences? Or is it, perhaps, a collection of strategies to have handy at big decision points ("Let's see ... I think Strategy No. 27 is the one to use in this situation")?

As we've seen, leadership is in fact something far more holistic. And in devoting themselves to studies of skills specific to their craft or business, to education that is more and more technical, leaders have lost an opportunity to develop the wisdom—the *practical* wisdom—that underpins real leadership ability. They have lost the perceptiveness and know-how that allowed Alexander, a good rider but by no means a professional horse-trainer, to determine why a particular stallion had resisted attempts at taming. Not only that, but given that most technical knowledge becomes outdated in a few years if not months, leaders have lost a foundation for learning and growing even within the bounds of their profession. Their training may fill a pail, but it doesn't light a fire.

Now, I'm not recommending that all would-be leaders rush off to get a degree in liberal arts. I do believe, however, that the *artes liberales* approach is valuable, indeed essential, for developing genuine leadership ability. Peter Drucker, the twentieth-century consultant and author who has been called "the founder of modern management,"[6] may have agreed. He wrote:

> Management is thus what tradition used to call a liberal art—"liberal" because it deals with the fundamentals of knowledge, self-knowledge, wisdom, and leadership; "art" because it is also concerned with practice and application.[7]

What would it look like to study leadership as a liberal art? The core of the approach is twofold: first, immersion in a wide range of time-tested ideas about how the world works and how human beings think and behave; second, opportunities to explore and engage with those ideas in a practical way. That sort of immersion and those sorts of opportunities are what *The Greats on Leadership* sets out to provide. And it won't take four years and your life's savings.

THE INGREDIENTS OF LEADERSHIP

The classics teach us that there's no pat formula—no Five Keys or Six Steps—for leading well. While leadership may indeed be that simple for a master with decades of experience, mastery is not so easily won. We can, however, list the many *ingredients* of good leadership, and such a list can provide a sense of what we are working toward.

Table I.1, The ingredients of leadership, is this book's theoretical framework. It is based on my 25 years' experience in the leadership training and consulting industry, during which time I reviewed or built some 40 leadership competency models for a wide variety of companies and industries; designed and developed about 30 leadership courses, both for specific clients and for broad markets; was head of Research and Development for The Forum Corporation, a global leadership training and consulting firm; and authored or co-authored three books and dozens of articles and white papers on leadership and workplace learning. I took the knowledge acquired from those years in the leadership development business and integrated it with my knowledge of classic books and authors deriving from a Master's degree in philosophy and a Bachelor's degree in philosophy and English literature.

The framework rests on three pillars: the business literature of the past few decades; classic works of political philosophy, history, psychology, and fiction; and my experience working with large organizations to educate their leaders. I intend it to be comprehensive rather than focused, a panoramic shot rather than a close-up. I believe it captures 80 to 90 percent of what a leader needs to know, do, and be.

Table I.1 The ingredients of leadership

BEHAVIORS that define true leaders	TRAPS that threaten leaders	CHARACTER TRAITS of effective leaders	CONCEPTS for leaders to grasp	LEVELS of leadership
Chapter 1	Chapter 2	Chapters 7, 12, 17, 22	Chapters 3–6, 8–11, 13–16, 18–21	Chapters 23–24
Going first	Ignoring blind spots	Courage	Change	Initiator
Creating hope	Being naïve about relationships	Integrity	Justice	Encourager
Focusing on people	Scorning the soft stuff	Resilience	Power	Cultivator
	Pursuing simplistic answers	Generosity	Authority	Mainspring
	Declaring victory too soon	Concern	Crises	
	Failing to adapt		Competition	
	Devaluing others' strengths		Dilemmas	
	Dominating and abdicating		Communication	
			Motivation	
			Personality	
			Decisions	
			Culture	
			Relationships	
			Accountability	
			Talent	
			Vision	

SOME COMMON CONCERNS

The idea of learning to lead from classic books may give rise to some concerns. Here are the seven I hear most often, along with my responses.

"I like great books, but I'm not a leader" You may not have a leader's title, but you don't need that in order to step into a leadership role. According to the American Management Association, the definition of "leader" is broadening: many organizations now consider people to be leaders based on their impact and the results they achieve, not on their position in a hierarchy.[8] (For a way to think about leadership levels in terms of impact rather than position, see Chapters 23 and 24.) Consider also that good leaders are needed in many contexts, including corporations, not-for-profits, professional firms, government, the military, communities, and households.

"The books you're talking about are over my head" I doubt it. The main reason these thinkers have stood the test of time is that their works are accessible, vivid, and useful to just about everyone. Of course, that doesn't mean they are quick and easy. They do make you think. You'll find, however, that *The Greats on Leadership* has done the heavy lifting of selecting the best books and highlighting the most interesting parts. All you need do is enter with an open mind, prepared to consider what these great authors have to say.

"*I need to know about* business *leadership*" *Business* is humans working together to imagine possibilities and solve problems. It has been going on for thousands of years. If you are a business leader or want to be one, I think you'll find the ideas and examples discussed here speak more powerfully than anything offered by the management gurus-of-the-moment. Of course, if your goal is to fill a specific educational pail, you'll be better off reading a book or attending a workshop on that topic. But if your goal is to light a fire—one that will illuminate and energize your path as a business leader for years to come—you're better off learning from the great thinkers found within these pages.

"I'm a woman, and most of these books are by and about men" One of the genuine drawbacks of learning leadership from the classics is that prior to the mid-twentieth century female authors were scarce, and female authors who wrote about leadership issues were even scarcer. I don't believe any book less than 50 years old can be judged a classic, so my options were limited. Even so, you'll find here three books by women (*The Chrysanthemum and the Sword*, by Ruth Benedict; *Frankenstein*, by Mary Shelley; and *Emma*, by Jane Austen) and several more with female main characters (*Antigone*, *Saint Joan*, and others), ensuring that women's perspectives and experiences are represented. Moreover, even the books with mostly male characters have been selected with an eye to their ability to speak to readers of any gender, nation, tribe, or time. That universality is, partly, what makes them classic. I do not believe that male authors can speak only to men any more than I believe female authors can speak only to women. So, to all my readers, I say: Read these classic books as if they were written for you, and you'll gain insights that are relevant to you as a leader.

"These books are all Western. What about Eastern literature and philosophy?" The classics of India, China, and Japan contain as much leadership wisdom as those of the West, if not more. The final chapter of this book uses one of the fundamental texts of Taoism, the *Tao Te Ching*, to shed light on a higher level of leadership than is revealed in the work of most Western thinkers. Eastern philosophy, however, is not the place to start when you're looking for leadership insights; it is the advanced course, not the introduction. For that reason, nearly all the books examined herein are drawn from the Western tradition. (For more leadership classics from a variety of authors, see my blog at JocelynRDavis.com.)

"These stories and ideas can be understood only in historical context" This concern is a variant of the previous two, and many scholars will agree. "All books are artifacts of their place and time," they'll say, "and must be read as such." They will, for instance, object to my treating Moses as a real leader with lessons to offer present-day leaders;

they will say the Exodus story can be approached only as a narrative whose purpose was to shape the identity of a particular Middle Eastern tribe of the sixth century BCE. While this approach has its merits, I've chosen another that has, I think, more value for readers outside academia; namely, reading these books as if they speak directly to us down the ages and across cultural divides—as indeed I believe they do. The reason Jane Austen's novels are still bestsellers is not that millions of people today want to make a study of the customs of the early nineteenth-century English gentry, but rather that millions of people today find Austen's characters and plots relevant to their lives.

I take it as undebatable that some books contain insights transcending time and place. I also take it as given (though not undebatable) that people are human beings first, individuals second, cultural products third, and gender or ethnic stereotypes a distant fourth. Leaders should divide their study time accordingly, making it their business to understand human nature deeply, individuals thoroughly, cultures adequately, and genders and ethnicities only insofar as they shed light on the first three. The classics featured herein are ideal for such a study plan.

"We know much more about leadership today, based on scientific research" There has indeed been a great deal of research on leadership in recent decades, some of it interesting and useful. Journals such as *Harvard Business Review* and *Psychology Today* will keep you up on the latest ideas and will often provide helpful tactics. My claim is not that classic books are more scientifically sound than contemporary research, but rather that reading and discussing classic books is a better way to *learn* to lead. In practice, leadership is more art than science. The "scientific management" attempts of the early twentieth century spawned a set of leadership theories that ignored much about the human mind and heart and as a result didn't work very well; half the business management articles published since the 1960s have been aimed at debunking those very theories. My recommendation is to study the latest research to learn about the science of leadership, but if you want to learn the *art* of leadership—if, that is, you want to become the sort of person whom others follow—study the classics.

Although I wouldn't lump all contemporary theorists together any more than I would all classic ones, I do believe the works of each group bear a family resemblance and foster a distinct outlook in aspiring leaders. The contemporary view, with origins in the "dismal science" of economics, reminds me (for the most part) of a concrete water tank: convenient to drink from, but a bit shallow, tepid, and apt to run dry. The classic view reminds me of a great lake: wide and turbulent, with deep waters feeding the rivers and streams that, ultimately, make our gardens grow. Age, said the philosopher Francis Bacon, is best in four things: "old wood best to burn, old wine to drink, old friends to trust, and old authors to read."[9]

Table I.2 on pages 14 and 15 presents, in highly simplified form, the contemporary and the classic view on each of this book's topics.

ONE MORE CONCERN AND THE RATATOUILLE PRINCIPLE

By now, I hope you're open to the idea that leadership is a liberal art that can be acquired through the study of great books and application of the wisdom therein. But you might be wondering: Does this mean anyone who engages in such studies can become a great leader?

Ratatouille is an animated film about Remy, a Parisian rat who yearns to become a great chef.[10] Although Remy has talent, he is blocked by relatives and colleagues who won't believe in his cooking abilities, nor even in his desire to cook, because he's, well ... a rat. Undaunted and determined to follow his dream, Remy draws inspiration from his idol Auguste Gusteau, a deceased chef-restaurateur and the author of a cookbook titled *Anyone Can Cook*. Throughout the film, various characters refer to that sentiment with either approval or scorn, and none more scornfully than Anton Ego, France's top food critic. He thinks the idea that "anyone can cook" is nonsense, and he reinforces the point by writing scathing reviews of restaurant meals prepared by chefs who don't measure up to his exacting standards.

In the end, however, Ego is moved to tears by a dish that Remy has designed and prepared for Restaurant Gusteau. He learns soon after, to his shock, that Remy is not only a culinary novice but also a rodent. That evening, Ego writes a glowing review of Gusteau's and its new talent in which he modifies his former opinion, stating, "Not everyone can be a great chef. But, a great chef can come from anywhere."

As with chefs, so with leaders. It's true: not every leader can be Great with a capital G. Really Great leaders are few, and undoubtedly they are born with some of the resources that propel them to greatness, not to mention are lucky enough to be in the right place at the right time. Nevertheless, to paraphrase Anton Ego's words, a great leader can come from anywhere. We needn't look only in the ranks of MBA students at prestigious business schools or among the politically well connected. We needn't look only at people who have corner offices or a million followers on Twitter. There are outstanding leaders in all walks of life, making a difference right now in offices and shops, museums and schools, city halls and suburban neighborhoods. Might you have the potential to be one of them? The Ratatouille Principle says you might.

And even if great leadership turns out to be beyond our reach, we can still aspire to better leadership, something every organization and community cries out for. All we need are some timeless teachers, a few fellow students, and a map for the journey.

Table I.2 *Contemporary vs. classic views of leadership*

TOPIC	WHAT TODAY'S GURUS TEND TO SAY	WHAT THE CLASSICS TEND TO SAY
A leader	Is a charismatic, visionary proponent of change	Is someone who goes first, creates hope, and focuses on people
Leadership traps	Threaten us when we aren't sufficiently confident, intelligent, or decisive	Threaten us when we prioritize being right over being effective
Change	Accelerates when a leader explains why the change is necessary and maps out new procedures clearly	Accelerates when a leader works with the natural phases of change and attends to people's emotions about it
Justice	Is mostly a matter of being objective and unbiased, applying the exact same rules to all	Is mostly a matter of knowing what is fitting or due to each person, even if that implies different treatment for some
Power	Is a negative thing and should not be pursued overtly; correlates directly with status	Is the ability to get work done and make things happen; does not necessarily correlate with status
Authority	Is the same as power and springs solely from one's title	Is separate from power and has three potential sources: rational/legal, traditional, and intrinsic
Crises	Demand that leaders make unhesitant decisions while operating "at the edge"	Demand the ability to keep learning and helping others learn in the midst of turmoil
Competitive advantage	Is based on finding uncontested space out in the marketplace	Is based first on a team's internal unity, agility, and excellence; then, on the wiliness to turn the tables on a competitor
Dilemmas	Are a species of problem arising in volatile environments and requiring cleverer than usual solutions	Are an eternal type of challenge, fundamentally different from problems and requiring management, not solutions
Communication	Means painting an inspiring vision of the future so that one's listeners will want to go there	Means painting a picture of the special enterprise to which one's listeners belong and what it demands of them

Table I.2 (cont.)

TOPIC	WHAT TODAY'S GURUS TEND TO SAY	WHAT THE CLASSICS TEND TO SAY
Motivation	Rests on basic human drives for safety and sustenance, which must be met before "higher" needs come into play	Rests on the basic human drive for meaning, which persists even when physical needs aren't met
Personality types	Are a way to appreciate people's differences	Are a way to appreciate people's differences *and* our own flaws and blind spots
Decisions	Improve when we become aware of, and guard against, dozens of cognitive biases	Improve only when we understand and act to mitigate the one fundamental bias that underlies the rest
Culture	Cannot really be understood by those outside it; the best we can do is learn rules of etiquette for various nations	Can be grasped through study and exploration; can be bridged with listening, empathy, and humility
Relationships	Are best seen as degrees of closeness along a single dimension from *strangers* to *friends*	Are best seen as points arrayed in two dimensions: *with or against you* and *conditional or unconditional*
Accountability	Is easily increased, as long as we are clear and uncompromising about what is expected	Is ambiguous and fraught with difficulties; efforts to increase it backfire unless accompanied by efforts to drive out fear
Talent development	Requires leaders to identify team members' improvement opportunities and work to close those gaps	Requires leaders to cultivate talents already present, helping team members become their best unique selves
Vision	Is something every leader should articulate and pursue	Is a risky game, to be pursued only when safer options have been exhausted
Character	Is simply a question of being authentic, true to personal values, and determined to reach goals	Is a question of balance or holding to a mean; consists of specific virtues, which are developed primarily through self-mastery
Leadership levels	Correspond to titles (manager, director, and so on); can be eliminated if an organization chooses to be "flat"	Correspond to the positive impact we make and the legacy we leave; exist even in "flat" organizations

part I

THE HEART OF LEADERSHIP

Better leadership begins with two questions: What are the behaviors that distinguish true leaders from misleaders? And, what are leadership's most dangerous traps?

Lofty questions, indeed, but lofty in the best sense: pondering them will lift you up above the daily turmoil—above, say, the five emails Diego sent you at 7:15 this morning about the problem in Accounting whose resolution requires the report Carol was supposed to have done yesterday, only she's out sick and said she'd hand it off to Ted, who you think is unreliable and who reports to Suzanne, who you suspect is trying to undermine you.

Whether you are new to leadership or an old hand, being in charge can feel like slogging through a swamp on a squelchy path with gnats buzzing round your head and pockets of quicksand threatening to engulf you. If you pause and look, however, you'll see a ladder here and there: a chance to ascend, take a breath, and gain some perspective before heading back down into the muck. *What are the behaviors that mark a true leader? What are the traps a leader should beware?* These questions are the first ladders we'll climb.

Chapter 1 looks at leadership myths and truths through the lens of one of the most ancient leadership stories: that of Moses, as told in the Old Testament book of Exodus. And Chapter 2 takes its cue from *King Lear*, Shakespeare's play about a leader who stumbles into a pit of confusion, descends into madness, and emerges, finally, to the light.

great author
MOSES AND EXODUS

This ancient story helps us see the holes in a pernicious and persistent myth about leadership.

The events of the Exodus story are traditionally dated to 1400–1300 BCE, but the archeological evidence suggests they actually occurred much later—if they occurred at all. Modern scholars believe the story was first recorded in the sixth century BCE, during the Babylonian exile of the Israelites, and then completed and revised over the next two centuries. While there is no indication of a population half a million strong departing Egypt at any time, there are a few documents that tell of a much smaller number of people being brought to Egypt as captives, being kept in slavery, and eventually leaving the region, all some time during the first millennium BCE. These incidents may be the wellspring of the tale.

The factual accuracy of Exodus, however, is not our concern. Everett Fox, translator and editor of *The Shocken Bible*, describes Exodus as "a mix of historical recollection, mythical processing, and didactic retelling"[1] and compares it to the semi-legendary accounts of the American founding—Washington and the cherry tree, the Boston Tea Party, and so on—whose purpose is not to present information but rather to educate readers in the ideals at the heart of a nation. Similarly, the purpose of the second book of the Old Testament is to bind a people together with a common understanding of who they are and what makes them special. Since conveying such an understanding is a key ability for leaders, Exodus is worth reading simply in order to see how that kind of storytelling works. More important, though, this partly mythical tale serves as a counterweight to an unhelpful myth that continues to skew our view of leadership today: that leadership is about charisma.

Read this in Exodus: Chapters 1–18 and 32–34.

chapter 1
ONE MYTH, THREE TRUTHS

The book of Exodus tells how a man with a speech impediment, shaky self-esteem, and a tendency to lean on his relatives is chosen by God to lead a nation of 600,000 people to freedom. Moses doesn't fit the standard conception of a great leader, yet his may be the world's best-known leadership story, given that the Bible is the top-selling book of all time and *The Ten Commandments* one of the top-grossing films. It's a good place to start, for if we have any preconceived or superficial notions about leaders—such as the myth described below—Moses' story is apt to clear them away, leaving us open to some deeper truths.

A CHARISMATIC EXECUTIVE

The word *charisma* comes from the Greek, meaning "a favor one receives without merit of one's own; a gift of divine grace." Today it has come to mean the ability to captivate people with an eloquently expressed vision of the future. The hallmark of the charismatic leader is the stirring speech delivered from a high perch: a horse, a cafeteria table, the deck of a sailing ship. The image runs deep in Western culture and, despite some debunking in recent years, in the world of leadership development. Job descriptions for senior leadership roles invariably list "executive presence" (code for charisma) as a key requirement, and leadership competency models usually include a section called Inspiring Others. Great leaders of the past, from Julius Caesar to Joan of Arc, are frequently described by history books as charismatic and their successes attributed to charisma. And in one of the first leadership seminars I ever attended, the instructor began by stating flatly, "Leadership is a matter of charisma. The trick is to figure out what charisma is."

None of this would be problematic if charisma were seen as icing on the cake of leadership ability and hiring decisions were made based on the quality of the cake. Too often, however, leaders are hired or promoted based on the icing, and that's when things go awry, as in the following example.

Oliver, a senior marketing professional, had just landed the top Consumer Affairs job at HomeCo, a global consumer products company.[2] In the cover letter to Oliver's interview packet, the executive recruiter had this to say: "His experience is impeccable, but more important, he's on the leading edge. When you speak with him, you'll see he's got some exciting ideas and knows how to drive change. Quite frankly, he's a visionary."

Oliver entered the company at a turbulent time. An organizational restructuring was underway, which meant, among other things, layoffs for about 30 of his group of 100. While the restructuring decisions hadn't been his, his employees badly needed communication about the ongoing changes—communication he failed to provide. Five months passed before he scheduled an all-team conference call, and during those months he held only sporadic one-on-one meetings with his direct reports. He mostly spent time with executives, and in those situations his charisma was on full display.

Oliver talked convincingly about the results he had achieved in previous jobs. He said the field of consumer affairs was mired in the past and needed to be redefined as part of an end-to-end customer experience. He spoke about the new technologies he planned to install, the new ways he would utilize social media, and the links to be forged with Marketing and Product Development. Most impressive of all, he talked like a businessperson, something no previous head of Consumer Affairs at HomeCo had been particularly good at. But when he took the same tack in his first team conference call, delivering an energetic spiel about the group's future and asking for questions, there was dead silence. Later, one employee explained the reaction this way: "You can't be absent for five months and then call a meeting and try to be all charismatic."

Oliver's departure was announced half a year after he had arrived. Given his obvious intelligence, one might wonder whether he was an effective business leader who simply lacked some warm fuzzies. It later transpired, though, that during his brief tenure he had significantly overspent his entire annual budget. A year later, the Consumer

Affairs group was still digging itself out of the financial hole. The consensus at HomeCo by then was that Oliver, though undeniably charismatic, was no leader.

It appears, then, that charisma isn't sufficient for effective leadership. But is it even necessary? Our first featured classic suggests not.

MOSES THE TONGUE-TIED

Moses, the central character of Exodus, doesn't fit the standard image of a great leader. Although by story's end his confidence has grown, throughout the first ten chapters he barely says a word except to express doubt that he'll meet expectations. Some modern observers have called him an introvert (see "On tall shoulders: Susan Cain on leadership myths and truths"); I'd go further and call him a Nervous Nellie.

In the film *The Ten Commandments*, Moses shows proud defiance as he's arrested and exiled for killing an Egyptian overseer; in the book, however, he simply runs away when he realizes his crime has come to light. "Surely the matter is known!" he says (Exodus 2:14), and flees the country in a panic.[3] In his new homeland he finds a wife and settles down as a shepherd, working for his father-in-law. For many years he displays no larger ambitions. Then one day he gets the big call: God appears to him in the burning bush and tells him to lead the Hebrews out of Egypt. These four statements are Moses' response:

> Who am I that I should go to Pharaoh, that I should bring the Children of Israel out of Egypt? (3:11)
>
> I will say to them: The God of your fathers has sent me to you, and they will say to me, What is his name?—what shall I say to them? (3:13)
>
> But they will not trust me, and will not hearken to my voice, indeed, they will say, YHWH has not been seen by you! (4:1)
>
> Please, my Lord, no man of words am I … for heavy of mouth and heavy of tongue am I! (4:10)[4]

on tall shoulders
SUSAN CAIN *on* LEADERSHIP MYTHS AND TRUTHS

In her book *Quiet: The Power of Introverts in a World That Can't Stop Talking*, Susan Cain writes in praise of introverts: those who are often described as shy but who might more accurately be called thoughtful. Introverts shun self-promotion and loud displays in favor of taking a quiet stand or making a quiet contribution.

Cain is a notable contemporary debunker of the leadership-as-charisma myth and champion of a different view of the behaviors that make a leader. She tells of history's many "limelight-avoiding" leaders, among them Rosa Parks, Steve Wozniak, Mahatma Gandhi, Eleanor Roosevelt—and Moses, who, she says, "was not the brash, talkative type who would organize road trips and hold forth in a classroom at Harvard Business School."[5] Instead, he climbed a mountain to speak with God one on one and wrote down, carefully, everything he learned on two stone tablets.

"We don't ask why God chose as his prophet a stutterer with a public speaking phobia," Cain says. "But we should."[6]

God tries to set Moses' mind at ease. He explains his identity, promises support, demonstrates how to work some magic to impress the Hebrews, and says not to worry about the public speaking because he'll tell Moses exactly what to say. After all that reassurance, Moses' fifth and final remark is essentially, "Can't you find someone else?"—whereupon God loses his temper. He tells Moses his brother Aaron can be the front man, and makes it clear the discussion is over.

Moses, probably seeing no alternative, packs his bags. He sets off for Egypt, meets up with Aaron, and informs him without enthusiasm of their assignment. God arranges ten plagues to persuade Pharaoh to free the slaves, and through the first nine, Moses says and does very little. Aaron does the talking and wields the staff that turns the Nile to blood and summons forth the frogs and gnats, while Moses stays in the background, relaying God's instructions. It's not until the approach of the tenth plague—the killing of the first-born of Egypt and the Passover of Hebrew homes—that Moses says more than a few words to Pharaoh or speaks at all to his own people. And, surprisingly, it is right *before* he makes this speech that his leadership status is noted for the first time: by now, the narrator says, Moses is "considered exceedingly great in the land of Egypt, in the eyes of Pharaoh's servants and in the eyes of the people" (11:3). Inspiring speeches clearly aren't the reason, for he hasn't made any.

The charismatic leader of myth is also a lone leader. It's always one general, not two, making the rousing speech from the back of the horse. It's Norma Rae who stands on the table in the textile factory holding up the UNION sign,[7] not Norma Rae and her sister. We tend to picture our leaders solo. In reality, though, leaders rarely stand alone, as we see in the rest of the Exodus story.

Gradually, during the departure from Egypt, the parting of the Red Sea, and the long trek through the wilderness, Aaron recedes into the background and Moses steps forward. By the time the people arrive in the region where Moses' wife and in-laws are still living, he has become the tribe's sole leader, and now his portrayal begins to jibe with his popular image: the robed and bearded patriarch standing on a rock, above and apart, communing with a higher power. But then—just as we start to feel that this is the Moses we know—he makes his first big mistake. His father-in-law, Jethro, calls attention to it:

> Moses sat to judge the people, and the people stood before Moses from daybreak until sunset. When Moses' father-in-law saw all that he had to do for the people, he said: What kind of matter is this that you do for the people—why do you sit alone, while the entire people stations itself around you from daybreak until sunset? (18:13-14)

Moses explains that the people bring their disputes to him because they know he has a direct line to God; nobody can judge as he can. Jethro doesn't disagree, but nevertheless insists that the arrangement won't work:

> Not good is this matter, as you do it! You will become worn out, yes, worn out ... for this matter is too heavy for you, you cannot do it alone ... you are to have the vision to select from all the people men of caliber ... every great matter they shall bring before you, but every small matter they shall judge by themselves. Make it light upon you, and let them bear it with you. (18:17-22)

Moses takes Jethro's advice and starts to hire and delegate. He chooses "men of caliber" and creates an organizational structure that would be familiar to any modern-day employee, with "chiefs of thousands, chiefs of hundreds, chiefs of fifties, and chiefs of tens" (18:25), each authorized to handle decisions of a certain magnitude. Steeped as we are in the myth of the heroic leader, we may find the whole scene strangely corporate: Moses the Seer must build an organization. A filmed version would show him drawing organizational charts and holding morning meetings with the chiefs.

So much for the charisma myth. Oliver's story shows that charisma is insufficient for effective leadership; Exodus shows us it's also unnecessary. Moses isn't the least bit charismatic, nor is he required or even encouraged to stand alone, yet thousands of people follow him and he achieves great things.

WHAT MAKES A LEADER?

None of this is to say that eloquent communication isn't helpful or that individual heroism isn't sometimes needed; it's just that these aren't the marks of a true leader. But if they aren't, what is? What is a leader, if not the charismatic star who rides at the head of the army? Put another way, how can we tell true leaders from false?

There are three clues, three behaviors that characterize a real leader. In this chapter I'll review them briefly, along with three corresponding types of "misleader." And in Part VI, I'll revisit these truths, expand on them, and use them to define a new set of leadership levels relating to impact rather than business title.

First of all, in the words of the 6-year-old daughter of one of my long-ago colleagues, ***leaders go first***. Good leaders step forward when others stay back. They speak when others stay silent.

They forge ahead where no path has been forged, and they set an example for others to follow. You won't always see them out in front; often they are found working alongside their team or taking up a position in the wings so their people can shine in the spotlight. But wherever they choose to stand at a particular moment, it won't be against a wall, butt covered, observing which way the wind blows. Conversely, there are plenty of high-status individuals who take just that stance, and though they may have leadership titles on their business cards, they aren't leaders, but *lackeys* (see "Assessment tool: Which misleader?").

assessment tool

WHICH MISLEADER?

Think of one of the worst leaders you know—a misleader. For each question below, select the statement that fits best. Then use the key at the end to interpret your results.

Repeat the quiz for some other misleaders, and finally, ask yourself: In your own worst moments, in which of the three directions do you lean? What might you do to avoid this tendency?

1. How does this person generally behave?
   A. Sticks to official rules and policies no matter what
   B. Takes whatever action will maintain or extend their power
   C. Does whatever the bigger bosses will approve of

2. What is this person's general demeanor?
   A. Businesslike; rarely makes eye contact; often too rushed to talk
   B. Often seems angry; yells and screams when things go wrong
   C. Pleasant to your face, but runs you down behind your back

3. How does this person spend most of their time?
   A. Checking up on employees and/or crunching data
   B. Often absent; when present, criticizing people's work or demanding explanations for errors
   C. Out of sight, seemingly doing very little

4. What does this person use to maintain control over subordinates?
   A. Systems and processes
   B. Spying and informants
   C. The authority of higher-level managers

5. What seems to be this person's overriding aim?
   A. To make sure people follow the rules
   B. To make sure people fear them
   C. To make sure people leave them alone and demand no decisions

Key

Mostly As This person is a *bureaucrat*
Mostly Bs This person is a *tyrant*
Mostly Cs This person is a *lackey*

Moses, despite his natural shyness, isn't a wall-leaner; on the contrary, he seems inclined to step forward. Having fled Egypt and settled down in Midyan as a shepherd, he goes out one day to tend his flock and sees something odd: a bush on fire that is not consumed. Another man might run away, or maybe just give a shrug and move on, but Moses says, "Now let me turn aside that I may see this great sight—why the bush does not burn up!" (3:3). Then, "when YHWH saw that he had turned aside to see" and calls Moses' name from out of the fire (now most people really would run), Moses says simply, "Here I am." Perhaps the incident was God's first leadership test: Is this a man who will go see? Is this a man who will go first?

Second, ***leaders create hope***. Leaders help us see the light at the end of the tunnel, or throw us a lifebelt when we're sinking under the waves. "A leader is a dealer in hope," said Napoleon Bonaparte, and the opposite of the hope-dealer is the fear-dealing *tyrant*. While some tough-minded political thinkers (most notably Niccolò Machiavelli; see Chapter 3) have argued that it's more important for a leader to be respected than loved, even they acknowledge that a leader who makes us feel terrible about the future is far less likely to succeed than a leader who inspires belief in a better day.[8]

Although you might suspect me of allowing charisma to creep back into our leadership definition, creating hope isn't usually about charismatic speeches to crowds. More often, it's about simple words and deeds. One of the most inspiring parts of the Exodus story is when Moses explains to the Hebrews, very briefly, how they must paint their door frames with lamb's blood so that God's "bringer of ruin" will pass over their houses on the night of the final plague, sparing their first-born, and how they must tell their children the story of that night (12:21-27). It's not a speech—just a set of instructions, really—but with it, Moses plants an image in the people's minds of God's awesome power, his astounding love for them, and the future they can anticipate thanks to that love. As a result, they "bow low" and do as he says, hope renewed.

Finally, ***leaders focus on people***. In the words of Grace Murray Hopper, computer scientist and rear admiral in the US Navy, "You manage things; you lead people." Naturally, there are plenty of managers who have excellent people skills. Management as a role, however, is primarily about using policies, systems, and processes to control the activities of an organization. Things are much easier to control than people, so for someone playing a pure management role, people are secondary to things. (Peter Drucker quipped, "Most of what we call management consists of making it difficult for people to get their work done.") Leadership, in contrast, is focused on human beings: developing them, mobilizing them, earning their trust.[9] When those in authority emphasize management over leadership, they may become *bureaucrats*: lords of procedure, oblivious to the humanity of their "human resources."

The Moses portrayed in Exodus is no bureaucrat. After some of the Hebrews decide to make a golden calf as an idol, breaking the first commandment, a wrathful God threatens to destroy the whole lot of them. Moses does not cower, nor does he argue legalities. Instead, he simply reminds God that these are *his own people*: "This nation is indeed your people," he says, and "we are distinct, I and your people, from every people that is on the face of the soil" (33:13-16). Moses almost seems to be encouraging God to act more like a leader than a manager: to focus on his relationship with the Israelites and on all they might become, rather than on the rules they have broken.[10] Moses prays for forgiveness, and then for permission to see God even more directly. The section ends with his prayers answered and his leadership of the Hebrews established, at last, beyond a doubt.

Going first; creating hope; focusing on people. These are the truths that replace the myth of the charismatic lone leader, and the signs by which to recognize a true leader. After Moses, says the Book of Deuteronomy (33:10–12), there were other prophets, but never one to equal the tongue-tied shepherd whom God spoke with face to face and chose to be his strong hand.

Next we explore eight common leadership pitfalls, all of which stem from one big mistake.

great author

WILLIAM SHAKESPEARE'S *KING LEAR*

Shakespeare drew the plot of *King Lear* from an old English folktale wherein an aging king decides to bequeath his wealth and lands to his three daughters and requires them to compete for their shares by explaining how much they love him. The two elder daughters make fulsome speeches claiming to love their father more than the whole world or more than life itself, thereby winning large portions. The youngest daughter, however, either remains silent or says something coldly opaque, such as "I love you more than meat loves salt."

In Shakespeare's version, written in 1608, the youngest daughter, Cordelia, says this: "I cannot heave my heart into my mouth. I love your Majesty according to my bond, no more nor less" (Act I, Scene i). She refuses to elaborate. Lear, furious at her apparent heartlessness, banishes her and rescinds her dowry. Cordelia leaves with her suitor, the King of France, who remains willing to marry her. Lear goes on to survive his own banishment, and after many misfortunes finally comes to understand: Cordelia loved him best.

Shakespeare adds a subplot about another father, the Earl of Gloucester, who, like Lear, trusts the wrong child. Both men are betrayed by their former flatterers, turned out of their homes, and left to wander insane (Lear) or blind (Gloucester). "All's cheerless, dark, and deadly," says the Earl of Kent in the play's final scene; nevertheless, by the end the two fathers have managed a partial escape from the sloughs into which they fell. They cannot be called happy, but they might be called free.

Read this in King Lear: Act I, which presents the main characters and the foundation of the story.

chapter 2

EIGHT TRAPS

That much of the world's unhappiness stems from bad leadership is obvious when you're thinking about an infamous tyrant on the world stage, less obvious when you're thinking about the person in the next cubicle. Yet for every Hitler or Stalin there are a million petty tyrants and ten million petty bureaucrats who in comparison can't be called evil, but who nevertheless go through life dispersing misery like a toddler spreads grape jelly. What makes these misleaders the way they are?

TRAPS FOR LEADERS

In an epilogue to *The Screwtape Letters*, C.S. Lewis's book about the art of temptation seen from a devil's point of view, we find senior devil Screwtape delivering a toast at a banquet in Hell. The menu has featured dishes of human souls, and Screwtape begins his address with nostalgic reminiscences of the days when guests would dine on spectacular evil-doers such as Casanova or Henry VIII. Those meals, he says, offered "something to crunch," while tonight's fare has consisted of nothing better than "a grubby little municipal authority with Graft sauce" and other flabby offerings.[1] He hastens to add, however, that Hell still has plenty to celebrate, for though the quality of the food may be wretched, the quantity has soared: "We never had souls (of a sort) in more abundance," he says.

Screwtape has a point. Today's institutions, though they don't afford really bad leaders the same scope for wickedness that ancient and medieval ones did, certainly allow more people to ascend to positions where they can exert destructive influence, even if it's only the chance to be on the Employee Activities Planning Committee and shoot down all proposed locations for the summer picnic. There may be fewer Stalins, but there are many more toxic supervisors and tiresome project managers. And, since more of us now have opportunities to be leaders, more of us must be concerned with avoiding the errors to which leaders are prone.

Of course, we all vow not to be like that bad boss we know: the one who throws temper tantrums, or that other one, the passive-aggressive one who refuses to make a decision and then blames subordinates for the ensuing mess. In making that vow, however, we miss a crucial truth: nobody gets up in the morning *intending* to be A Terrible Manager. Just like us, ATM gets out of bed intending to do a good job, accomplish a few things, and earn others' respect.

But the road to Hell, as Screwtape could tell us, is paved with good intentions. "I meant well" is not enough. Leaders who want to avoid becoming misleaders must watch out for these eight traps:

1. Ignoring blind spots
2. Being naïve about relationships
3. Scorning the soft stuff
4. Pursuing simplistic answers
5. Declaring victory too soon
6. Failing to adapt
7. Devaluing others' strengths
8. Dominating and abdicating

Before we dive deeper, let me make two general points.

First, these eight errors may be understood as versions of one overarching error: *choosing rightness over efficacy*. This is the über-trap, the mistake that engenders the rest. As a leader, you must commit to one or the other—being right or being effective—because very often you cannot be both. In fact, it is possible be "right" on every step of the way down to disaster. A bit of doggerel from a book I owned as a child makes the point memorably:

> Here lies the body of William Jay,
> Who died maintaining his right of way.
> He was right, dead right, as he sped along,
> But he's just as dead as if he'd been wrong.[2]

Second, while each trap may eventually become extreme and therefore obvious, each tends to present itself as a perfectly natural, even laudable, leadership behavior. This means it's easy for us to trundle along, satisfied in our course and repeating fine-sounding justifications for our actions, even as we go sliding unawares into a hole (see "On tall shoulders: Marshall Goldsmith on leadership traps").

Trap 1: Ignoring blind spots (What it sounds like: "I'm certain") This first pitfall may be the most difficult to avoid, since avoiding it usually means opening our eyes to things we don't want to see.

Shakespeare's King Lear is a prime example of a leader whose blind spots destroy him. When we read or watch the famous first scene of the play, in which Lear gleefully tells his three daughters that they must compete for shares of his kingdom by describing how much they love him, we may find it incredible that he doesn't see Goneril and Regan's speeches for the nauseating flattery they are, nor Cordelia's quiet protestations as clear evidence of her love and fidelity. But Lear is blinded by ego, along with a set of fears—loss of job, diminishment of prestige, approaching death—that make ego all the stronger. His commitment to being right, as opposed to effective, is unshakeable; when the Earl of Kent tries to intervene and open Lear's eyes to the truth about his daughters, the king will have none of it: "Come not between the dragon and his wrath," he cries, and a little later, "Out of my sight!" (I.i). Lear knows what he knows and, like many of us, is loath to admit he might be missing something.

What helps most with this pitfall is seeking out and listening to people who are different from us—sometimes radically different. When I first saw *King Lear* I was puzzled by the large part given to the Fool, who starts out as court jester and later becomes Lear's companion and protector in homelessness. Most of the Fool's speeches are weird to the point of opacity. It is the riddles and harangues of this weirdo, however, that begin to tear the scales from Lear's eyes and set him on a more enlightened path. Chapter 15 provides further insight on how diverse perspectives can mitigate our blind spots (see Table 2.1 and "Planning tool: Trap avoidance").

on tall shoulders

MARSHALL GOLDSMITH on LEADERSHIP TRAPS

Forbes magazine has named Marshall Goldsmith one of five "most-respected executive coaches." His books—including *What Got You Here Won't Get You There* (2007) and *Triggers* (2015)—focus on increasing our awareness of the personal traps and quagmires that beset us as leaders.

Goldsmith is one of a few contemporary business authors who appreciate how horribly difficult it is to perceive our flaws and change our behavior and, at the same time, how seductively easy it is to "make guilty of our disasters the sun, the moon, and the stars," as if we were "villains on necessity, fools by heavenly compulsion" (as Edmund son of Gloucester puts it in *King Lear*, Act I, Scene 2).

Goldsmith uses 360-degree feedback to jolt his Armani-suited tutees out of that sort of it's-not-me thinking. But he knows that, in the end, avoiding leadership traps comes down to the zero-degree feedback we are willing to give ourselves. In *Triggers* he writes, "How can we strengthen our resolve to wrestle with the timeless, omnipresent challenge any successful person must stare down—becoming the person we want to be?"[3]

Trap 2: Being naïve about relationships (What it sounds like: "They love me!") Most leaders don't know that their relationships can be grouped into four broad categories: friends, foes, allies, and adversaries.[4] The friend and foe relationships are unconditional: a friend supports you no matter what, while a foe works against you no matter what. Allies and adversaries, in contrast, are with you or against you based on *interests*, which are conditional and transitory. Chapter 18 takes a look at these four relationship types and at the most common form of this trap: mistaking allies for friends and mistaking adversaries for foes.

King Lear mistakes allies for friends, and fails to recognize his true friend. Believing Goneril and Regan's over-the-top declarations, he gives up all his wealth and authority to them. He fails to see that their love and obedience up to that point depended entirely on

Table 2.1 More on the leadership traps

LEADERSHIP TRAP	SEE CHAPTER	KEY CONCEPT
1. Ignoring blind spots	15	The Star Chart
2. Being naïve about relationships	18	Relationship types
3. Scorning the soft stuff	13	Workplace climate
4. Pursuing simplistic answers	10	The structure of a dilemma
5. Declaring victory too soon	3	The Change Road
6. Failing to adapt	8	Crisis Zones
7. Devaluing others' strengths	20	Two views of talent
8. Dominating and abdicating	5	The King's Paradox

their desire to get hold of his riches and grow their own power; in other words, they were his allies, not his friends. Cordelia's words could have given Lear a clue that she is the *real* friend: "I love your Majesty according to my bond," she says (I.i), meaning her bond to him as his child—an unconditional relationship that will never alter, even if interests do.

Trap 3: Scorning the soft stuff (What it sounds like: "Get over it") This trap is for leaders who expect hearts to be checked at the office door. They fail to see that denying people's emotional connection to their work is one of the fastest ways to squash an organization's spirit.

In the fourth scene of Act 2, Goneril and Regan refuse to accommodate their father's train of knights; earlier they had promised to allow him 100, a number fitting to his royal status, but now Goneril, noting that she has plenty of servants to tend to his needs, cuts it to 50. A moment later she slices that quantity down: "What need you five-and-twenty? ten? or five?" And Regan brings the matter to an icy conclusion with "What need one?" The king is devastated. In his last speech to the pair, before rushing out into the storm, he chastises them not for denying him money or servants, but for humiliating him under the guise of prudent household management—what today we might call rightsizing.

planning tool
TRAP AVOIDANCE

Think about a leadership opportunity or challenge you're facing. As you work on that opportunity, which of the eight traps should you be on the watch for? Construct your trap avoidance plan by answering the questions below, or ask a colleague to talk through the questions with you.

Trap to watch for: ______________________________

1. What are three things you'll be sure to do in order to avoid the trap?

2. What are three things you'll be sure not to do?

3. What will be a warning sign that you are slipping into this trap?

4. Which of your habits or beliefs might tend to pull you down?

5. What help or advice might you need, and from whom will you get it?

Use Table 2.1 to find the chapter and key concept that address your selected trap, and use these as a resource for your plan.

Here's an example of a contemporary leader who scorned the soft stuff and paid a price for it. Pinecone, a midsized public relations firm with headquarters in California, had recently been acquired by Hanover, a global marketing and advertising conglomerate based in Sydney. Founded in the 1980s, Pinecone had for decades attracted employees in a competitive labor market thanks to a collaborative, upbeat culture and a mission in which people took pride. Within the "Pinecone family" celebrations were frequent: large sales, birthdays, and promotions were all marked with cake and applause. Clients felt the warmth, too. On surveys, they consistently cited "great people" as their main reason for choosing Pinecone for their PR needs.

After the acquisition, Rona, a senior manager from another Hanover business, was brought in to take the helm. Although Pinecone had always been profitable, its operating margin was low compared to other Hanover companies, and Rona, a believer in numbers, was convinced the employees needed a few stern lessons in business thinking. In her first presentation to the entire staff, she included a slide that read:

Pinecone's mission is to deliver profit to Hanover.

This statement met with a dismayed silence, which later gave way to much talk around the water coolers. There followed several years of declining morale, layoffs, shrinking revenues, and the resignation of many long-term employees. Eventually, Hanover sold Pinecone to a new owner, and Rona was invited to leave. Of course, the causes of the problems were numerous and complex; when asked what had gone wrong, however, many Pinecone alumni would refer to the moment when Rona's "mission" slide had appeared on the screen. "That," said one, "was when the spirit left the building."

Trap 4: Pursuing simplistic answers (What it sounds like: "It's obvious") Should Rona have ignored Pinecone's unacceptable financial performance and let the company amble happily along? Of course not, but neither should she have fallen into the trap of seeing every difficulty as a stark either/or. She saw her choice as "*either* I pop these people's self-satisfied bubble right now *or* they'll go on for ever with their weekly birthday celebrations and crappy results." Most leadership challenges, though, are not either/or problems but dilemmas.

A dilemma is an issue with two sides, each with benefits to be maximized and drawbacks to be minimized. Dilemmas are managed, not solved (we'll explore their structure in Chapter 10). There's a set of classic dilemmas that most organizations face, among them centralized vs. decentralized, long term vs. short term, and planning vs. action. When Rona took charge, Pinecone was facing dilemmas of profit vs. growth and efficiency vs. engagement. Rather than simply trying to stamp out the problems, she could have acknowledged the benefits that had resulted from the firm's collaborative culture and meaningful mission—benefits such as company longevity, employee retention, and growth potential—and sought ways to hold on to those positive aspects while at the same time fostering some new ones.

Trap 5: Declaring victory too soon (What it sounds like: "My work is done") The most competent of leaders can fall into this trap; in fact, it's often the competent ones who do. Avoiding it requires knowledge of the way in which change initiatives typically unfold. The Change Road, as we'll see in Chapter 3, comprises five phases: the start, the rapid ascent, the plateau, and finally either the gentle rise or the cliff. Many leaders make the error of declaring victory in the middle of the rapid ascent. "With the wonderful progress we've made and the goal within reach," they think, "surely the foot soldiers can take it from here." What they fail to anticipate is the plateau that will appear at the top of the climb, stretching for miles to the actual destination.

Perhaps the most famous example of this error is when President George W. Bush, on May 1, 2003, stood on the deck of the USS *Abraham Lincoln* in front of a "Mission Accomplished" banner and announced the end of major combat operations in Iraq. King Lear falls into the same trap when he announces his retirement and hands over his kingdom to his children in a matter of minutes, apparently expecting that all concerned will accept this drastic change immediately. Whatever the mission and however successful the launch, leaders would do well to survey the terrain ahead before making such confident announcements.

Trap 6: Failing to adapt (What it sounds like: "This is the way") In the Introduction we saw how great leaders have a keen appreciation for circumstances and adjust their approach accordingly. King Lear, for all his flaws, does learn. He reaches his nadir out on the heath in the storm (III.iv), but it is also in that storm, with the Fool and Kent, that he begins to examine his former behavior and seek to mend his ways. The Earl of Gloucester (the play's other irate father) also reflects on his errors and is eventually redeemed. Some leaders, though, never learn.

"The Procurator of Judea," a famous short story by Anatole France, provides a compelling picture of a leader caught in this pitfall. The leader is Pontius Pilate, erstwhile financial administrator of the Roman Empire's region of Judea and that same administrator who ordered the execution of Jesus Christ. For Pilate, the correct way to do anything is in accordance with Roman law and interests. This maxim would seem to allow for a fair amount of latitude, but as he recounts his many past grievances to his friend Aelius Lamia, we see how inflexible his interpretation of "Roman interests" is.

Pilate puts down rebellions—only to find that his boss, Vitellius, favors the rebels and that the Roman emperor (surprise!) favors Vitellius. Pilate also has the idea of building an aqueduct for Jerusalem: he calls in mechanical experts, sweats every detail, draws up regulations to prevent "unauthorized depredations," and initiates construction—only to find that the inhabitants of Jerusalem consider the structure impious and want it torn down, which leads to still more civil unrest and headaches for Rome, and more rebukes from Vitellius. Pilate forges ahead, never stopping to wonder whether the "right way" might be all wrong for this particular situation.

Trap 7: Devaluing others' strengths (What it sounds like: "I'm the expert") What makes leaders susceptible to this trap is a tendency to see others as if through the wrong end of a telescope: appearing smaller than they are and with less potential than they have. Pilate, for example, has a bored contempt for his Jewish constituents reminiscent of the contempt some present-day managers seem to feel for their team. When his friend Lamia points out that "the Jews celebrate rites which their very antiquity renders venerable," Pilate merely shrugs. "They have very little exact knowledge of the nature of the gods," he says.[5] He proceeds to give examples of the Jews' supposed confusion and ignorance about divine matters, thereby revealing his own confusion about Jewish religious practices and his own ignorance of the impact Judaism has had on how the world thinks about

God. Lamia's playful suggestion that an actual god might someday come out of Judea and threaten Roman authority brings a fleeting smile to Pilate's face, but he quickly dismisses the idea as fanciful. A *god, from those people? Seriously?*

At the end of the story, Lamia has a vague recollection of the man who turned out to be the most important Jew of that era (some would say the most important person of all eras) and asks Pilate what happened to him, saying, "His name was Jesus; he came from Nazareth, and he was crucified for some crime, I don't quite know what." Pilate probes his memory, but "cannot call him to mind."[6]

Trap 8: Dominating and abdicating (What it sounds like: "Not unless I say ... Oh, whatever") This eighth and final trap is about failing to find the right balance between direction and involvement. The best leaders know how to bring the two together so that team members feel both clear on where they're going and engaged in the process of getting there. Less effective leaders, on the other hand, tend to oscillate between domination and abdication.

The word domination may call to mind the stereotypical bad boss who stomps around issuing orders and threats as a way to goad people into action. More commonly, though, the attitude of the dominating leader is not "Do as I say" but "Not unless I say." Driven by fear, this leader wants above all to make sure that nothing goes wrong and, if something does, to make sure that he or she is not blamed for it. Inaction, therefore, is preferred to any sort of action, and the worst occurs when people are doing anything, even speaking, *without permission.*

King Lear's greatest wrath in the first scene of the play falls on the Earl of Kent, who tries to speak on Cordelia's behalf. Kent has barely opened his mouth before Lear shuts him down, and when Kent refuses to be cowed—insisting that "to plainness honor's bound when majesty falls to folly"—the threats and insults escalate, until Lear finally falls back on the boss's prerogative to declare subordinates insubordinate and fire them. Kent is banished.

Notice, however, that the starting point for Lear's dominating behavior isn't a grab for power but, rather, an abdication: his announcement that he'll step down from the throne and cede power to others. But when he kicks off his "how much do you love me" competition and then flies into a rage when things don't go as planned, we can see that he's still clinging to control. He's caught in the same pattern as that modern-day manager who is absent and unreachable—until he's suddenly in your face, inspecting every detail and making you undo all the work you did while he was away. Abdication to domination, and back again.

"I'm certain."
"They love me!"
"Get over it."
"It's obvious."
"My work is done."
"This is the way."
"I'm the expert."
"Not unless I say... Oh, whatever."

These are the thoughts running through the minds of leaders who are willing to destroy their organizations, and sometimes even themselves, before letting go of the need to be right. It's easy to say we'd stay out of these leadership traps. It's easy to say we'd never be like Rona, Pontius Pilate, King Lear—or William Jay, who died maintaining his right of way.

But I have to admit: If I could see the thought bubbles over my head as I go through my week, I know I'd often see one of those eight phrases floating there.

The Prince, Niccolò Machiavelli's famous manual for leaders, sheds light on what drives change and what impedes it, and this is where we go next.

part II

POLITICS

Now we turn to more specific questions of leadership. Part II is about politics: the arena of plots and power plays, steep rises and equally steep downfalls. We'll explore the topics of change, justice, power, authority, and character.

Politics is a good place to begin an investigation of leadership practices, given that one can't be in a leadership role for half a day without running into some type of political challenge. No matter what your sphere, political issues will present themselves and will potentially make or break you as a leader. Politics is the very air leaders breathe.

In recent decades it has become fashionable for people at the top, even actual politicians, to declare that they "prefer to avoid politics" or that they "hate dealing with all the politics." But you won't hear the best leaders saying such things. Otto Von Bismarck, the Prussian imperial chancellor and diplomat who in 1871 unified most of the German states into one empire, called politics "the art of the possible." He might have said: A leader's job is to turn possibilities into actualities. We can eschew politics in favor of high ideals if we like, but ideals on their own don't make things happen. If the mission is actually to be accomplished, if the new land is actually to be reached, and if actual people are to be involved—which of course they always are—then leaders must master the sometimes messy but always necessary art of politics.

Many classic political works were written as how-to manuals for leaders. We'll begin with a look at the most famous of these, Niccolò Machiavelli's *The Prince*, and then travel some 1,900 years back to the seminal work of political philosophy, Plato's *The Republic*. Next come Sophocles' *Antigone* and Shakespeare's *Julius Caesar*, which are explorations of power, authority, the difference between the two, and the price paid by those in opposition. Finally, we'll look at some essays on leadership character by Winston Churchill, the great twentieth-century statesman who won a Nobel Prize in Literature for being, said the prize committee, "a Caesar who also has the gift of Cicero's pen."

great author

NICCOLÒ MACHIAVELLI'S *THE PRINCE*

> It should be considered that nothing is more difficult to handle, more doubtful of success, nor more dangerous to manage, than to put oneself at the head of introducing new orders.[1]

That statement sits at the heart of Niccolò Machiavelli's *The Prince*, at once the most famous and most infamous book of leadership advice ever written. Dedicated to Lorenzo de' Medici, a member of the cunning and powerful Medici family who ran Renaissance Florence, *The Prince* was regarded for several hundred years after its 1513 publication as a how-to book for tyrants, dripping with sinister advice. In recent decades, however, it has been defended as a work of supreme pragmatism: an unflinchingly honest examination of what works and what doesn't for a leader who wants to make and sustain big changes.

Given that "Machiavellian" is a word used only pejoratively (if ever) by today's management consultants, it's surprising to see that many of Machiavelli's ideas anticipate the very advice those consultants offer. Here are a few of *The Prince*'s maxims for would-be conquerors.

Get to know the people If you know little about the territory, it's best to go live there and make yourself accessible. Your subjects will know more about you, so they will have greater cause to like or at least respect you. Also, you'll be able to learn the customs of the country and check any disorder before it gets out of hand. Even better, bring some of your own most trusted people to live there, too, and help them blend in with the existing populace.

If you must act harshly, do it quickly If you notice discontent, address it right away; don't let problems continue in hopes of avoiding conflict. And it's better to get rid of rebellious lords altogether than to demote them and keep them around, for they won't forget the insult even if you're conciliatory later on. As for any necessary harsh actions, make sure they are done at a stroke and then quickly and obviously turned to utility for your subjects. Cruelties that grow with time are an invitation to mutiny.

Base your rule on competence and good intent It's best to acquire a principality through your own cleverness and virtue. Buying people's loyalty with money or threatening them with punishment will only take you so far. People will always mistrust anyone new, but the more competent you are and the more you act in your subjects' best interests, the more quickly you'll gain their trust and the more easily they'll accept the changes you install. If, on the other hand, you upset a lot of them and they grow to hate you, beware. You won't be around for long.

❀ *Read this in The Prince:* Chapters I–IX, XV–XIX, XXI, XXIII, *and* XXV.

chapter 3

CHANGE

Every leadership effort—whether it's launching a product, getting a team to embrace a different way of working, or helping one individual learn and grow—is about helping somebody move toward some sort of new reality. In these journeys leaders must go first and bring others along, which implies they must understand what makes people embrace or reject change.

THE CHALLENGE OF CHANGE

Machiavelli's *The Prince* has been described as the first treatment of politics as it is rather than as it should be. It is certainly the first to be utterly frank in its assumption that all rulers want to acquire power, and to explain how to do just that.

More important, *The Prince* explains how to *maintain* power, for much of it concerns the mistakes leaders make that get them kicked out on their ear, or more likely in Machiavelli's day, get their ears removed along with their head. "Making a change is hard," we might imagine him saying, "but sustaining a change is harder." Present-day change management gurus would agree—their research suggests that individuals are only persuaded to try a change if the promised state of affairs appears to them twice or thrice as good as the current state; moreover, studies show that on average, 50–70 percent of change initiatives fail in the long run.[2] If the status quo has a pull three times stronger than the new and if most change efforts end in a ditch, we must wonder why so many leaders embark on change initiatives with hardly more thought than if they were heading to the beach on a summer's day. Have we got the drinks cooler, umbrella, and towels? Do we have the address of the restaurant where we're having lunch so we can plug it into the GPS? Kids, no fighting in the back seat! Away we go!

Unfortunately, a little planning and a bit of firm direction are nowhere near enough to make change happen. Although some leaders wonder why their team can't simply get on board ("We're paying them, for goodness' sake"), Machiavelli was keenly aware that that sort of thinking is unhelpful. The fact is, change is hard and people rarely like it. Those who benefited from the old order naturally won't like the new, but on top of that, Machiavelli says, even the people who might benefit from the new order will be only lukewarm supporters, because, first, they fear revenge should the old guard return to power, and second, they can't really believe in a new regime until they have some actual experience of what it will do for them. Therefore, a leader seeking to bring about a major change must put enormous strategic effort into getting and sustaining buy-in, or at least acquiescence, from all involved. Unlike on a beach trip, you can't just throw everybody in the minivan and flip the childproof door locks.

From *The Prince*, we take away two keys to leading change successfully: knowing the Change Road and attending to people factors.

KNOWING THE CHANGE ROAD

The first thing a leader of a change must do is anticipate its stages. There's a pattern to change that predicts how a project will unfold, how a business will grow, how an industry will evolve, even how a civilization will rise or fall. Sometimes called the S-curve, this pattern has been studied by social scientists and belongs to that small group of contemporary leadership concepts that are truly illuminating (see "On tall shoulders: George Land on patterns of change"). Understanding it is like having a pair of binoculars that allows you to look down a road and see the landforms ahead; for that reason, I call the pattern the Change Road and refer to its five phases as terrains (see Figure 3.1). Anticipation and skillful management of these terrains—and of the *plateau*, in particular—are essential to a successful change effort.[3]

1. ***The start*** At the beginning of the road, enthusiasm is high. People anticipate an exciting journey and set out with good will.
2. ***The rapid ascent*** Assuming the leader has put at least some effort toward gaining buy-in, progress in the early days is fast and everyone feels a sense of momentum.

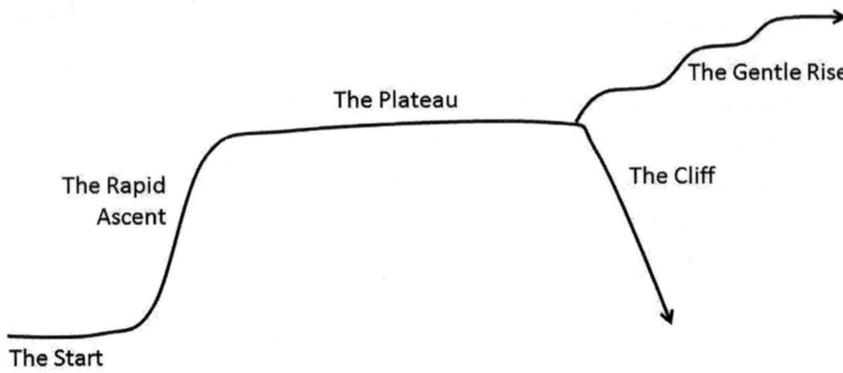

Figure 3.1 The Change Road

3. ***The plateau*** Here is where the pace slows and spirits dampen. Often unanticipated and misunderstood, the plateau is what kills most change initiatives.
4. ***The gentle rise or the cliff*** Some leaders know how to get off the plateau and onto a gentle rise where the gains of the initiative can be sustained over the long term. Others don't, and their initiatives will, eventually, plummet off the cliff.

"The nature of peoples is variable," says Machiavelli, "and it is easy to persuade them of something but difficult to keep them in that persuasion."[4] A leader must be ready, he adds, for the inevitable time when people "no longer believe." This is the plateau: flat, cold, barren, and long. It's when the initiative has become old hat, quarrels have broken out, and people are sick to death of hearing you talk about Customers First or The Power of One or whatever the big new thing is called. What do you do then? Tell everyone to put their head down and keep going? Strive to paint a more inspirational vision? Or perhaps simply drop the whole thing and move on to something new?

Machiavelli's advice is to be ready to "make them believe by force," which sounds unpleasant. If we read on, however, we find that he's talking about not just armed force but, more broadly, what one might call magnetic force: something substantial that will hold fast the wavering believers and draw in the unbelievers. (A "permanent sticking charm," as Harry Potter fans might say.) To illustrate that the strongest force for cementing belief is the leader's own virtue, or efficacy, Machiavelli tells the story of Hiero of Syracuse, a man of neither status nor fortune who gained and hung on to a crown purely through competence and careful cultivation of friends and allies. "[W]hen he had friendships and soldiers that were his own," Machiavelli says, "he could build any building on top of such a foundation."[5]

It's surprising to see such an emphasis on friendship coming from the author infamous for the phrase "better to be feared than loved," but Machiavelli seems well aware that the real "force" that will keep people moving through a period of waning belief is neither the threat of punishment nor an airy vision, but something much more positive and concrete: a belief in you, their leader, and in your intent to help them.

on tall shoulders

GEORGE LAND *on* PATTERNS OF CHANGE

George Land's *Grow or Die: The Unifying Principle of Transformation* was published in 1973. It's a book little known to the business world that nevertheless has had a profound effect on that world. Land's theories engendered many of the terms, images, and metaphors we use today to talk about strategic planning and change management.

The drive to *grow*, says Land, is the basis for natural processes—chemical, biological, psychological, and social—and gives rise to patterns common to all those arenas. At the heart of his transformation theory is the so-called S-curve, representing three phases of growth: experimentation, characterized by the attempt to gain a foothold in the environment; replication of success, characterized by fast growth; and finally reinvention, an opening up to new information, resources, or strategies that were rejected in the previous phases. Before Phases II and III is a breakpoint where the system makes the leap to the next phase (and continues to grow) or fails to do so (and dies).

Many leaders see change as either a quick jaunt or a smooth ride. George Land and Machiavelli know it is neither quick nor smooth but, rather, a long journey on a bumpy road.

Besides building loyalty early on, there's something else a leader can do to get people through the plateau: create milestones, and celebrate reaching each one while being very clear that the entire mission is not yet accomplished. Unaware of the importance of milestones, less effective leaders tend to make one of two errors on hitting the plateau: either they exhort their team to keep going, doing all the same tasks and using all the same approaches, or they decide the whole effort wasn't worthwhile after all, drop it, and move on to the next thing. Effective leaders, however, understand that aiming for a series of milestones provides people with constantly renewed focus and energy while maintaining their commitment to the ultimate goal. Not to mention, says Machiavelli with his usual bracing practicality, that pursuing a series of milestones keeps your subjects happily occupied so they won't have time to cook up plots against you.

One more thing to know about the Change Road: once you reach the gentle rise, you'll find that it, too, is a series of mini ascents and mini plateaus. If the gains of the change are to be sustained, you should think of your goal not as the destination where everyone comes to a permanent halt, but rather as the point beyond which you and your fellow travelers, made fit by the journey and grown accustomed to the climbs, will find it easy to keep going (see "Team tool: Anticipating change terrains").

ATTENDING TO PEOPLE FACTORS

The second key to leading change is recognizing that it's the "people factors" that matter most. Mapping out the change and lining up the necessary technologies and systems are important, of course, but not nearly as important as ensuring the support of those affected. I like to point to the unused paths on university campuses: campus administrators and their landscape architects put much effort into planning and installing lovely paved walkways that wind from building to building, but one look at the well-trod tracks cutting straight across the fields from the dorms to the dining hall tells you just how little power those administrators and architects have to keep students on the approved pathways. Similarly, leaders of organizations may issue flowcharts all day long, but if people don't *want* to do things the new way, gesturing more firmly toward the flowcharts isn't going to help.

This general point has been made so many times in leadership books and articles, one would think most managers by now would have accepted its validity and taken the advice to heart. In my experience, however, leaders of large-scale change initiatives still tend to show much more concern for how the new software is designed than for how people feel about the new software. Such managers may believe emotions are "soft" and therefore have no place in business or may worry about appearing insufficiently business-minded—that is, weak—should they be caught paying attention to how their subordinates *feel* about a change. The toughest manager in the world, however, need have no qualms about taking advice from Machiavelli, the original hard-ass. Let's see what he has to say about attending to people's feelings:

> Whoever believes that ... new benefits will make old injuries be forgotten deceives himself.[6]

> [A] prince should take little account of conspiracies if the people show good will toward him; but if they are hostile and bear hatred for him, he should fear everything and everyone.[7]

> For a prince it is necessary to have the people friendly; otherwise he has no remedy in adversity.[8]

> When a prince who founds on the people knows how to command and is a man full of heart ... and with his spirit and his orders keeps the generality of the people inspired, he ... will see he has laid his foundations well.[9]

What we learn from these and many other statements in *The Prince* is this: Subordinates' emotions, far from being soft and fluffy, are like a bristling array of swords that will either cut you down or back you up.

team tool

ANTICIPATING CHANGE TERRAINS

Select a change project, large or small, of which you are the leader.

Prepare for your next meeting with the project team by drawing the outline of the Change Road (see Figure 3.1) on a flipchart page or whiteboard (or, if the team is not co-located, on a slide or virtual whiteboard) and mentally noting the point on the road that you think the project has reached.

In the meeting, or over the course of several meetings:

1. Explain to the team the Change Road and its five terrains.
2. Ask each team member to mark on the diagram where he or she thinks the project is now.
3. Discuss the various opinions, and reach a consensus about the current terrain.
4. Discuss (a) likely problems and challenges for the project, given the current terrain; (b) things the team could do to mitigate those terrain-specific challenges; and (c) things the team could be doing now to prepare for upcoming terrains.

More than any other philosopher, Machiavelli understood the raw power of people's feelings, the imprudence of ignoring them, and the necessity of harnessing them to your advantage. When he talks about how one gains or loses people's support, his words are strong, almost violent: *love*, *hatred*, *hostility*, *injury*, *heart*, *deceit*. We may start to suspect that today's tough-minded business managers are right to roll their eyes at their consultants' advice to "build commitment" and "engage change agents." Such phrases do sound namby-pamby, but not because emotion is soft; on the contrary, it's because they don't do justice to the strength of emotion. Emotion can be a tidal wave that sweeps through a technocrat's tidy world of process and procedure and knocks it all flat in an instant. In the end, people's feelings about a change (and its leader) are what will propel it forward or send it over a cliff.

FASTTRACK GRINDS TO A HALT

Declaring victory too soon and ignoring people factors often go hand in hand, guaranteeing a failed change initiative. Consider the following example.

Arthur, an experienced operations and IT executive, was the recently hired COO for AmDel, a package-delivery and logistics company that operates within the United States. With the blessing of AmDel's CEO, Arthur set out to overhaul the company's transportation network and tracking systems. "With a modernized fleet of trucks, some new planes, and up-to-date tracking software, we'll be able to compete head to head with the global delivery companies," he enthused in his presentation to the management team. He dubbed the initiative FastTrack, and true to its name it got off to a blazing start. Within a few months, new trucks rolled up to the distribution centers and new handheld tracking devices were issued to every driver. Cameras and data recorders were installed in vehicles and warehouses. Each employee who handled packages went through an intensive training session, the centerpiece of which was Arthur's pride and joy: the FastTrack Manual, 500 shiny pages that mapped out every procedure, method, and step associated with the new processes.

Arthur extolled the improvements that would come from all the data flowing in. And, after six months, he was able to report some impressive results: a 10 percent reduction in late deliveries, for example. In month seven, he paid an outside media firm to produce a cinema-quality video touting FastTrack's success and thanking all AmDel employees for their support. A famous actor did the video's narration.

Around month nine, however, the improvements began to slow. Some even reversed. When the root causes were investigated, it turned out that the main problem was a steady increase in delivery truck breakdowns. Arthur and the executive team were mystified, until someone finally suggested they interview a few of the maintenance managers.

It turned out that Maintenance had been completely ignored in the FastTrack rollout; its staff had received no training and were never asked their opinion on any aspect of the changes. They went unmentioned in the thank-you video. Moreover, of the oceans of capital spending, not one cent had gone into upgrading the systems that affected their work. As a consequence, the entire maintenance staff now assumed that their contributions weren't valued, and their morale was at an all-time low. They had pretty much stopped bothering to look for or report warning signs of impending mechanical problems; they simply waited until a truck broke down and then fixed it.

Arthur immediately embarked on a "listening tour" to hear from Maintenance and a few other groups that, it turned out, had also been overlooked. But as he read over the transcripts of the interviews, he had a sense that it was too little, too late. One maintenance worker's statement said it all: "The trucks break, I fix the trucks. That's what you're paying me for."

We can condense Arthur's story and Machiavelli's advice into two critical principles for change leaders: Understand the phases of change, and attend to people factors more than technical factors. Even more critical, however, are these two principles' negative corollaries: Don't announce "Mission accomplished" when you're only halfway up the first hill. And don't sit in your tent drawing flowcharts while emotions simmer away in the camp outside.

Next we ask ourselves: What is justice? Plato's *The Republic* offers answers to this not so easy question.

great author
PLATO'S *THE REPUBLIC*

In *The Republic*, Socrates, Plato's teacher and famous "gadfly" of Athens, asks: "What is justice?" While modern readers might expect a discussion about criminal law, Socrates has something much broader in mind. He wants to know the best way for human beings to live and work together, and he leads his friends into a far-ranging conversation about government, societal structures, and leadership practices.

As *The Republic* opens, Socrates and a companion are leaving downtown Athens when they are stopped by their acquaintance Polemarchus, who invites them to his house. There they find Polemarchus's friends and brothers along with his father, Cephalus. Socrates is eager to talk philosophy with anyone willing, and soon finds himself in a discussion with Cephalus about the meaning of justice. Cephalus says that justice is giving back what you've taken, but Socrates cites the case of a madman who, clearly, shouldn't be given back the weapons you borrowed from him. Justice, Socrates says, must be something else.

Polemarchus says that justice is giving to each what is owed, which translates to helping friends (who presumably deserve help) and harming enemies (who presumably deserve harm). Socrates rejects this definition too, noting that when people are harmed they become less virtuous. Justice is aimed at making people better, not worse, he says, so justice can't consist of harming anyone, even enemies.

Polemarchus's friend Thrasymachus now bursts into the conversation. "Wake up, Socrates," he says. "Justice is the advantage of the stronger." A city's rulers set down laws to their advantage, he continues, and those laws are what everyone calls justice. Socrates takes Thrasymachus's argument apart by pointing out that good rulers actually work for the advantage of the ruled, in the same way that good doctors work for the advantage of the patient.

Thrasymachus becomes even angrier and says no, what he meant was that injustice is more profitable than justice. Socrates counters by showing that injustice creates faction, discord, and failure among groups and even within individual souls, while justice creates harmony, strength, and efficacy; therefore, he says, "the just soul and the just man will have a good life, and the unjust man a bad one" (sect. 331a).[1] Whether profitable means the same thing as good—an interesting issue for today's business leaders—is a question left for later in the conversation.

✯ *Read this in The Republic: Book I, which is a capsule version of the entire dialogue.*[2]

chapter 4
JUSTICE

Brown or tufted capuchins are small primates with rough fur, a short thick tail, and black hands and feet. They live in and around the Amazon River Basin. Known for their social and cooperative ways, these creatures were selected for a study performed in 2003 at the Yerkes National Primate Research Center in order to see whether some non-human animals might have a sense of fairness.[3]

In the study, capuchins were placed in pairs and trained to give a small rock to a human handler in exchange for a piece of cucumber. After a period of reliably consistent rock-cucumber swapping, the handlers revised the deal: now, if one capuchin handed over a rock, they gave both it and its partner some cucumber, even if the partner had done nothing. Sometimes they would even give the partner a grape—which to a capuchin is like getting a significant pay raise. On witnessing slackers getting the same rewards as they were or better, the wronged capuchins showed striking reactions: they refused to work (no more passing of rocks), rejected their pay (no more eating of cucumbers), and aired their grievances (flinging of cucumber bits at the handlers' heads). In short, they preferred revenge without rewards to unjustly distributed rewards.

This study, along with several others of primates and their responses to "unfair" treatment, suggests that a sense of justice is not just an artifact of human culture or convention but something embedded, touchily, in our animal brain. Leaders tread on people's sense of justice at their peril. If an aggrieved monkey hurls food, what might an aggrieved human do?

JUSTICE IS RENDERING WHAT IS DUE

Some leaders recognize the importance of justice but nevertheless take a simplistic approach to the whole issue. They think they know what it means to be just: they must give people what's owed them under the rules and contracts to which everyone has agreed.

They're like the leaders I mentioned in the previous chapter, who, when advised to build their team's buy-in to a change, reply impatiently, "But we're paying them." Think of Don Draper, in the television series *Mad Men*, who responds to an employee's complaint that he never says thank-you with "That's what the money is for!" Such leaders are like a slime-flecked handler trying to talk sense into a sulky capuchin: "I gave you a bit of cucumber in exchange for the rock, exactly as we agreed, so what's your problem? So what if Buster got a free grape?"

For finding out what justice really is and why it matters so much to us, there is no better guide than Plato's *The Republic*, the first work of political philosophy and to many minds still the best. The book consists of one long conversation between Socrates, the famous teacher of ancient Athens, and a group of his friends and followers. Their aim is to understand what justice is and why it is better to be just than unjust.

The stage is set when Socrates and his friends make a visit to the home of Cephalus, father of one of the young men in the group. Socrates asks Cephalus to describe what life is like at his advanced age: Is it a hard time, or not? And what makes old age easy or hard? Cephalus, with some prompting from Socrates, admits that wealth makes it much easier to have a pleasant old age, but he adds that it is not the money itself that makes the difference; rather, having money makes it easier to avoid committing injustices. These, he says, are the chief cause of unhappiness at the end of life:

> Now, the man who finds many unjust deeds in his life often even wakes from his sleep in a fright as children do, and lives in anticipation of evil. To the man who is conscious in himself of no unjust deed, sweet and good hope is ever beside him. (354a)

As he continues his musings, Cephalus equates injustice with cheating, lying, and failing to pay what is owed. Socrates quickly picks up on this assumption and uses it as an occasion to pose the central question of the dialogue: "What is justice?" Justice can't be simply telling the truth and paying one's debts, he says, offering the example of someone who borrows weapons from a friend. If the friend goes violently insane and then demands the weapons back, obviously you don't hand them over. That's a silly example, we might think, but actually it goes to the heart of the matter: justice can't be defined as sticking to the letter of contracts and laws, because we can always think of special circumstances, often having to do with the character or intentions of the people in question, that would demand a more flexible interpretation of the contracts and laws touching us and them. As the dialogue continues, we see Socrates encouraging his friends to explore a broader idea of justice, something more like "rendering what is due."

The Republic unpacks the unexpectedly complex idea of *what is due* to different groups, different individuals, and even different parts of oneself. For present-day leaders, the key point to grasp is that although we might adhere to all company policies and honor all contracts, if we don't give people their due—that is, what is owed them given their character and the circumstances—we'll be perceived as unjust. "Sounds unfair to the leader," you might say, "and after all, shouldn't a leader be impartial?" Maybe so, but "I treated everyone impartially and according to company policy" will never hold up as a defense against accusations of injustice. On the contrary, leaders who deviate from policy *when the situation calls for it* are the ones whom we tend to hold up as exemplars of justice.

Consider how the big life insurance companies in the United States reacted to the events of 9/11. Soon after the planes hit the buildings, writes Robert Gandossy in the *Journal of Business Strategy*,[4] some of the companies issued statements reminding their customers of the war exclusion clause (that deaths caused by acts of war are not covered is a standard element of insurance policies), and most of them stuck to their standard claims process: wait for a claim to be submitted, request a death certificate and other documentation, analyze the claim, and pay if appropriate. One company, however, behaved differently. Before noon on September 11, Northwestern Mutual announced that it would not invoke the war exclusion clause and would accept non-standard forms of confirmation of death.

Moreover, rather than wait for customers to contact the company, Northwestern began processing claims proactively, using flight manifests and employee lists to determine the families who had suffered a loss. The industry average time to pay a claim is 30 days; in the aftermath of 9/11, Northwestern processed 157 claims in 5 days. There was nothing standard about how it handled the situation. Instead, its staff based their actions on what they thought they owed their customers in those special circumstances. Several years later, they were still being cited in the press as an admirable example of fair dealing.

How should a leader think about what is due to his or her team members? The key is to think beyond the money or rank owed to someone based on their performance rating or seniority. Handling money and rank unfairly may certainly offend an employee's sense of justice, but most of the time, justice is about intangibles: Does Alison deserve to be heard on this point? Ought I give Rowan the benefit of the doubt in this case? How much of my time and attention do I owe the team in Beijing? Has Carmela earned this assignment, and is it a good fit for her? Should I reply to Gunther's question with an email or a phone call? Neither perusing employment contracts nor knowing salary bands would help you make those sorts of decisions, but a well-developed sense of justice might.

By the end of Book I, Socrates and his friends have had a deep conversation about two questions: What is justice? Is the just person happier than the unjust? Both of these serve to expand our view of the issue. We may start out, with Cephalus, seeing justice as a simple matter of telling the truth and paying one's debts (that is, refraining from lying, cheating, or stealing), but eventually we come to understand it as something much broader, something we might describe as "the proper arrangement and management of a community or organization whereby everyone behaves and is treated in a fitting way, resulting in success for all." That's a tall order for a leader; much harder than paying people's salaries on time and turning over any contractual disputes to Legal. But then, leadership is not for those who want an easy life.

JUSTICE IS INDIVIDUAL

Notice, also, the words that people use when they talk about justice and injustice: "I expected more from you." "She, of all people, deserves better." "He had it coming." "I owe my success to you."

Justice is about individuals. People's complaints of injustice don't generally focus on how senior management, that faceless blob, failed to apply policy correctly or made a decision contrary to the good of the company. Grievances tend, rather, to sound like this: "*That* person treated *me* (or *him*, or *her*) unfairly." Even when the issue is one that affects an entire organization, such as blowing the whistle on a major ethics infraction or negotiating a union–management dispute, people typically talk about injustice in personal terms: somebody is being wronged, and the wrongdoers are low-down cheats who deserve to be pelted with rotten tomatoes (or pieces of cucumber, if you're a capuchin). For a leader, therefore, defining general rules and applying them without undue bias, though important, is only the beginning of justice. Stop there, and you'll end up treating individuals unjustly—or at least, the individuals will see it that way. Full justice means understanding individuals' strengths, weaknesses, histories, and relationships with you and others, and treating them accordingly; with *due* bias, if you will (see "Communication tool: How do they want to be treated?").

Most modern Western societies are highly egalitarian in outlook, if not always in practice, and even in hierarchical organizations the view that "everyone is the same and the same rules apply to everyone" tends to prevail. While Western leaders easily accept wage and title differences based on performance evaluations and length of tenure, both of which are thought to be fair yardsticks, they have a harder time accepting the idea that people's different talents, contributions, and vulnerabilities may cause them to deserve different treatment. Management consultants, too, have until recently been unanimous in their advice that leaders should apply the same standards and policies to all subordinates lest they be seen as unfair. Marcus Buckingham and Curt Coffman, authors of *First, Break All the Rules*, were the first consultants to adopt, perhaps unknowingly, a more Platonic version of justice and to advocate applying it in the workplace (see "On tall shoulders: Marcus Buckingham on breaking the golden rule").[5]

communication tool

HOW DO THEY WANT TO BE TREATED?

If you're a good leader, you break the golden rule all the time: instead of treating others as you would like to be treated, you treat others as *they* would like to be treated.

Asking your people about their goals, preferences, and needs is one of the easiest ways to improve as a leader. Plenty of management books provide templates for such conversations, but the exact questions aren't important; what is important is simply that you ask, and listen to the answers. Here are a few to begin with:

- What would you like to be doing a year from now? In five years?
- Think about the day at work in the past three months when you felt you were performing at your best. What were you doing? What did it feel like?
- What things can you consistently do well? Where do you consistently struggle?
- How do you like your good work to be recognized? What kinds of reward are most meaningful to you? What kinds are not meaningful?
- What types of behavior or treatment make you especially angry or frustrated?
- What kinds of help do you need and appreciate from me? What help do you not need or appreciate?

on tall shoulders

MARCUS BUCKINGHAM *on* BREAKING THE GOLDEN RULE

In *First, Break All the Rules* and *Now, Discover Your Strengths*, Marcus Buckingham argues that the best managers don't try to treat everyone the same; instead, they revel in individuality.

These managers know how to capitalize on each employee's strengths—or, to put it another way, how to give to and demand from each employee what is fitting. Buckingham's books are filled with stories of managers who masterfully suit the person to the role and the role to the person, sometimes bending policy so that someone with definite talents but equally definite weaknesses can make the greatest possible contribution to the enterprise. "Everyone is exceptional," says Buckingham, which means both that everyone has unique strengths and that everyone will demand different things of a manager. "The best managers reject the Golden Rule. Instead, they say, treat each person as *he* would like to be treated, bearing in mind who he is."[6]

This doesn't mean, of course, that leaders should blithely ignore rules, but it does mean that appropriate flexibility is sometimes the essence of fairness, not to mention the key to team success.

One of the more extreme yet brilliant examples offered by Buckingham and Coffman focuses on "Marie S.," the head of a property insurance agency who had to deal with an agent who was tremendously productive but also tremendously egotistical. Every time Agent Ego (you know the type) was in the office, he would roam around running his mouth and driving his colleagues crazy. Most managers, trying to be "fair," would have lectured him about company values or perhaps sent him along with the entire staff to a teambuilding class. But this staff didn't need to work as a team, and this agent wasn't messing up projects or customer relationships; he was simply a pain. Marie's solution was to cut a new door in his office wall opening onto the external hallway and put his name on it in gold lettering. As Buckingham and Coffman write, "With one stroke she not only fulfilled his ego needs, she also diverted him directly into his office and away from his negative wanderings."[7] Was it unfair that he got a golden nameplate while nobody else did? Maybe. But Marie knew that nobody else in the agency cared about nameplates. They were, however, delighted that Agent Ego was out of their hair.

One of the hallmarks of totalitarian states is their emphasis on sweeping ideas about "social justice" and their utter disregard for individual differences. I once saw a photograph of some mass games put on in North Korea in celebration of a national holiday. The image consisted of about 200 teenaged girls, standing row upon row, identically dressed, with identical posture and expression; they even seemed to be all the same height and weight. The effect was chilling.

By the end of Book VII of *The Republic*, Plato has given us a picture of exactly that sort of state, a picture that results from Socrates' relentless drive to flesh out the nature of a perfectly just society—if "perfectly just" is taken to mean "no special treatment of individuals." He paints a picture of a city-state where everyone is treated exactly the same, where the good of the community is the only good, and where social policy reigns supreme. The argument becomes a *reductio ad absurdum*, for it is plain that no one would wish to live or work in such a horribly unjust, tyrannical place as the "perfectly just" city that Socrates conjures up. In fact, the realization of such a city would be impossible, as it would have to eliminate or deny most of the relationships and goals that human beings care about. Clearly, for Plato, something is deeply wrong with that particular version of justice.

For today's leaders, then, what does it mean to be just? Some of us will get by with the light-hearted approach of Cephalus, who avoids outright lying, cheating, and stealing and sleeps soundly at night as a result. Some of us will aim a little higher and earn a reputation for applying company rules and policies impartially. But the only leaders who will be praised as truly fair-minded are those who strive for a kind of justice that is at once sounder and more flexible: the kind whereby individuals get what they (truly) deserve.

Leaders need power to accomplish their goals, but the pursuit of power can backfire, as we see in the next chapter.

great author
SOPHOCLES' *ANTIGONE*

Other dramatic works may portray the dilemmas and pitfalls of leadership more thoroughly or with more nuance than *Antigone*, but none as concisely or with such agonizing emotion.

Antigone, daughter of Oedipus, is a noblewoman of the city-state of Thebes. When her brothers Eteocles and Polyneices kill each other in a battle for the city (the first defending, the second attacking), the recently crowned King Creon refuses to bury Polyneices, calling him a traitor to his home and family, hence undeserving of the last rites. Creon sets sentries around the body. Polyneices will be carrion.

Antigone, believing that Creon's judgment goes against divine law, decides to bury Polyneices' body herself. She reveals her intention to her sister, Ismene, who begs her not to risk being executed for defying the king's order, but Antigone says she prefers death to participation in the shame and evil of leaving her brother unburied. When Creon catches Antigone in the act, he sentences her to be walled up alive in a cave. Creon's son Haemon, who is engaged to be married to Antigone, makes a plea for leniency, pointing out that the people of Thebes are on her side and accusing his father of blind stubbornness. The city elders weigh in, backing Haemon and expressing pity for the princess, but Creon insists that his judgments are correct and refuses to listen. With each rejection of counsel he increases his isolation from his family, advisers, and subjects and hastens his own demise. By the time the prophet Teiresias convinces Creon to change his mind and reverse the sentence on Antigone, it is too late. The damage is done.

Creon seems to think that a ruler's power lies essentially in the ability to kill or otherwise erase troublesome people. When Antigone asks, "Do you want anything beyond my taking and execution?" he replies, "Oh, nothing! Once I have that I have everything" (line 542).[1] It's an ancient error, and one that modern leaders—who usually can't order executions but can crush subordinates in other ways—would do well to avoid. For if all a king can accomplish is to destroy his subjects (and this is, in fact, all that Creon achieves in the play), how much power does he really have?

chapter 5
POWER

While Socrates was talking philosophy with the future leaders of Athens, Sophocles was writing dramas for their entertainment. He based his play *Antigone* on an ancient Greek myth; French playwright Jean Anouilh created a modern adaptation in 1944. We could look at many of the leadership questions in this book through the eyes of Antigone, who defies King Creon's command to leave her brother's body unburied outside the walls of Thebes. The play is especially insightful on the question of *power*: what it is, how a leader ought to use it, and what happens when a leader abuses it—or perhaps just misunderstands it.

POWER IS THE ABILITY TO ACCOMPLISH WORK

Leaders generally dislike talking about power, let alone admitting that they seek it. Today, any prominent leader who replied to the question "Why did you pursue this position?" with "Because I wanted power!" would risk being booted out of said position, or at least would be required to issue an extensive apology in the media. Power has a bad reputation, and rightly so: when we look at the pain and suffering that have been inflicted to various degrees down the ages by people in power, from the Spanish Inquisition of the sixteenth century to the Holocaust of the twentieth to the financial meltdowns of the twenty-first, we must acknowledge that leaders who lack a healthy distrust of power often wield it in terrible ways. We should be grateful that naked grabs for power are seen in more and more regions and cultures as unacceptable, and grateful that this disapproval serves as something of a deterrent to the abuse of power. An even more effective deterrent, however, is the knowledge of what power really is. Leaders who have a good understanding of the true nature of power are both less likely to abuse it and, ironically, more likely to gain and maintain it.

I say less likely to abuse it, but of course, there are leaders who understand power very well, amass much of it, and choose to employ it for evil ends. This, however, is relatively unusual. It is far more common to see (or to be) a leader whose intentions are good, but who, in failing to grasp the nature and workings of power, becomes the proverbial bull in the china shop. In any case, convincing my readers not to pursue evil ends is beyond my own power as a writer. I must stick to a more modest task: clarifying what power is and how it is acquired.[2]

The word *power* comes from the Latin *posse*, meaning "to be able." Its first definition in the *Oxford English Dictionary* is "to do or effect something, or to act on a person or thing." We tend to think of power this way when we talk about it as the muscular power lifting a weight or the electrical power driving an engine. In the physical realm, power is simply the ability to accomplish work: to make something happen or change or move. And by that definition, the leader with real power—let's call it productive power—is not the one with a big title or a big staff, but the one who can get big things done (see "On tall shoulders: Dale Carnegie on power for all"). But when we turn from muscles and electricity to leadership and politics, we often grow confused, mixing up the idea of power with the idea of status.

It is true that status often boosts power. People tend to go along with commands given by those who outrank them; when we look at one of the pyramids of ancient Egypt, erected not because ten thousand slaves willed it but because one pharaoh did, it's obvious that a person who sits at the top of a pyramid-shaped organizational hierarchy can typically accomplish more work than a person who sits at the bottom of that pyramid. And desire for status and desire for power often go hand in hand, which can lead us to conflate the two. Even so, *status* is nothing more than the ability to issue directions to people and count on their superficial acquiescence. It is a mistake to equate status with productive power, which is present only when others don't just smile and nod, but strive to carry out your intent.[3]

on tall shoulders
DALE CARNEGIE on POWER FOR ALL

Simply type "How to" into the search field on the Amazon.com home page (or "How to win" into Google) and the first suggestion that pops up is *How to Win Friends and Influence People*. Eighty years after it was first published, Dale Carnegie's classic self-help book ranks #1 in the communication and leadership categories and well within the top 1,000 books on Amazon as a whole.

Carnegie's genius lay in combining two long-standing formats: the advice manual for aristocrats looking to govern a state and the etiquette book for average Joes and Janes looking to rise in society. He thereby announced that anybody, not only fat cats, can wield real power in the world. How to do it? Not by throwing your weight around, but by winning others over. Among the "Twelve Things the Book Will Do for You," writes Carnegie, are "Help you to win people to your way of thinking" and "Increase your influence, your prestige, your ability to get things done."

That last phrase, along with Carnegie's evident fondness for engineering terms, makes me think he might have approved of my definition of power: *the ability to accomplish work.*

A PROCLAMATION LACKING POWER

In the play *Antigone*, King Creon confuses his status, which no one disputes, with his power, which someone does. That someone is Antigone, a princess of Thebes who is soon to become Creon's daughter-in-law. When Creon proclaims that Polyneices, Antigone's brother and the commander of an army that attacked Thebes, is to be treated as befits a dead traitor and left to rot on the battlefield, he is absolutely certain that his edict is correct, that he has the right to issue it, and that anyone who disobeys it will deserve death. "Such is my mind in the matter; never by me shall the wicked man have precedence in honor over the just," he says (line 225). Creon also assumes that the only reason anyone could have for defying his orders is a base one: greed. At the end of his first speech, when the city elders insist that no one would be foolish enough to earn death by disobeying the king's command, Creon drily points out that people have been known to do ruinously foolish things for the sake of money. He can imagine a greedy person flouting the proclamation for a bribe; he can also imagine a heedless person having missed the proclamation altogether. What he cannot imagine is a well-intentioned, diligent person knowingly defying the proclamation in the sincere belief that it is wrong.

When Antigone, having made an attempt to bury Polyneices with the proper rites, is brought before him, Creon—like Lear—is thrown for a loop by his kinswoman's recalcitrance:

> CREON ... Now, Antigone, tell me shortly and to the point, did you know the proclamation against your action?
>
> ANTIGONE I knew it; of course I did. For it was public.
>
> CREON And did you dare to disobey that law?
>
> ANTIGONE Yes, it was not Zeus that made the proclamation; nor did Justice, which lives with those below, enact such laws as that, for mankind. I did not believe your proclamation had such power to ... override God's ordinances. (490–499)

If Creon is shocked at Antigone's "insolence" in breaking the law ("the established laws," as he puts it, implying that an executive order issued by him the day before is equivalent to a great body of legislation built up over time), he is still more shocked that she doesn't try to deny her action; indeed, she defends it. He can't comprehend that a subordinate might genuinely adhere to an idea of the good that is different from his own. Instead, he sees her attitude as pure arrogance: "She boasts of it, laughs at what she did," he says incredulously (527).

Creon's attitude is reminiscent not only of King Lear, but also of Thrasymachus in *The Republic* (see Chapter 4). Like Thrasymachus, Creon believes that justice and the ruler's will are one and the same. Since Antigone is following a version of justice different from the king's will, she must be unjust, a traitor deserving of death. As the play continues and we see other individuals, including Creon's own family members, begin to question and defy his decisions while he forges ahead with Antigone's execution, we can see he has mixed up three different things: first, what he *ought* to do (his duty); second, what his position gives him the *right* to do (his authority); and third, what he can *actually* do or make happen (his power). These things may be the same for a leader, sometimes; but they aren't necessarily the same.

By the end, Creon's wife, son, and son's fiancée are dead and the people of Thebes have turned against him. It emerges that Antigone was right about at least one thing: there was no real power in his proclamation. In fact, it has been his undoing. A self-described "vain silly man," he asks his servants to lead him away.

THE KING'S PARADOX

Creon, like many leaders after him, was caught in the King's Paradox (see Figure 5.1). This phenomenon was described by nineteenth-century German philosopher G.W.F. Hegel, who called it the "master and slave problem." The gist of the paradox is this: The more a master (ruler, leader) treads down his slaves (subjects, employees), asserting dominance over them and seeking to control what they do, the more weak, indecisive, and unimpressive they become, until, finally, the master is nothing more than a "master of slaves"; that is, first among the weak, indecisive, and unimpressive. As attempted dominance rises, actual power falls.

You can find a modern example by looking around your own organization for the biggest bully of a manager, who typically has the most dysfunctional and ineffective team. This sort of leader, unable to bear the thought of subordinates outshining him or her, not only fails to empower the team but goes so far as to squelch its talent, wreck its harmony, and undermine its plans. Leaders, as we saw in Chapter 1, don't stand alone; their power consists of the ability to accomplish work with and through others. The leader with a mess of a team, then, is the least powerful leader around (see "Assessment tool: How powerful are you, really?").

assessment tool

HOW POWERFUL ARE YOU, REALLY?

Use this assessment to get a sense of your current level of productive power. Where a rating is from 1 to 10, 10 is high.

A. Number of people you have mentored and who would credit you, in part, for their professional achievements (0–20): ___

B. Average annual performance rating of all your team members (1–10): ___

C. Average level of team member commitment to team goals and projects (1–10): ___

D. Percentage of projects you lead that are completed on time and achieve the results intended (10–100%; divide percentage by 10 to get an integer 1–10): ___

E. Rating of how well your team collaborates compared with other teams in the organization (1–10): ___

F. Number of "executive decisions" you make each month over the objections of your team (0–10); now make that a negative number: -___

G. Number of people who have chosen to quit an organization while reporting directly to you (0–20); now make that a negative number: -___

Key

Total your score, being sure to subtract, not add, the numbers for F and G.

-26–5 You have hardly any productive power.
6–15 You have a small amount of productive power.
16–25 You have a moderate amount of productive power.
26–50 You have a great deal of productive power.
51–60 You're likely overestimating yourself and your team. (Ask a team member or two to provide you with more objective power ratings.)

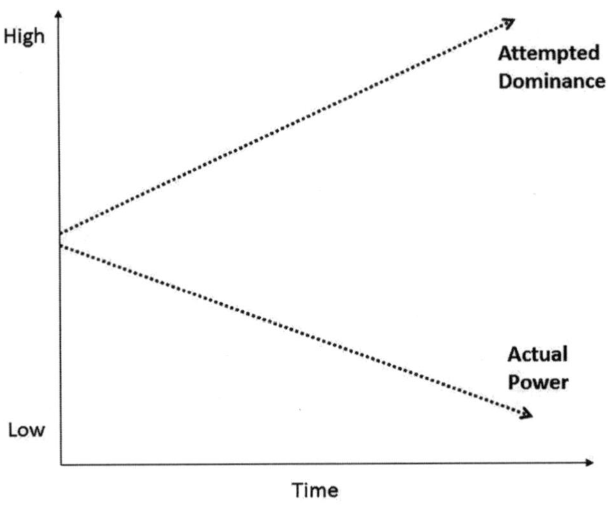

Figure 5.1 The King's Paradox

Here's a contemporary example of the King's Paradox. Kyle and Robert were co-directors of the Malory Institute, a London-based thinktank focused on educational policy that offered a variety of research services, publications, and conferences to subscribers. A few years back, the institute's founder (a theoretical sort with no interest in managing the place) had appointed the two to joint leadership positions because of their complementary skill sets: Kyle held a doctorate in education and was in charge of the institute's research and content, while Robert, with an MBA, had authority over marketing activities. They started out working cooperatively enough, but the seeds of conflict were sown when Robert asked for control over the schedule for Malory's flagship publication, a quarterly journal called *Lyceum International*. "It's critical from a marketing standpoint that we have *LI* to distribute at our semi-annual conferences," Robert said in an executive meeting, "and due to slow editorial approvals, we didn't have it at the last one." Kyle reluctantly agreed to allow Robert "some input" into the schedule for *LI*, but insisted on retaining absolute control over its content. Nothing was said about the firm's other publications.

Thus began a swift descent into dysfunction on both sides of the house. Research associates started to receive weekly emails from

Robert demanding to know when their article for Newsletter X or Bulletin Y was going to be done. When they contacted Kyle to ask for his signoff, they'd get an earful about how it was he, not Robert, who was in charge of content and how he wouldn't approve the article unless numerous changes were made. Robert then decided to "recategorize" several of the institute's publications as marketing collateral; he directed his staff to set a schedule for those pieces and to send them out on time, with or without editorial approval. When one unfortunate associate hit "Send" on a newsletter that turned out to contain some faulty data, Kyle called her into his office and yelled for a good ten minutes. Within a matter of months, the entire staff was in a state of paralysis. The next issue of *LI* came out three months late, the blog and newsfeeds were riddled with errors, and two senior writers simply stopped writing. Subscriber complaints went through the roof, and a grant that supplied half the institute's funding was not renewed.

FEAR OF TREACHERY

Although it would be easy to blame fuzzy lines of authority for the Malory Institute debacle, the real issue was the co-directors' failure to see that, as they were clawing their way out the line of attempted dominance (see Figure 5.1), their actual power was sinking. Of course, if you ask leaders like Kyle and Robert what they're trying to do, they will say, along with Creon, that they are simply "upholding high standards" or "insisting on what's good for the organization." And, fair enough: as leaders, they are in charge. It is their job to make certain decisions and see that those decisions are carried out, to set certain standards and enforce them. Who knows, perhaps Creon is right to make an example of Polyneices, who did after all lead an attack on his home city and kill his own brother in battle.

But Creon's mistake lies not in issuing an edict and expecting obedience to it, nor even in punishing someone who disobeys. Rather, his mistake lies in the belief that any challenge to that edict, any questions as to its rightness or arguments for another plan, are to be interpreted as direct attacks on his authority, or treachery.

This belief causes him to hear the words of Antigone, whose intent in burying her brother has nothing to do with toppling Creon, as if they were the war cry of an enemy. It causes him to hear his son Haemon's report that the people of the city are backing Antigone as if it were news of a mutiny: "Should the city tell me how I am to rule them?" he huffs. Leaders such as Creon have tucked away in their mind, if not in their desk, "a long list of traitors who don't understand" (to quote a lyric by pop star Taylor Swift). It is a list of those who questioned orders, who talked back, who showed a distressing tendency to act according to their own best judgment. The threat of such "treachery" keeps these leaders in near-constant terror that their orders will not be carried out; that their power will be diminished, even destroyed.

Note that one doesn't have to be power mad to think this way. One just has to be ignorant of what power is and, consequently, susceptible to the King's Paradox. True power lies in having truly powerful—that is, efficacious—people who are willing to follow you. Leaders who fail to understand this fact will try to build their own power by suppressing that of others. They will see signs of growing power in a subordinate as a reason to stamp down harder. And they will keep moving farther out along the attempted dominance line while the actual power line, unseen through a red haze of frustration, drops lower and lower.

An understanding of power's essence tells us that we should use our power as leaders to build the power (or efficacy) of our people, for in so doing we will not only avoid power's abuses but also gain and maintain productive power for ourselves. Of course, this isn't just a matter of puffing your people up and letting them fly; like balloons you've inflated but failed to knot, they'll only hurtle around making offensive noises before collapsing in rubbery heaps on the floor. There's an art to developing and channeling the power of others so that it's put to good use and sustained over time without leading to disorder or rebellion. (Machiavelli has much to say about this art; see Chapter 3.) But leaders should begin with the simple yet profound words of advice that Haemon, Creon's son, offers his father:

Do not bear this single habit of mind, to think
that what you say and nothing else is true.
A man who thinks that he alone is right,
or what he says, or what he is himself,
unique, such men, when opened up, are seen
to be quite empty. For a man, though he be wise,
it is no shame to learn—learn many things ...
Yield something of your anger, give way a little. (760-774)

In the next chapter, two Roman rulers and their violent demises teach us where authority comes from and what triggers mutiny.

great author
WILLIAM SHAKESPEARE'S *JULIUS CAESAR*

Julius Caesar is king of Rome in all but name, and a group of senators—including the cynical Cassius, the treacherous Casca, and even the conscientious Brutus, whose dreams of restoring the Roman Republic have shaken his loyalty to his dearest friend—are plotting against him. Although Caesar three times rejects the crown that Marc Antony offers him in front of the throng at the public games, Cassius persuades the others that Caesar secretly aspires to be emperor and must be killed in the name of freedom. The conspirators fix the date as the "ides of March." Despite dark omens and the pleas of his wife to stay home, Caesar goes to the Senate on that day, is attacked in the hall, and dies of 13 stab wounds. His last words are: *Et tu, Brute*? ("You also, Brutus?")

The killers don't have long to celebrate Rome's liberation. Antony, whose life Brutus and Cassius have spared in hopes he will join their cause, uses his impressive oratorical skills to rouse the people, reminding them of Caesar's virtues and hinting at the piles of money left to the people in his will, all the while claiming he has no wish, no, none at all, to criticize the assassins—"for Brutus is an honorable man." The anarchy that Antony unleashes is crystallized in the third scene of Act III, in which an innocent man is mistaken by the mob for one of the conspirators and murdered no less viciously than Caesar:

> FIRST PLEBEIAN Tear him to pieces! He's a conspirator!
> CINNA I am Cinna the poet! I am Cinna the poet!
> FOURTH PLEBEIAN Tear him for his bad verses! Tear him for his bad verses!
> CINNA I am not Cinna the conspirator.
> THIRD PLEBEIAN Tear him, tear him!

Acts IV and V show us the struggle for that same crown Caesar rejected. Antony joins and then falls out with Octavius, Caesar's great-nephew and adopted son; Brutus joins and then falls out with Cassius. The battles and quarrels rage on, until it becomes clear who will be Rome's emperor.

✾ *Read this in Julius Caesar: Acts III, IV, and V (aftermath of the assassination)*

chapter 6

AUTHORITY

Leaders need power, but power by itself is not enough. Leaders also need authority, which is the legitimate right to rule or judge. For example, a mob may have the power to execute a convicted criminal, but only a court of law has the authority to do so. Power is the might, authority is the right.

POWER AND AUTHORITY ARE SOLD SEPARATELY

Think of power and authority as two circles in a Venn diagram. Leaders with plenty of power but no authority are strongmen or con artists; they can push people around or use charm to get their way, but sooner or later they are exposed as illegitimate—and toppled (see "On tall shoulders: Frank Abagnale on power without authority"). Leaders with plenty of authority but no power, on the other hand, are figureheads; they may have big titles, but they can't get much done, so their rule, too, is shaky. As a leader, you want to be in the overlapping part of the circles, where authority and power come together.

We saw one example of a much-authority-not-much-power leader in Chapter 5: King Creon of Thebes, who assumed that his ruling position would cause his subjects to carry out his edicts and was stunned when one of them, Antigone, refused to do so. Another is Ron Johnson, the man who developed Apple's hugely successful retail stores and who, in 2011, was brought in by J.C. Penney to lead the struggling department store chain back to profitability.

As Jennifer Reingold reported in an article for *Fortune*, Johnson came in with the idea of transforming drab, stodgy Penney into a home for high-end brands and modern design that would attract young, well-heeled customers.[1] Along with a totally new product mix and store layout, he introduced a new pricing strategy: instead of the constant sales and clearances to which, in his view, Penney was addicted, there would be one low price for pretty much everything all the time.

on tall shoulders

FRANK ABAGNALE on POWER WITHOUT AUTHORITY

Frank Abagnale's autobiography, *Catch Me If You Can*, is the story of a great conman.[2] Later made into a Hollywood film, the book tells how Abagnale, beginning at age 16, posed as a PanAm pilot, a college professor, a physician, a lawyer, and more. In each role his authority was nil but his power substantial; he was able, for example, to cash $2.5 million in bad checks. Like all con artists, he excelled at winning friends and influencing people (see Dale Carnegie in Chapter 5) and cared little about his right to wield that influence.

Eventually the law caught up with him. At 21 he was arrested in France, stood trial and served time in several countries, and finally was extradited to the United States and sentenced to 12 years in federal prison. But he was released after four years on condition he help the feds nab other scammers, and soon afterward he founded a consulting firm to advise banks, corporations, and the FBI on fraud prevention.

So Abagnale the crook became Abagnale the authority. Going legit seems to have modified his views: in the book's Q&A section, he argues for tougher penal systems.

Ron Johnson had the full backing of the board of directors, most of whom seemed awed by the celebrity CEO and his vision. No one questioned him, not even when he announced an incredibly fast schedule for the transformation: three months to unveil the new brand look and the pricing, four months to roll out new advertising, twelve months to revamp hundreds of stores.

One board member did ask when the new pricing would be tested. "Johnson scoffed," says Reingold. "Never mind that other retailers had tried such pricing only to see customers vanish. He had made his decision."[3]

With his authority unchallenged, Johnson forged ahead. He hired a new leadership team who held long-time staffers in low regard; one executive allegedly referred to the veterans as DOPES, for "dumb old Penney's employees." This team shielded their CEO from the skepticism that was percolating. "In Johnson's mind," says Reingold, "everybody was behind him."[4] But the financial results were not encouraging. In May 2012, same-store sales were 19 percent less than a year before. Penney's old customers were deserting. It turned out they had liked the sales that were now verboten. They missed the private-label brands that had been eliminated. They were put off by the new advertising. As for the younger, hipper customers that Johnson assumed he would entice: they were not lured in.

Johnson insisted it was just a matter of time. The customers had to be educated, he said in an interview. By the end of 2012, however, it was becoming clear that the customers weren't open to education. Results for the year were abysmal, and board members started to lose confidence. Johnson resigned on April 8, 2013.

It's not uncommon for top leaders to assume (as did Creon and Johnson) that their authority automatically confers power over other people's volitions: to assume that subordinates, colleagues, and even customers will think what they're told to think. It's also not uncommon for leaders to assume that if they're powerful, people will automatically recognize their authority to lead; that is, their legitimacy. In fact, authority and power are sold separately, and successful leaders cultivate both.

WHO GETS TO CLAIM A VACANT THRONE?

Shakespeare's play *Julius Caesar* tells the story of a group of men who overthrow a ruler and later find that only one of them has sufficient power and authority to take his place. Analyses of the play have tended to focus on the conspirators' plans and motives for the assassination, but notice: Caesar is killed at the beginning of Act III, so more than half the play is about the later events, the struggle for leadership among Brutus, Cassius, Marc Antony, and Octavius. It seems Shakespeare was concerned with what happens not just in the lead-up to a rebellion, but in the aftermath, when a legitimate ruler has been ousted and a throne is left vacant. What sort of person, in the end, gets to claim the throne?

The answer, in Shakespeare's story, is Octavius: the man who eventually becomes Augustus Caesar, founder of the Roman Empire and one of its longest-lasting rulers. Each of the other principal characters tries to take charge, and each has significant talents and virtues—not to mention money and position—to bolster his claims. Brutus is a conscientious man who wants above all to do the right thing. Cassius is a political man, psychologically aware, with deep powers of persuasion. Antony is passionate and a great orator, able to sway crowds with words. Octavius, in contrast with these others, seems somewhat flat. He appears late, in Act IV, having taken part neither in the conspiracy nor in the competition for the crowd's loyalty directly after the assassination (when Antony gives his famous "Friends, Romans, countrymen, lend me your ears" speech). He teams with Antony to fight Brutus and Cassius, but while Antony continues to wax eloquent at every turn, Octavius says little, and what he does say reveals his battle plans rather than his inner thoughts. In the very last scene, Antony delivers a flowery eulogy to Brutus ("This was the noblest Roman of them all"), while Octavius gives the terse orders for Brutus's burial (Act V, Scene v).[5]

But Octavius has one big advantage over the others: he is Julius Caesar's son. Caesar adopted him in his will, and although this practice of posthumous adoption may seem strange to us today, it was not unusual in ancient Rome and was certainly considered legitimate. The adoption is first mentioned at the start of Act V: Octavius refers to himself as "another Caesar"; that is, he has the same surname as his adoptive father. After he breaks with Antony, all acknowledge him as "Octavius Caesar" and Julius's heir. Though Brutus be ever so conscientious, Cassius ever so persuasive, and Antony ever so passionate, none of them has the authority—the *right* to succeed Julius—that Octavius has. He unites power (or efficacy) with authority (or legitimacy). As a result, he ascends the throne and stays there.

THREE SOURCES OF AUTHORITY

OK, good for Octavius. But most of us aren't going to be adopted by a monarch, so how do we ordinary leaders acquire authority to go with our power? One answer comes from Max Weber, the German socialist and economist (1864–1920). He outlined three types of authority: *rational/legal* authority, which derives from written laws, rules, and charters; *traditional* authority, which derives from custom or long-established social structures; and *charismatic* authority, which derives from a leader's innate ability to inspire belief. (For reasons discussed in Chapter 1, I prefer to call the third type *intrinsic* authority.)

It is important for leaders to understand their major source of authority and to avoid undermining that source. The most obvious example is leaders in a large organization who derive their authority from their position in the organizational hierarchy and therefore must support that hierarchy or risk weakening themselves. Something that Brutus and Cassius fail to grasp is that Caesar's death is a severe blow to the sociopolitical structures from which they, as senators of Rome, derive *their* right to govern. Brutus seems to hope that in the wake of Caesar's death, a republic will reemerge spontaneously and he will still have a place as senator therein; Cassius's hopes are apparently for something like an anarchy, in which clever individuals such as he can wield power in the absence of a government. But both their hopes are vain: the people of Rome have become accustomed to a single ruler, a "Caesar," and the Senate's authority now derives mostly from him. If the current Caesar is eliminated, another must take his place, and the only question is who.

Any leader today who derives authority from an organizational structure and seeks to overthrow that structure must be prepared to face the situation Brutus and Cassius were in: an authority vacuum that will be filled, but not necessarily, nor even probably, by the ones who did the overthrowing.

Then there's intrinsic authority, the most mysterious of Weber's three types and the one Marc Antony tried to tap. The majority of leaders do just fine without it, relying instead (as did Octavius) on rational/legal or traditional authority, either of which is a perfectly solid platform for leadership. Leaders who stake their claim on intrinsic authority are few, which may be why they stand out in our minds: Mahatma Gandhi, Martin Luther King, Jr., Joan of Arc. A more recent example is Malala Yousafzai, the Pakistani schoolgirl and Nobel Peace Prize winner who was the target of a 2012 assassination attempt by the Taliban in retribution for her advocacy of girls' education. What all these leaders have in common is their ability to connect people to, or at least make them *feel* connected to, a higher cause. Some leaders use charisma to achieve this effect—King, for example, did it with supremely eloquent speeches—but charisma is by no means the only way. Joan of Arc, for instance, seems to have done it with an unshakeable, blunt-spoken belief in her own rightness that struck her hearers first as sheer madness, then as shocking conceit, and finally as a force that would unite France and save them all (see Chapter 21).

Some people would argue that noble causes led by such figures turn out badly more often than not; that there are more little Hitlers than little Gandhis. Intrinsic authority is certainly a more slippery platform than the other two kinds. Nevertheless, it's important for leaders to understand *all* their potential sources of authority and, if rational/legal and traditional authority are unavailable to them, to know that there is a third source, independent of external structures, that they can cultivate: their intrinsic ability to inspire belief.

TRIGGERING MUTINY

So, suppose you're a leader who has done a good job of combining power and authority. Your power is productive: you have steered clear of the King's Paradox (Chapter 5) and worked to enhance not only your own efficacy but also that of your team. You understand the major basis for your authority (rational/legal, traditional, or intrinsic), and you are careful to avoid undermining it. Surely your position is secure and you have nothing to fear?

Well, yes and no. Yes, the combination of productive power and well-grounded authority is difficult to assail, and few people will be inclined to try. But no, you're not entirely secure, for even a firmly placed leader can make the fatal mistake that triggers a mutiny (see "Assessment tool: Is your authority at risk?").

A mutiny is an attempt, generally within a military organization, to overthrow a legitimate ruler. Mutinies are enlightening case studies for leaders, because nowhere are lines of authority clearer and power more thoroughly developed than in the military. While of course any army or navy will contain some mere strongmen and some mere figureheads, most militaries are quite efficient meritocracies, in which leaders rise based on their efficacy and are granted authority backed by the immense weight of tradition, law, and structure. Mutinies, therefore, are rare, since they depend on individuals mustering the will to oppose abundant power plus clear authority, a formidable combination. But they do happen, and when they do, they are not always caused by sweeping historical forces or by circumstances outside a leader's control. Often, the spark for a mutiny is one particular leadership mistake.

That mistake is to humiliate one's subordinates. The historical examples of a connection between humiliation and mutiny are many, from the infamous mutiny on the *Bounty* against Captain Bligh—who rarely resorted to whipping but insulted his men at every turn[6]—to the Indian Mutiny of 1857, triggered when British officers of the Indian Army introduced a new type of ammunition requiring the sepoys to bite off paper cartridges for their rifles, cartridges rumored to be greased with beef and pork fat, considered vile by Hindus and Muslims.[7]

assessment tool

IS YOUR AUTHORITY AT RISK?

Leaders' authority can be weakened by subordinates (when they rebel or withdraw their support) or by leaders themselves (when they undermine their own sources of authority). Although most of us are not at much risk of assassination, our authority can still be diminished or even lost entirely if we fail to cultivate it.

Overleaf is a list of leadership actions and behaviors that can weaken your authority. Check all that you may indulge in, even a little bit or occasionally. (If you find yourself thinking, "Oh, they don't mind" or "It's all in fun," think again.) Then, assess your risk of mutiny using the key underneath.

1. You tease your team members about their personal habits, appearance, or mannerisms, or give them "funny" nicknames.
2. You find subtle ways to make it clear to your team members that you are smarter or more competent than they are.
3. You berate team members in front of their colleagues or subordinates.
4. You grill team members in order to expose their ignorance or flaws in their work.
5. You check your email or social media accounts when team members are speaking to you.
6. You disparage your direct manager in front of your team members.
7. You disparage other leaders and teams in front of your team members.
8. You undermine your direct manager in small ways.
9. You make cynical comments at work about your organization, its leaders, its goals, or its customers.
10. You dwell silently on your direct manager's stupidity and incompetence.

Total your checkmarks on items 1–5:

- **0** You're doing a good job of cultivating your authority; your team likely respects and supports you.
- **1–2** Your team members may not admire you as much as you think they do.
- **3–5** "Beware the ides of March"; your team members resent your behavior and want you gone.

Total your checkmarks on items 6–10:

- **0** You're doing a good job of supporting your sources of authority.
- **1–2** Although your negative feelings may be justified, be careful: you may be inadvertently undermining the people and structures on which your authority depends.
- **3–5** Start planning your exit. Your days as a leader in the organization are numbered.

A vivid literary example of the phenomenon appears in *I, Claudius*, Robert Graves's historical novel about the first three Roman emperors as seen through the eyes of the fourth, Claudius, a grandson of Augustus Caesar.[8] Born with a stutter and a limp and considered an idiot as a youth, Claudius spent his first five decades being ignored by his aristocratic family as they plotted and schemed in the orgies of political intrigue that marked the reigns of Augustus, Tiberius, and Caligula.[9]

Caligula's mad cruelties and lascivious excesses made him feared and hated by his subjects. Given his appalling behavior, it's not surprising that he, like Julius Caesar, was eventually assassinated. What *is* surprising is that his murder was orchestrated not by one of the many citizens whose entire family he had had executed, nor by someone whose wife he had raped, nor by an opponent whose money and lands he had stolen. The mutiny was led, rather, by a captain within his Royal Guards, Cassius Chaerea (a different Cassius from the one who plotted with Brutus). In Graves's version of the story, Caligula reneges on Cassius's promised promotions and makes him perform all sorts of unpleasant tasks. Cassius, an old soldier accustomed to obeying his superiors, makes no protest—until Caligula goes too far. One of Cassius's duties is to come to the emperor daily to receive the password for the troops, and Caligula decides to have some fun with this:

> [The watchword] had always been "Rome" or "Augustus" . . . or something of the sort, but now to annoy Cassius, Caligula would give him absurd words like "Stay-laces" or "Lots of Love" or "Curling-irons" or "Kiss me, Sergeant," and Cassius had to take them back to his brother officers and stand their chaff. He decided to kill Caligula.[10]

Cassius leads a mutiny and is the first to plunge a dagger into his boss's chest. He does it not because Caligula was a tyrant who terrorized thousands, but because Caligula was a petty bully who made his employees say humiliating things such as "Kiss me, Sergeant."

You may recall Machiavelli's caution in *The Prince*: just about the most dangerous thing you can do as a leader is to give offense to the people whose support you need. However strong your power and authority may be, their passionate resentment is likely to be stronger, and mutiny may be the result.

Next we explore leadership character via Winston Churchill's essays on famous and infamous leaders of his day.

great author

WINSTON CHURCHILL'S *GREAT CONTEMPORARIES*

"[N]ot only the actors but the scene" is what Churchill aims to present in these essays, written between 1929 and 1937. Here are 20 leaders from Britain and other nations—statesmen, politicians, military captains, intellectuals—all of whom shaped the events and ideas of their time. Two of the most interesting pieces describe infamous misleaders: Kaiser Wilhelm II and Adolf Hitler, arch-enemies of Britain and instigators of two world wars. The essay on the Kaiser is written with hindsight; the one on Hitler, with (some) foresight.

A great deal of the essays' value lies in the details. Churchill knew many of his subjects well, hence is able to share personal anecdotes that reveal their nature as no official accounts could. Even the men he viewed mostly from a distance are described with a vividness that makes us feel we are up close: watching the Kaiser, for instance, seated splendidly on his warhorse during military maneuvers, or T.E. Lawrence lighting a fuse to blow up a Turkish railway in an Arabian desert.

Although these leaders lived their lives on big stages, the writings as a whole convey a sense that "great leadership" is, in the end, not a matter of making grand speeches, plotting government overthrows, or directing vast armies. It is, rather, a matter of promises kept or broken, decisions made judiciously or rashly, and opinions stated with a sneer or a smile. In short: it's a matter of character.

Read this in Great Contemporaries: *Essays on Lawrence of Arabia, the ex-Kaiser, George Nathaniel Curzon, Adolf Hitler, the Earl of Rosebery, Herbert Henry Asquith, and Georges Clemenceau.*

chapter 7
CHARACTER, DEFINED

The practical wisdom of a leader comprises three qualities: perception, insight, and efficacy. Perception is about seeing situations for what they are, and insight is about knowing what to do. Seeing and knowing, however, only take you so far; brilliant as your plans and decisions may be, they'll come to nothing if you can't execute them. Efficacy, for a leader, means execution. And execution requires, more than anything, strength of character.

Management books are full of stories of freshly minted leaders who thought that execution would be the easy part. The typical new manager knows that he or she needs to learn about the technical and strategic aspects of the job and eagerly signs up for classes or seeks advice on industry knowledge, competitive analysis, and the like. But I've never heard a new manager say: "Actually, I tend to drop the ball a lot; is there a class for that?" Or, "I've noticed my plans often collapse because I can't get my team's commitment." Yet it's these sorts of issues on which most of us need the most help.

We need help because execution is difficult, and it's difficult because it's messy. Execution means taking a lucidly written strategy document or a neatly drawn process map and throwing it up against a wall of people: real people with likes and dislikes, aspirations and fears, family troubles, health problems, bad moods, and bad hair days. And, of course, all that messiness applies to us, as well: we have our own bad hair days to cope with. Just as no battle plan survives contact with the enemy, no work plan survives contact with the workplace and its human inhabitants. It's easy to make a nice clean decision and write it up in a PowerPoint presentation. It's much harder to present that decision (*am I hitting the right points?*) in the post-lunch session at the company offsite (*half the audience is napping*) and take questions on it (*I never anticipated these sorts of reactions*), all alone on stage (*my co-presenter called in sick*), with the projector not working properly (*stupid technology!*), and your boss finally grabbing the microphone to say, "This plan is only preliminary, and clearly some course corrections will be needed" (WHAT?). Your nice clean decision just went splat against a wall of humanity.

Perhaps you've heard this old riddle: Six frogs are sitting on a log. Four decide to jump off. How many are left?

Six, because deciding is different from doing.

CHARACTER TRAITS OF EFFECTIVE LEADERS

Character is the muscle that backs up effective execution, allowing leaders to put their insights and decisions into action. The five character traits of effective leaders are *courage*, *integrity*, *resilience*, *generosity*, and *concern*.

Each of these traits is the midpoint of a continuum or, as Aristotle puts it, the "mean" between two extremes, one of which is a deficiency of the trait and the other an excess (see Figure 7.1).[1] *Courage* is the mean of timidity (too little) and rashness (too much). *Integrity* is the mean of deceit and offensiveness; *resilience*, of obstinacy and vacillation; *generosity*, of severity and slackness; and *concern*, of indifference and mania. At each extreme we find leadership behaviors that are at best unproductive; at worst, evil.

Nearer the center of each continuum, sitting on either side of the mean, are two other traits: let's call them the *near-means*. It's difficult to hit the exact midpoint of the line, so most of us tend to lean a little toward one side or the other. We don't automatically slide off toward the extreme end point; instead, we settle fairly comfortably on one of the near-means and make it our modus operandi. In the case of the courage continuum, for example, some of us tend toward responsibility, which is a slightly tepid form of courage but is obviously a good thing most of the time; others of us tend toward boldness, which is a slightly overdone form of courage but, again, is often helpful.

A perfectly courageous person would integrate responsibility and boldness, striking the perfect balance every time. In the same way, each of the other four character traits represents an integration of two near-means, uniting the best of each. Integrity unites discretion and honesty; resilience unites perseverance and flexibility; generosity unites attentiveness and tolerance; and concern unites

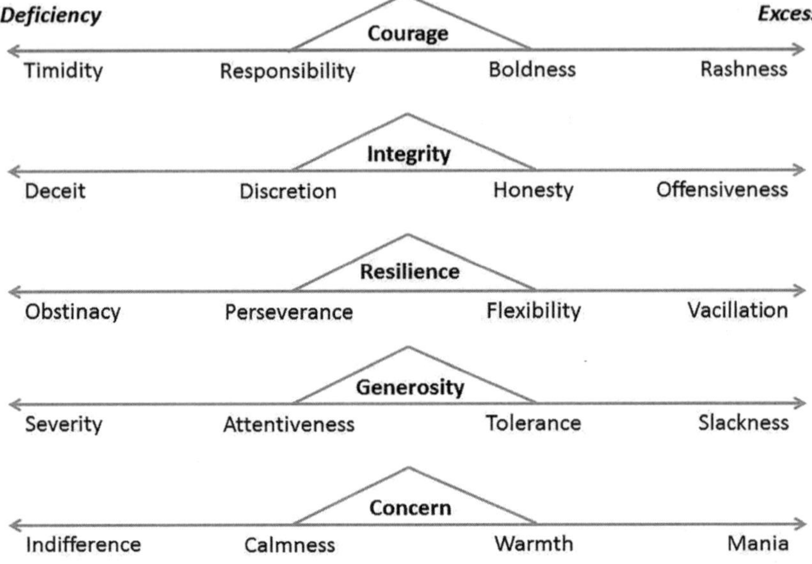

Figure 7.1 *Five character traits of effective leaders*

calmness and warmth. The average leader tends to gravitate toward one side or the other: discreet *or* honest, persevering *or* flexible, and so on. But the very best leaders manage, in their behavior and manner, to meld both sides and hit the mean (see "Planning tool: Finding the mean").

Churchill's *Great Contemporaries* is a collection of essays on prominent European figures of the late nineteenth and early twentieth centuries, rich with observations about each man's character and how it contributed to his successes, struggles, and, in a few cases, ultimate downfall. As we consider these portraits in light of the character continuums, four types of leader emerge: the Loose Cannon, the Sociopath, the Lightweight, and the Champion.

planning tool
FINDING THE MEAN

Select an upcoming difficult action you need to take as a leader. Pick one character continuum (courage, integrity, resilience, generosity, or concern) that seems especially relevant to that decision or action. Referring to Figure 7.1, write down the two near-means and the mean on that continuum:

Near-mean left:

Near-mean right:

Mean:

Reflect on how you might handle the decision or action. Suppose you leaned toward near-mean left: What would you do? Suppose, instead, you leaned toward near-mean right: What would you do? Now suppose you centered yourself on the mean: What would that look like, and what do you think the results would be?

Either record your thoughts or talk about them with a colleague. Be as detailed as you can in describing each scenario.

THE LOOSE CANNON: "LURCHING TO CATASTROPHE"

"The Ex-Kaiser," the second essay in *Great Contemporaries*, is about Emperor Wilhelm II, ruler of Germany during World War I. Churchill attended some German military displays in 1906 and 1908; he contrasts the Kaiser then, "surrounded by Kings and Princes while his legions defiled before him,"[2] with the Kaiser 12 years later, a "broken man hunched in a railway carriage" waiting for permission to cross the border and escape his defeated country. Churchill wonders whether this fate was the result of guilt or incapacity and comes down on the side of the latter: "It is indeed impossible to exaggerate the fecklessness which across a whole generation led the German Empire in successive lurches to catastrophe."[3] From the time he ascended the throne, Wilhelm committed a string of offenses more suited to junior-high than a monarchy—rude comments, impulsive messages, bossy interference—which resulted in the estrangement of all Germany's closest allies. Eventually,

> an enormous latent coalition had been formed in the center of which burned the quenchless flame of French revenge … It remained only for William II to offer Austria, in the sultry atmosphere of July 1914, a free hand to punish Serbia for the Sarajevo murders, and then to go away himself for three weeks on a yachting cruise.[4]

Loose Cannons, such as the ex-Kaiser, lack control over their character as leaders. They swerve wildly around the continuums (Figure 7.1), one moment obstinate, the next vacillating; one moment deceitful, the next offensive. There is no question of their holding to any particular character trait, let alone to the mean. They're especially prone to the eighth leadership trap: swinging between domination and abdication (see Chapter 2). When Loose Cannons trundle in your direction, it's best to get out of the way. Confusion, anger, and dismay follow in their wake, the results of their unpredictable behavior.

Churchill thought that Kaiser Wilhelm's actions, despite their dreadful outcomes, were generally well intentioned and, indeed, the typical Loose Cannon often means well. As someone once said to me about a feckless but benign leader we both knew who had unwittingly caused a massive problem for his team: "He doesn't *know* he's a bozo."

THE SOCIOPATH: "BORNE ONWARDS BY CURRENTS OF HATRED"

Sociopaths, in contrast, know exactly who they are and what they're doing.[5] Nowadays Adolf Hitler is the all too obvious example of a sociopathic leader, but what's interesting about Churchill's essay on Hitler is that he wrote it in 1935—four years before the onset of World War II eliminated any doubts about the dictator's nature.

In 1935, there were still doubts: although Hitler's campaigns of aggression were already underway and condemned by many people, some opined that he was raising a great nation from the dust and expressed admiration for his "patriotism." Churchill notes, "History is replete with examples of men who have risen to power by employing stern, grim, and even frightful methods"[6] but whom we now regard as great leaders. He wonders how Hitler will turn out and claims to be reserving judgment, but as the essay continues, we get the sense that at the time of writing he wasn't entirely blinded by "the vital force which enabled [Hitler] to challenge, defy, conciliate, or overcome all the ... resistances that barred his path."[7] Although it would take the start of the war to open Churchill's eyes completely, he had already begun to see Hitler for the Sociopath he was.

Sociopathic leaders, unlike Loose Cannons, are masters of their behavior, but they make no attempt to strike the mean—to be generous, for example, or courageous—*unless* it is expedient to do so. They play the character continuums like a game board, picking whichever trait suits them (see "On tall shoulders: Martha Stout on sociopaths"). If harshness will help them prevail, they are harsh; if honesty is the quickest means to an end, they are honest. Persevering or flexible, timid or rash, it all depends on what serves their purpose. "He makes speeches to the nations," says Churchill of Hitler, "which are sometimes characterized by candor and moderation."[8] Just so, for when candor and moderation are the ticket, the Sociopath displays them. The one character trait that is often not in the Sociopath's control, and hence can be his undoing, is mania (the extreme excess of concern). "Passion" is the veil a Sociopath throws over mania, disguising hatred for certain groups of people or an obsession with certain ideas. But Churchill seems to see through the veil:

> If, as I have said, we look only at the past, which is all we have to judge by, we must indeed feel anxious. Hitherto, Hitler's triumphant career has been borne onwards, not only by a passionate love of Germany, but by currents of hatred so intense as to sear the souls of those who swim upon them.[9]

on tall shoulders

MARTHA STOUT on SOCIOPATHS

"Imagine—if you can—," writes psychiatrist Martha Stout in *The Sociopath Next Door*, "not having a conscience, none at all, no feelings of guilt or remorse no matter what you do ... no struggles with shame, not a single one in your whole life."[10] Now recognize that because everyone assumes that conscience is universal among humans, you have no trouble hiding the fact that you are conscience free.

This is the sociopath: the individual with antisocial personality disorder, a condition defined as a total lack of empathy for others or remorse for hurting them. Guiltlessness, says Stout, was the first personality disorder to be recognized by psychiatry, and in her book she takes a long, close look at these aliens among us. Their pathology means they can do *anything at all* (though most aren't violent), yet their "strange advantage" over the majority tends to go undiscovered.

But does this so-called advantage lead to happiness, or even success? Stout's portrait of a sociopath-next-door named Tillie—who stirs up fights with the neighbors, sits alone and drunk every night, and in the end is unable to take down even a groundhog—suggests not.

THE LIGHTWEIGHT: "BESPANGLED WITH EVERY QUALITY"

"Few careers in modern British politics are more worthy of examination than George Nathaniel Curzon,"[11] says Churchill. "Here was a being gifted far beyond the average level: equipped and caparisoned with glittering treasures of mind and fortune"—and yet, a being who ultimately failed to achieve his life's ambition. Curzon, born into a noble and wealthy family, was a brilliant student at Eton and Oxford. His reputation as an up-and-comer preceded him into the House of Commons, and there he continued to impress with his polished speeches, sagacious analyses, and attractive manner. Yet something was lacking:

> You could unpack his knapsack and take an inventory item by item. Nothing on the list was missing, yet somehow or other the total was incomplete ... the House considered him from the earliest day of his membership as a light weight.[12]

Lightweight leaders, like Curzon, are replete with virtues that don't quite gel. Lightweights are always a little off-key, being responsible when boldness would be better or passionate when circumstances call for calm. While they don't veer off to the continuum extremes, neither do they find the center and convey the balance and depth that only come from centeredness. They read as flimsy and superficial, and the result is a lack of influence. Churchill admires Curzon's "superfine performances" in the House of Commons but notes that "simpler people with rugged force within them ... made homely halting speeches which counted for more."[13] Another thing about Lightweights is that they don't behave the same way with everyone: Curzon's generous hospitality to friends was renowned, but so were his harsh rebukes to subordinates. Were he around today, he would be the sort of person who is rude to waiters. And in the end, Curzon's dream of becoming prime minister of England came to naught:

> Bespangled with every quality that could dazzle and attract, he never found himself with a following. Majestic in speech, appearance and demeanor, he never led. He often domineered; but at the center he never dominated.[14]

THE CHAMPION: "HOLDING ONE OF THE MASTER KEYS"

Last we have the Champion: the leader who possesses attractive qualities and knows how to put them all together. Like Sociopaths, Champions are in full control of their behavior; unlike Sociopaths, they adjust their behavior with intent to serve rather than trample. As the label Champion implies, they are winners, but as it also implies, they are winners who fight for others, who advocate for the cause of those less able to advocate for themselves. They are also centered. While the Loose Cannon careens up and down the character continuums and the Lightweight leans tentatively and a little pompously this way and that, the Champion strikes the mean with consistency and vigor.

Churchill shows us a quintessential Champion in his piece on T.E. Lawrence, aka Lawrence of Arabia. The well-known film of that name is a sweeping, romanticized view of the young Lawrence's exploits in World War I, focusing on his role in the Arab Revolt against the Turks, a campaign that was essential to the Allies' ultimate victory.[15] In Churchill's brief essay, we get a more intimate and subtle picture of the man. It was 1919 when the two first met, and at that point Lawrence had long been committed to the Arab cause; his steady goal throughout the war had been to place Faisal, son of the Grand Sharif of Mecca, at the head of a unified, free Arabian state with its capital in Damascus. Using a combination of military prowess, shrewd negotiating, and personal magnetism, Lawrence drew and held together an army of disparate Arab tribes who fought and overthrew the Turks and conquered Greater Syria.

Yet their success was short-lived. In his memoir *Seven Pillars of Wisdom*, Lawrence describes his mental agony on finding at the war's conclusion that the British and French governments, despite their support of his campaigns, never intended to cede any of the formerly Turkish territory to the Arabs but planned, rather, to divide it among themselves. With a new world dawning, he says, "the old men came out again and took our victory to re-make in the likeness of the former world they knew. We stammered that we had worked for a new heaven and a new earth, and they thanked us kindly and made their peace."[16] In the months afterward, he continued to advocate tirelessly for Faisal, accompanying him and pleading his case in meetings with government leaders in London and Paris. It was of no use. After the peace treaty was signed and Syria was handed to France, French troops threw Faisal out of Damascus and repressed all further Arab resistance. Lawrence, his spirit crushed, retired from public life for a time.

It was Winston Churchill who persuaded him to step back in. In 1921, Churchill was put in charge of straightening out the mess in the Middle East that had been building up over the past two years. Among the problems (which will sound familiar to twenty-first-century readers) were bloody rebellions in Iraq requiring 40,000 British troops to maintain order, and growing strife between Arabs and Jews in what was then called Palestine. Churchill formed a new department of the British Colonial Office to seek solutions. As its nucleus he recruited half a dozen "very able men" who had served in the region during the war, and he proposed adding Lawrence to their number. The new recruits were aghast—not because they didn't respect Lawrence, but because they thought his temperament entirely unsuited to the patient politicking that was going to be required. Churchill asked him nevertheless, Lawrence accepted at once, and to everyone's astonishment he turned out to be the epitome of tact and collaboration: altogether the perfect diplomat for a thorny transnational situation. Churchill says:

> Here is one of the proofs of the greatness of his character and the versatility of his genius. He saw the hope of redeeming in a large measure the promises he had made to the Arab chiefs and of re-establishing a tolerable measure of peace in those wide regions. In that cause he was capable of becoming—I hazard the word—a humdrum official.[17]

As a "humdrum official," Lawrence at last achieved his purpose. After a year of steady effort by the team, Faisal was placed on the throne of Iraq, another Arab emir was given rule of Trans-Jordania, and something like peace settled over the Middle East.

An anecdote in Churchill's "Lawrence of Arabia" essay shows exactly what I mean by leadership character and is a good way to end this chapter. In the spring of 1919, says Churchill, he invited Lawrence to a lunch party, during which one of the other guests "rather mischievously" told a story about Lawrence refusing to accept a medal from the King of England at a public ceremony. Churchill saw this refusal as disrespectful grandstanding and chided Lawrence for it. Years later, he learned that the incident was not at all as the guest had portrayed it; the refusal actually happened privately, in an impromptu conversation, and Lawrence's behavior was blameless. But at the luncheon, Churchill says, "whether or not Lawrence saw

I had misunderstood the incident, he made no effort to minimize it or to excuse himself. He accepted the rebuke with good humor" and went on to explain, briefly and pleasantly, his rationale for refusing the decoration.[18]

How many people, placed in a similar situation, would have thought it necessary to be "honest"—to vindicate themselves with the true story—and ended up merely being offensive and ruining the party? How many others would have played the toady, "discreetly" agreeing with everything their powerful host said? But Lawrence struck the mean between honesty and discretion, speaking and acting with perfect integrity. In this situation and in many others, says Churchill, "he held one of those master keys which unlock the doors of many kinds of treasure-houses."[19]

How do the best leaders manage crises? In the next part, the greatest news story of modern times and a Shakespeare play provide clues.

part III
BATTLES

La Conquistadora, the oldest continuously venerated statue of the Virgin Mary in the United States, was so named by Spanish captain Don Diego de Vargas in thanksgiving for her help in his troops' retaking of the city of Santa Fe 12 years after the Pueblo Revolt of 1680. But her name referred, he later said, not to her assistance with crushing a rebellion, but to her benevolent generalship over her followers' hearts. And indeed, many leaders who set out to conquer others discover that the real struggle lies in conquering oneself.

Part III revolves around leadership battles: external or internal, with swords or with words. Our specific topics are crises, competition, dilemmas, communication, and character development.

We begin with Shakespeare's play *Henry V*, which contains not only a great motivational speech but, even more instructive, an up-close look at a leader's attempts to understand his own motives in the thick of conflict and crisis. Next we'll examine the campaigns of six legendary captains through the eyes of Theodore Dodge, a soldier turned military historian; and then a campaign of words, *The Federalist*, written by James Madison and Alexander Hamilton to push for ratification of the Constitution of the United States. After that we have two great addresses aimed at sustaining a nation in wartime: one by Athenian statesman Pericles and the other by US president Abraham Lincoln. And finally, we revisit the leadership character traits we explored in Chapter 7 and learn from Plutarch, chronicler of the ancient Greeks and Romans, how these traits are developed by philosophy and the right attitude toward our enemies.

Note that while many of these books talk of "history," their historical precision will not be our concern. No doubt a historian could point out numerous exaggerations and inaccuracies in all of them; we, however, will approach them not as historians seeking facts but as leaders seeking wisdom—and finding it, most often, in the story.

great author
WILLIAM SHAKESPEARE'S *HENRY V*

Many of Shakespeare's plays have intricate plots and unforgettable secondary characters, but the plot of *Henry V* is straightforward (Henry takes England to war against France, wins battles on French soil against great odds, and eventually makes peace by marrying the French king's daughter), and its secondary characters are relatively flat and not much dwelled on. The story's focus and main source of interest lie in King Henry: how he thinks, what he does, why he wins.

Knowing Henry's back story, recounted in *Henry IV Part 2*, helps us see and appreciate his growth as a leader. As Prince Hal, he spends most of his time carousing with his lowlife friends. But when his father dies, he sheds his irresponsible ways and grows thoughtful: he inquires, he reflects, he examines his conscience and weighs his options. This new version of Henry leads a small and mostly amateur army against a large and formidable enemy, and prevails. Then in the aftermath, although France is defeated and some people advise him to press his advantage, he ceases campaigning; instead, he sets up lasting peace by wooing and marrying a French princess.

As king, Henry taps into his introverted side and balances his penchant for risk-taking with an almost Hamlet-like taste for introspection and caution (see Chapter 14 for more on extraverts and introverts). Very much unlike Hamlet, however, Henry maintains a talent for motivating a team, especially at times when things look bleakest. He is the quintessential dealer in hope, continually painting a picture of the triumphs awaiting not just him, but us. Observe how he does it in the famous "Saint Crispin's Day" speech, delivered on the field of Agincourt to a ragtag troop of soldiers outnumbered by the enemy and wondering why they came:

> This day is called the Feast of Crispian:
> He that outlives this day and comes safe home,
> Will stand a-tiptoe when this day is named,
> And rouse him at the name of Crispian.
> He that shall see this day, and live old age,
> Will yearly on the vigil feast his neighbors
> And say, "Tomorrow is Saint Crispian."

Then will he strip his sleeve and show his scars,
And say, "These wounds I had on Crispin's day."
Old men forget; yet all shall be forgot,
But he'll remember, with advantages,
What feats he did that day …
And Crispin Crispian shall ne'er go by,
From this day to the ending of the world,
But we in it shall be rememberèd—
We few, we happy few, we band of brothers;
For he today that sheds his blood with me
Shall be my brother …
And gentlemen in England, now abed,
Shall think themselves accursed they were not here;
And hold their manhoods cheap whiles any speaks
That fought with us upon Saint Crispin's day. (Act IV, Scene iii)

✯ Read this in *Henry V*: Act IV, which contains the speech above and other scenes of interest to leaders.

chapter 8
CRISES

Troubles, trials, hardships, turmoil, hot water, exigencies, crises. Whatever we call them, eventually we'll face them: difficult situations that test our ingenuity and resilience. Some gurus call this "leading at the edge,"[1] but the best crisis managers strive to get their teams *away* from that adrenaline-charged borderland of unthinking action, back to a calmer place where learning can occur.

CRISIS LEADERSHIP

The sinking of the *Titanic* has been called the greatest news story of modern times.[2] It is also a quintessential illustration of how, during a crisis, some leaders veer from complacency to panic while others manage to find a sweet spot—a mean, to use the language of the previous chapter—that allows them and their people to keep moving forward, calmly and swiftly, even as the waters threaten to engulf them.

The many familiar examples of complacency aboard the "unsinkable ship" include the inadequate lifeboats; the absence of safety drills; the missing binoculars for the crow's-nest lookouts; and above all Captain Smith's decision to speed up, never mind the threat of icebergs, in hopes of reaching New York a day early as a fitting capstone to his career. The crew's frenzied evacuation efforts are also infamous. Less well known are the events aboard the other two ships sailing the north Atlantic on the night of April 14, 1912.

The *Californian* was the nearest, less than 10 miles away and the best placed to launch a rescue, but its crew members, like those of the *Titanic*, spent the first few hours of the crisis in relative idleness. Although the *Titanic* fired rockets for hours, the deck watch of the *Californian* assumed that the rockets' color (white, not red) meant a party with fireworks, so they watched unperturbed. As the ship sank, the *Californian*'s second officer remarked casually on its odd appearance, but decided it must simply be sailing away. No one on board the *Californian* investigated anything until the wireless operator woke at dawn and discovered the *Titanic*'s distress messages, which triggered a frantic rescue effort, but too late. In short, both ships' leaders lurched from complacency to panic, and some 1,500 people died.

Contrast all this with what happened aboard the *Carpathia*, 60 miles away. That ship's wireless operator, who had his earphones on while undressing for bed, received the *Titanic*'s first distress call at midnight. He woke Captain Rostron, who instantly ordered a reverse in course. The *Carpathia* raced to the disaster site (with lookouts increased so icebergs could be spotted early) and arrived fully prepared for rescue operations, the entire crew having been set to tasks such as swinging out lifeboats, collecting blankets, and rigging chair slings for the injured.

But one small detail says even more about Rostron as a leader. When he got the call, he ordered the *Carpathia*'s new course immediately, before checking the message and before calculating the *Titanic*'s location, and then, after they were under full steam, he verified the report, calculated the ships' relative positions, and adjusted course. In other words, he neither sat on his hands nor became unhinged, but rather moved, evaluated, adjusted, and kept on moving. The *Carpathia* arrived on the scene at 4:10 a.m., in time to save the 700 people in the lifeboats. It seems that Rostron, alone of the three ship captains, knew how to dance with a crisis.

FOUR CRISIS ZONES

That sweet spot that Captain Rostron found and the other captains didn't is the *learning zone*. Ronald Heifetz, founding director of the Center for Public Leadership at the John F. Kennedy School of Government at Harvard, writes eloquently of the learning zone and its importance to teams and organizations in crisis (see "On tall shoulders: Ronald Heifetz on adaptive leadership"). The idea is compelling, but much less has been written by Heifetz or anyone else about *how* to stay in the learning zone. The "how" is crucial, so I've sought to build on Heifetz's theory and make it a little more actionable with a framework called the Crisis Zones (see Figure 8.1).

on tall shoulders
RONALD HEIFETZ on ADAPTIVE LEADERSHIP

Treating leadership as an activity rather than a position or set of qualities, Ronald Heifetz is known for his study of organizations in volatile, unpredictable situations. He calls his approach adaptive leadership.[3]

Heifetz originated the idea of a "crisis lifecyle" defined by movement in and out of three zones: comfort zone, danger zone, and learning zone. During normal times, he says, we coast along in a state of equilibrium, the comfort zone, where stress is low and everyone tries to keep it that way. An emergency will kick us into the danger zone, where high stress levels create energy for the fast action and laser-beam focus necessary to survive a fight-or-flight situation.

But neither comfort zone nor danger zone helps us deal with the world's turmoil—which, you may have noticed, shows no sign of stopping. The place to be, says Heifetz, is the *learning zone*: the spot where we're alert and energetic, but not driven to ineffectual rage or panic. The learning zone is the adaptive zone.

The two axes of the framework are *unity* and *agility*; as a leader, you want both to be high, especially during and after a crisis.[4] When unity is high and agility low, you and your team are in the upper left box, the complacency zone, where signs of impending crisis and suggestions for adaptation are met with a chorus of "Around here, we always ..." Conversely, when agility is high and unity low, you're in the disconnection zone, where each person's priority is saving their own skin: when the ship starts to go down, there's a stampede for the lifeboats and devil take the hindmost. And when *both* unity and agility are low, you're in the blame zone, where everybody's main concern is to make sure all fingers are pointed firmly at somebody else. In each of these boxes, people's thoughts and utterances tend to begin with just one pronoun—either *we*, or I, or *they*—and to be declarative: *We always ... I will ... They are ...*

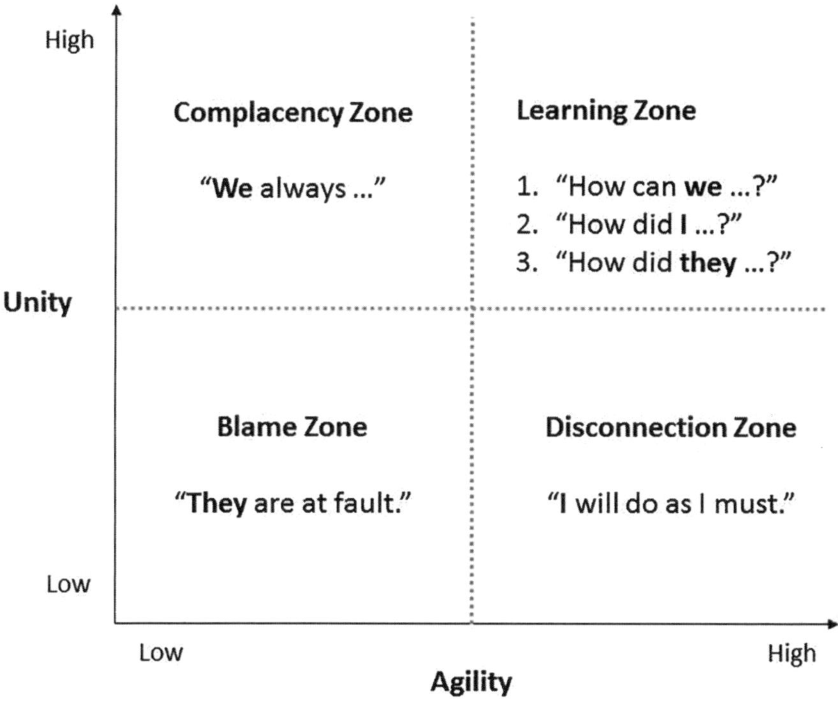

Figure 8.1 Crisis Zones

In the learning zone, in contrast, the focus is on all three pronouns and the tone is one of inquiry. The single most important thing a leader can do to keep his or her team in the learning zone, both during and after a crisis, is to ask these three questions:

1. How can *we* resolve these difficulties and move forward as a team?

2. How did I contribute to the difficulties, and how can I ensure I don't make the same mistakes again?

3. How did *they* (my team members) contribute to the difficulties, and how can I coach them so they avoid the same mistakes and are better prepared for the next crisis?

The questions' order is critical. Leaders who begin with Question 3 will find it difficult to take up Questions 1 and 2; consequently, the original problem will remain unsolved, their own contribution to it will remain unacknowledged, and their team members will put their energy into deflecting blame now and covering their rears later. With nobody learning anything, the team will settle back into whichever zone is habitual and wait for the next crisis to come along—or more likely, the same crisis to repeat (see "Planning tool: First we, then I, then they").

planning tool
FIRST WE, THEN I, THEN THEY

Consider a tumultuous or troubling situation you and your team are facing right now or faced very recently; not a "bolt from the blue," but a crisis that perhaps could have been avoided or mitigated had people behaved differently. Help keep your team in the learning zone by reflecting on the questions below. You may choose to ponder the questions on your own or, better still, discuss them with your team.

Important: Answer the questions in the given order, and allow at least 24 hours between reflections on each one. This will ensure you give sufficient consideration to the first two questions ("we" and "I") before moving to the third one ("they").

1. How can *we* resolve these difficulties and move forward as a team?

2. How did *I* contribute to the difficulties, and how can I ensure I don't make the same mistakes again?

3. How did *they* (my team members) contribute to the difficulties, and how can I coach them so they avoid the same mistakes in future and are better prepared for the next crisis?

HENRY V: THE LEARNING KING

In Shakespeare's *Henry* V we find a leader dedicated to promoting both unity and agility. In the Saint Crispin's Day speech, King Henry paints a picture of the honor and glory to be gained by the "band of brothers" about to fight a foe 20 times their number. Would-be deserters change their minds, and the English army pulls together and wins the day. But earlier, when he lays siege to the French town of Harfleur (II.ii), Henry takes a very different approach. He knows the Dauphin of France has refused to send troops to help the town, so he plays the fear card, bellowing threats of death and torture so dire—"Why, in a moment look to see ... Your naked infants spitted on pikes"—that the terrified governor of Harfleur yields the town with barely a protest. Constantly throughout the play we see Henry calculating the odds, figuring out not only how to keep the troops on board (unity) but also how to turn the circumstances to England's advantage (agility).

Again, integration is critical. The pursuit of unity and agility as separate goals can take you bouncing between the complacency and disconnection zones (see Figure 8.1), but thanks to the level of inquiry he sustains, Henry avoids this trap. He is one of the most reflective of Shakespeare's princes—we see him constantly examining his own and others' motives and considering various options for action—yet he never suffers from analysis paralysis. Rather, he asks questions in order to learn, and then applies that learning, quickly, to the situation at hand.

Consider two examples. In the second scene of Act I, we see Henry questioning his archbishops about the validity of his claim to a section of France. Keenly aware of the blood that will be shed if he invades, he charges the bishops not to obfuscate or make the case with trickery, but to be scrupulously honest. He then cuts off the Bishop of Canterbury's pettifoggery with a terse question that reveals his desire to conform not only to the letter of the law but to its spirit: "May I with right and conscience make this claim?" (I.ii). Later, on the night before the big battle with the French (IV.i), he walks disguised through the army camps to discover the men's mood—and what they think of him. The overheard conversations, not all of which are flattering, lead him to consider deeply what it means to be a king, with cares that overshadow all the power and gold. He ends up praying for forgiveness, aware that as king he "takes on" the sins and errors of many others and must accept responsibility even for things he didn't personally do. Henry's eve-of-battle musings reveal the uncertainty often felt by a leader in the learning zone, where *our* mistakes, *my* mistakes, and *their* mistakes are pondered as one interconnected whole.

HENRY IN THE LEARNING ZONE: THE WILLIAMS INCIDENT

Henry's stroll in disguise among the campfires sets off a strange sequence of events that reveals much about how a leader can stay in the learning zone even amid the fire and smoke of battle. He encounters an English soldier named Michael Williams, and the two fall into a debate about the king's character. Williams, a cynical hothead, states that the king plans to be captured and ransomed while all the common foot soldiers are killed. Henry disagrees. Williams won't let the argument go and challenges Henry to a fistfight, not knowing, of course, that it's the king he's talking to. Henry accepts the challenge. Since it's the middle of the night, they vow to pick up the quarrel next day after the battle, and exchange gloves. Each will recognize his opponent by his own glove stuck in the other's hat.

In the morning the battle proceeds and the English defeat the French. Henry has only just confirmed his victory and has myriad demands on his attention, but in the midst of everything he catches sight of Private Williams (IV.vii). He calls him over, asking him why he has that glove in his hat. Williams, as belligerent as ever, explains loudly that the glove belongs to a "rascal" whom he has sworn to "box on the ear." Henry expresses mild interest and dismisses him.

Then comes the strange part: Henry has his most faithful captain, Fluellen, stick Williams's glove in his (Fluellen's) hat. He tells Fluellen an elaborate lie about how the glove belongs to a French lord and how the man who will attack Fluellen on seeing the glove is a traitor; then he sends Fluellen off on an errand guaranteeing he'll cross Williams's path. We wonder if this is going to turn out to be a not-very-funny joke on Fluellen and a vicious trap for poor Williams.

Immediately, however, Henry sends two of his earls after Fluellen, charging them to "see there be no harm between them." Henry himself follows close behind.

Williams and Fluellen do run into each other, and Williams does attack Fluellen, who is in high dudgeon by the time the lords show up (IV.viii). Henry now reveals with some drama that it's his own glove in Williams's hat—and that he, the king, is the very man Williams vowed to fight! Williams is horrified. He stammers out that he meant no offense against the king; that last night he didn't *know* it was the king and it's his intent that really matters, for "all offenses come from the heart." He begs for pardon, and Henry gives it—along with the glove, filled with gold coins. Henry then tells Fluellen to "make friends" with the man, and Fluellen steps up to the mark by giving Williams 12 pence and a slap on the back.

What are we to make of this episode? Let's think about the options Henry has for dealing with Williams. He could dismiss the incident as a trivial one not worth his attention (especially not in the middle of a war), toss away the glove, and leave Williams to assume that his unknown adversary was killed in the battle. He could let Fluellen thrash Williams, thereby ensuring that a loudmouth gets his comeuppance while he, Henry, keeps his hands clean. He could make the whole thing a terrible "gotcha" by wearing the glove, letting Williams attack him, revealing himself as the king, and then having Williams banished or executed for treason—something like a CEO who secretly monitors an employee's email and, on reading a few mildly insulting comments about himself, fires the employee for misconduct.

But Henry does none of these things. Instead, by arranging for Williams to run into Fluellen, glove in hat, he makes the blusterer follow through on his bluster. By sending the two earls to observe, he makes sure nothing too terrible happens. By revealing himself finally as the king, he gets Williams to apologize and to think twice (no doubt) before picking another pointless fight with a stranger. By pardoning Williams and giving him a gloveful of gold, he makes his magnanimity as a leader evident to all. And finally, by giving Captain Fluellen a chance to be magnanimous as well, he makes his direct report look good and demonstrates once again the value he places on unity among his team members.

In a crisis, whether a battle or simply an unexpected competitive threat, good leaders keep people in the learning zone. Where another king might wield a sledgehammer, Henry wields a teacher's pointer as he deals with a case of what some would call treachery. At least five people are witnesses to the Williams dust-up, and surely dozens if not hundreds more will hear the story as it traverses the English camps that evening, stirring up laughter and admiration: "Just listen to what the king did now ... Didn't he teach that guy a lesson!"

Incidentally, Henry's generous treatment of the hotheaded soldier stands in sharp contrast to his swift order in Act II for the execution of three real traitors. He knows, like Williams, that the heart's intent makes all the difference.

Next, the campaigns of two great military captains teach us about competitive advantage.

great author

THEODORE DODGE'S *THE GREAT CAPTAINS*

As a young man, Theodore Ayrault Dodge saw action in the Civil War; he eventually rose to the rank of colonel in the US Army and by his death in 1909 had produced a comprehensive body of work on the history of warfare. *The Great Captains* contains his lectures on the campaigns of three great military leaders from ancient times—Alexander, Hannibal, and Julius Caesar—and three more from modernity—Gustavus Adolphus, Frederick II, and Napoleon.

The names Alexander, Caesar, and Napoleon remain famous today; the names Hannibal, Gustavus, and Frederick have faded somewhat. Hannibal (247–182 BCE) was supreme general of the forces of Carthage, the great civilization based on the northern coast of Africa that wrestled with Rome for power over the Mediterranean world for 100 years. Gustavus Adolphus (1594–1632) was King of Sweden during the Thirty Years' War, which at first pitted the Protestant and Catholic states of Central Europe against each other and then developed into a more general conflict across the continent. Frederick II (1712–86), later dubbed Frederick the Great, was King of Prussia and led his armies to success in the Seven Years' War, which involved all preeminent world powers of the time.

Dodge's thesis is that "the art of war owes its origins and growth to the deeds of a few great captains. Not to their brilliant victories ... but to their intellectual conceptions."[1] His six lectures in *The Great Captains* trace the evolution of warfare *from* a simple matter of drawing up two armies in parallel and having them hammer away until one side surrendered, *to* a sophisticated matter of battle formations, moves and countermoves, resources, logistics, training, and above all the sustaining of morale. In Alexander's improvements to catapults and ballistas (the equivalent of modern artillery), in Gustavus's invention of the fortified supply chain by which troops are kept equipped, and in Napoleon's uniting of military theory and practice in his campaigns, we see the development of strategy as "the highest grade of intellectual common sense."[2] But more than that, we see how these leaders engaged their troops to carry out their plans. In the final analysis, says Dodge, a great captain is produced not just by extraordinary intellect but by equal force of character—character that infuses "confidence and spirit into the solider, who will be strong and victorious, feeble and beaten, according as he thinks he is."[3]

Dodge is the only author featured in this book who has been almost entirely forgotten by present-day readers. It's time to dust off his works, which are unmatched for their deep yet concise analyses of great military campaigns and the men who led them.

✯ *Read this in The Great Captains: The essays go best in ancient-modern pairs: first Hannibal and Gustavus Adolphus, then Alexander and Napoleon, and finally Julius Caesar and Frederick the Great.*

chapter 9

COMPETITION

A long time ago, my parents had a friend named Teddy Newbold—I called him Uncle Teddy—who was known for winning games. I'm not talking about strenuous sports (though he was good at those, too), but board games, card games, parlor games, and lawn games. Whether it was checkers or croquet, bridge or Botticelli, Uncle Teddy came out on top. When asked his secret, he would say, "I play for myself." He meant that when presented with a choice between two possible moves, he chose the one that would move him ahead rather than the one that would set an opponent back. In a board game, for instance, he would advance one of his own pieces rather than bump someone else's piece back to Start. While the other players were slugging it out, he would just keep moving forward, racking up points until he won the game.

FIGHTING WITH INTELLIGENCE

For a leader, few topics are more interesting than how to beat the competition. After all, if groups of human beings didn't have to compete—whether for land, market share, trophies, brand recognition, grant money, or any other type of prize—we might not need leaders at all. Leaders are supposed to fight for their team: to help their team succeed in a world where not all teams can be equally successful. This is not to say inter-team cooperation is bad or that business is the same as warfare; rather that a leader must know something about competitive strategy, which essentially means knowing how to defeat an opponent of equal or greater strength. Happily for the small and outnumbered, brute force doesn't guarantee victory. As Uncle Teddy demonstrated, often the winner of a contest is not the side better able to bash and thrash, but the side that does the better job of keeping its internal sense of purpose and confidence high. The loser, meanwhile, is often the side that falls apart from within.

"War is as highly intellectual as astronomy," said war historian Theodore Dodge. "The main distinction between the one and the other lies in the fact that the intellectual conception of the general must ... call for the exertion of the moral forces of his character, while the astronomer's inspiration stops at a purely mental process."[4] From Dodge's essays on six superb generals, we can glean four factors that enable a David to take down a Goliath.

FIRST: UNITY

We saw in the previous chapter how King Henry capitalized on team unity to beat a stronger foe. The point bears repeating: *If a team is less aligned or more subject to faction than its opponent, it will eventually lose.* It's amazing how many leaders, forgetting this truth, put no effort into unifying their team and even pit team members against one another in a misguided effort to increase their own power. This sort of "competitive strategy" only guarantees defeat.

Dodge emphasizes the value of unity in all his great-captain essays, but especially in his account of the Swedish king Gustavus Adolphus, who in the seventeenth century defended his own country and a large part of Protestant Germany from the aggression of the Hapsburg Empire, all while lifting the art of war out of the confusion in which it had languished through the Middle Ages, and with far fewer resources than his enemies. Gustavus was the first European king to create a standing national army and to equip and pay them well; previously, rulers going to war would recruit troops from the swarms of mercenaries milling about the continent, pay them with opportunities to plunder, and fire them once the fighting was done. The Swedish troops' salaries improved not only their own morale but also their image with potential allies: the people of the provinces through which Gustavus passed tended to see him as a liberator, not a marauder, and hence supported his cause.

Like Alexander the Great, Gustavus was renowned for sharing the same dangers and hardships experienced by his troops: "Always in the thickest of the fray, he led his men in person."[5] He also shared with his men a purpose that rose above mere monetary or political gain: he was fighting to save the Protestant world from the yoke (as he saw it) of Catholic oppression, and "his army partook his enthusiasm, as it shared his earnest religious feeling, and was devotedly attached to him as man and king."[6] In aims, culture, and beliefs, the Swedish troops were a force united.

SECOND: AGILITY

We've seen agility come up before, too. King Henry battled a French prince one year and married a French princess the next. Great captains, says Dodge, are able "to take advantage of as well as to make circumstances."[7] They're able to take context into account, and adapt.

Next to the superior maneuverability of their armies (based on battle formations more flexible than the enemy's), the most telling form of agility that Dodge's six warlords possessed was their extraordinary awareness of which military stance to take—offense or defense, advance or retreat—without reference to traditional rules of strategy. Here's how Dodge describes Gustavus's overall campaign in the German provinces:

> Herein is a peculiarly intelligent adaptation of work to existing conditions. From the king's landing to the passage of the Elbe, while securing his base, a cautious, but by no means indecisive policy; from crossing the Elbe to Nürnberg, while moving upon the enemy, a singular quickness and boldness, but by no means lacking in intelligent and methodical caution; from Nürnberg to Lützen an alternation from caution to boldness as circumstances warranted ... There was an entire freedom from blind subservience to the rules of war as then laid down.[8]

One of the rules of war laid down in those days was that an enemy's entrenched camps could not be successfully attacked. It was considered foolish even to try, yet Gustavus tried several times and showed it could be done. In April 1632, in Bavaria, his army encountered 40,000 imperial troops dug in behind earth walls on the opposite side of the river Lech. The foe's Austrian commander was Count Tilly, a general renowned for his military skill. Tilly refused to be drawn out, so Gustavus devised an audacious plan. First he set up a battery of cannons and, under cover of their fire, sent some of his men across the river in boats. They in turn built a bridge over which he marched his entire infantry, while at the same time his cavalry forded the river some distance away and rode down on the enemy's flank. Under direct attack, Tilly was forced to send part of his army out to defend the camp, but the combination of Swedish cannon fire, infantry, and cavalry was too much for the Austrian detachment; they lost their nerve and fled, taking cover behind their breastworks. With morale damaged, the imperial army soon retreated altogether and allowed the Swedes to take possession of much of Bavaria.

Gustavus, however, modified his plans once again: finding Bavaria's population hostile, he decided not to waste energy on an occupation and withdrew his forces east, turning his attention to other fronts and more promising allies.

Leaders such as Gustavus teach us that the race goes to neither the steady nor the swift, neither the cautious nor the bold. It goes to the adaptable. The winning side often isn't the one with the most brilliant plan, but rather the one that sees most clearly how the brilliant plan ought to be adjusted, and makes those adjustments without hesitation.

THIRD: TEAM EXCELLENCE

Fast-forward four centuries to another kind of battle.

Super Bowl XLVIII, played on February 2, 2014, at MetLife Stadium in Rutherford, New Jersey, was eagerly anticipated as a contest between the National Football League's best offense and best defense: Denver Broncos vs. Seattle Seahawks. Most commentators agreed that the Broncos had the edge. Their quarterback, Peyton Manning, was a 16-year veteran who had led his team to two straight 13–3 seasons while setting new NFL records for touchdowns and winning the league's Most Valuable Player award for the fifth time. But the game began badly for Denver, with a snapped ball that flew over Manning's head and gave Seattle an immediate two-point lead, and continued badly, with Denver unable to score a point until the end of the third quarter. The Broncos were overwhelmed from beginning to end, and the Seahawks ultimately won 43–8, the largest margin of victory at the Super Bowl in 21 years.

Manning was clearly the better and more experienced quarterback (compared to Seattle's Russell Wilson, who was good, but only in his second season), so the Broncos were a safe bet to win. But here's the problem with that reasoning: although Manning was the better quarterback, the Seahawks were the better team.

Having top-notch skills yourself isn't enough. Even having top-notch lieutenants isn't enough. Dodge's six great captains, like all good leaders, focused on building skill, intelligence, and discipline at every level of their organization. To take Gustavus Adolphus again as an example: he was, as I mentioned, the first ruler to create a standing national army. On top of that, he kept his troops in training exercises year round, devised drills that matched his intended battle maneuvers, and insisted on strictly merit-based promotions (no nepotism). He also invented a lighter musket and taught his men how to load and fire in 95 motions, which sounds absurdly slow until you learn that the standard number of motions at the time was 160. Thanks to the systemic excellence he created, Gustavus could count on not only the obedience but also the intelligence and initiative of his soldiers in battle. Meanwhile the generals of the Hapsburg imperial forces, sitting atop a relatively untrained and wholly self-interested group of mercenaries, had to put much more effort into maintaining discipline and couldn't count on anything should that discipline fall apart.

All leaders would do well to think more about the excellence of their foot soldiers than about their own excellence. If they don't, then like Count Tilly—and Peyton Manning, nearly 400 years later—they may find their impressive personal skills of little use when confronted by a foe with a more impressive team.

FOURTH AND LAST: WILINESS

Finally we come to the competitive factor that many leaders find most interesting: wiliness. The hope of outfoxing the competition has sold millions of leadership books with titles like *The Lords of Strategy* (Walter Kiechel) and *Competitive Advantage* (Michael Porter). One reason we gravitate to such books is that they promise to show us how to beat competitors without breaking a sweat; that is, without

on tall shoulders
W. CHAN KIM *and* RENÉE MAUBORGNE *on*
MAKING THE COMPETITION IRRELEVANT

In 2005, W. Chan Kim and Renée Mauborgne published *Blue Ocean Strategy*.[9] The book paints an enticing picture of the pristine "blue ocean"—uncontested market space—that awaits business leaders clever enough to escape the shark-mobbed "red ocean" where most organizations struggle for survival. Kim and Mauborgne offer a robust set of analytical tools for making that escape to the blue.

Many readers will pick up the book hoping to find a magic spear gun for all those sharks; or maybe a magic anvil to drop, like Wile E. Coyote, on their enemies. What they'll find instead is a way to spend less energy worrying about enemies and more energy creating leaps in value for customers; a way, perhaps, to be more like my Uncle Teddy, who in a game of croquet never wasted time knocking away someone else's ball when he could knock his own far out on the pristine green lawn.

taking on the long, hard work of creating a unified, agile, excellent team. Unfortunately, if you don't have unity, agility, and team excellence in place, the cleverest strategy won't be of much use. But if you do, then the fourth and final key to competitive advantage is the ability to turn the tables on an opponent, transforming his or her strength into weakness and your weakness into strength (see "On tall shoulders: W. Chan Kim and Renée Mauborgne on making the competition irrelevant").

Hannibal son of Hamilcar was a master of the art of table turning. He was commander of the forces of Carthage, the great civilization that challenged the Roman Empire for supremacy around the Mediterranean. He's still famous today for taking his entire army across the Alps to invade northern Italy in 218 BCE. Up to that time, only tiny bands of merchants had ever crossed those formidably high and snowy mountains; Hannibal did it with 59,000 men and 37 elephants. Dodge's essay on Hannibal, however, focuses not on that Alpine march (which he describes as "probably the most daring enterprise ever set on foot"), but rather on a battle that took place two years later: the battle of Cannae, in which Hannibal pulled off a feat of military jiu-jitsu that crushed an enemy more than twice his size.

The scene was the river Aufidus, which swoops south in a U near the village of Cannae in Italy. The Roman army, comprising some 80,000 foot and 7,000 horse and led by the consul Varro, lay on the north side, while Hannibal's 32,000 foot and 10,000 horse faced them on the south. Hannibal's main weakness was his much smaller infantry: if he drew up all his troops facing the enemy, one part of his line—left, right, or center—would have to be much thinner than theirs. His main strength was his cavalry, which was more numerous than that of the Romans, had larger and better-armored steeds and riders, and was better trained. It was also led by an exceptionally able captain named Maharbal.

Hannibal began by fording the Aufidus in two columns, covering his advance with archers and slingers in front of the main body. He placed his cavalry on his left, directly facing the enemy's cavalry; he knew that his heavier horse could crush theirs, thereby cutting off any attempted retreat to the Roman camps and eventually permitting an open ride around their rear to attack them from behind. As for the infantry, lacking the numbers for a uniformly strong line, he made the left and right flanks thick but left the center very thin.

Then came the stroke of genius. Hannibal arranged that rather weak center in a chevron, thrusting out toward the enemy. His plan was

> to withdraw his centre before the heavy Roman line—to allow them to push it in—and then to enclose them in his wings and fall on their flanks. This was a highly dangerous manoeuvre, unless the withdrawal of the centre could be checked at the proper time; but his men had the greatest confidence in him; the river in his rear would be an aid, if he could but keep his men steady ... Hannibal had fully prepared his army for this tactical evolution, and rehearsed its details with all his subordinates.[10]

And everything unfolded exactly as planned. Varro, seeing the thinness of the Carthaginian center, poured more and more men into his own center in an attempt to overwhelm the foe. Hannibal's chevron now began to withdraw, very gradually, maintaining just enough tenacity to encourage the Romans to keep advancing. "Varro now insanely ordered still more forces in from his wings to reinforce his centre, already a mass so crowded as to be unable to retain its organization," says Dodge. "He could not better have played into Hannibal's hands."[11] The Romans pressed on, becoming more jumbled at every moment, and the Carthaginians fell back, morphing from a chevron, to a straight line, to a concave crescent. Hannibal now had his left and right wings start advancing slowly, edging the Romans into a cul-de-sac that they, still shouting of victory, did not perceive. All this time, Maharbal and the cavalry had been doing their job, and so, finally:

> The decisive moment had come … Arresting the backward movement of the centre, which still had elbow-room to fight, as the Romans had not, [Hannibal] gave the orders to the wings which they were patiently awaiting. These veteran troops, in perfect order, wheeled inward to right and left, on the flanks of the struggling mass of legionaries. The Roman army was lost … for, at the same instant, Maharbal, having finished the destruction of the cavalry, rode down upon its rear.[12]

Hannibal ended up losing barely 6,000 men, while the entire Roman army of 87,000 was annihilated.

Dodge calls the battle of Cannae "a consummate piece of art, having no superior, few equals in the history of war."[13] It is a stunning example of how brain, not brawn, can be used to enact a scheme that turns an opponent's strengths against him. Today, the best leaders know how to do the same (see "Planning tool: Ten questions to turn the tables").

There is one more thing to notice about Cannae: The successful execution of Hannibal's plan depended entirely on his prior success in building unity, agility, and disciplined excellence throughout his army. A leader who tries to compete solely on wiliness, without the firm foundation of the other three factors, is only blowing smoke.

planning tool
TEN QUESTIONS TO TURN THE TABLES

Consider a competitive challenge your organization is facing right now. It could be something that cropped up recently, such as a startup entering the market with a new technology or product; or a long-standing situation, such as the ongoing need to compete against a larger or better-established firm.

Reflecting on Hannibal's battle of Cannae and using the questions below, create a strategy for turning the tables on your competitor.

1. What are your competitor's top three strengths with respect to this challenge?
2. How might these strengths be transformed into vulnerabilities?
3. Of these three transformations, which one seems most feasible?
4. What are your own organization's top three vulnerabilities with respect to this challenge?
5. How might these vulnerabilities be transformed into strengths?
6. Of these three transformations, which one seems most feasible?
7. Based on your analysis, how might you turn the tables on your competitor? Summarize your overall strategy in a sentence or two.
8. What specific steps must be taken to put your strategy into effect?
9. Which aspects of your strategy depend heavily on team *unity*, *agility*, and *excellence*?
10. How might those three factors need to be improved if your strategy is to work? What will you do to improve them?

Don't get caught in the trap of treating dilemmas as if they were problems. The latter can be solved; the former must be managed, as we discover in the next chapter.

great author

ALEXANDER HAMILTON AND JAMES MADISON'S *THE FEDERALIST*

The collection of 85 newspaper articles published under the title *The Federalist* contains more than 50 by Alexander Hamilton, nearly 30 by James Madison, and 5 by John Jay. While the authors' ostensible purpose was to persuade the people of New York to support the new Constitution of the United States (nine states' approval being needed to ratify), their even more ambitious goal was to offer a defense of the principles of federalism, a system of government that divides power between one central and many local authorities. The centralization vs. decentralization dilemma has confronted societies since ancient times and continues to bedevil organizations today.

All through the sweltering Philadelphia summer of 1787, the delegates to the Constitutional Convention had wrestled not only with that dilemma but with a number of related ones: majority rule vs. minority rights, security vs. liberty, stability vs. adaptability, and more. While the document they produced was wrongheaded on a number of issues (the most glaring example being the perpetuation of slavery), it nevertheless became a strong platform for later improvements, mostly because it provided a voice for each side of each dilemma. Take the so-called Connecticut Compromise that balanced the interests of big and small states by specifying, for the House, representatives apportioned by population, and for the Senate, equal representation for each state. At the time, the equal setup of the Senate made the less-populous Southern states willing to join a union with a strong central government; some 50 years later, however, proportional representation in the House gave the non-slave-owning Northern states the power they needed in order to pass the Thirteenth Amendment, abolishing slavery. Skillful dilemma management doesn't ensure that an organization will get everything right from the start. Rather, it lays a foundation for better answers to emerge over time.

In Essay 10, perhaps the most famous in the collection, Madison addresses the dangers of faction, the tendency for an organization to disintegrate into rival parties blind to the good of the whole. A faction is a group of people, whether a majority or a minority, who plant their feet on one side of a particular dilemma and refuse to budge. At best, factions lead to organizational dysfunction; at worst, to riots and death squads. Madison lays out with elegance all the possible methods for controlling faction without sacrificing liberty, and makes the case for a federal republic as the one type of government that works in this regard. Essay 10 is a must-read for any leader seeking to keep an organization united in purpose yet vibrant in debate.

✯ Read this in *The Federalist*: Essays 10, 39, 45, and 62.

chapter 10
DILEMMAS

Strategy isn't always about competing with an opponent. Sometimes it's about reconciling competing priorities or competing versions of the good. In such cases, the strategic thinkers are not those who take a side, but those who weave two sides together.

A MIRACLE IN PHILADELPHIA

> *February 21, 1787.* Resolved that in the opinion of Congress it is expedient that on the second Monday in May next, a Convention of delegates who shall have been appointed by the several states be held at Philadelphia for the sole and express purpose of revising the Articles of Confederation ... as shall, when agreed to in Congress and confirmed by the states, render the federal constitution adequate to the exigencies of Government and the preservation of the Union.[1]

As 1787 began, the United States of America was not a nation but a confederation: 13 states that had banded together to end British rule but thereafter remained a collection of self-governing entities. The Continental Congress, to which each state sent representatives, had no serious authority. The country as a whole was trying to do business under the Articles of Confederation, with poor results: the national currency was worthless, public and private credit held no confidence, and the peace treaty with Britain signed four years earlier was unenforceable. European aristocrats at their dinner parties scoffed at the idea of the "United States." Yet, despite the obvious deficiencies of the Articles, advocates for strengthening them could expect angry reactions: Are you saying our state should hand back its hard-won freedom to a tyrannical central government? Are we to be taxed to death, as before? Are we to bend the knee again to a king?

The delegates to the Constitutional Convention, who began assembling in Philadelphia on May 14, knew that their task would be thorny. They did at least all agree that tweaks to the Articles would not do: a brand-new document was needed. James Madison, of the Virginia delegation, had drafted a plan in advance and managed to persuade some of the early arrivals to back it, at least in principle. That document therefore became the starting point for deliberations. Even so, disputes broke out immediately. Especially fraught was the question of how many representatives each state would have in the new US Congress: the smaller states insisted they should have representation equal to that of the larger states (after all, their statehood was just as valid, and they weren't up for being trampled by the likes of New York and Pennsylvania), while the larger states insisted the number of representatives should be in proportion to each state's population. To each side, its view seemed clearly fair and the other side's clearly unfair. A compromise was proposed early by Connecticut but rejected out of hand, and it wasn't until the second month that that same compromise was revisited and, finally, adopted. In the lower house of Congress, the number of representatives would be proportional to population, while in the upper house, the Senate, the number would be the same for each state.

They argued and negotiated all through the summer. Finally, on September 17, the new Constitution was presented to the public for endorsement—and then the debate *really* heated up. Although later generations would call the convention's outcome "Miracle in Philadelphia," no one at the time was calling it that. The press was deluged with citizens' letters heaping praise or condemnation on the document. Some called it overly nationalistic; others, not nationalistic enough.

Into the fray stepped "Publius." Over the next seven months, he published 85 newspaper articles in defense of the Constitution and, more generally, of *federalism*, that type of government in which power is divided between a central authority and constituent political units. These were collected in a book titled *The Federalist* in June 1788, and Publius was then revealed to be not one person but three: Alexander Hamilton, James Madison, and John Jay. The trio had offered a thorough analysis of the Constitution and the federalist principles underpinning it. They argued persuasively that those principles were indeed "adequate to the exigencies of Government and the preservation of the Union."

DILEMMAS ARE NOT PROBLEMS

Taken together, the Constitution of the United States and the essays in *The Federalist* supporting its adoption exemplify the art of dilemma management.

First, we must distinguish dilemmas from problems. A *problem* is a challenge with a potential solution; you find and apply the solution, and the problem goes away. For instance, my old house is heated by a steam boiler. Every few weeks, the water in the boiler drops below the required level, and the system shuts down. The house grows cold. Perceiving the problem (for some reason I never seem able to anticipate it), I walk down to the boiler room, turn a handle on a pipe, and fill up the tank to the appropriate level. The boiler comes back on, and the house starts to warm up. I sing a celebratory verse of "Steam Heat" and go about my business. I had a problem; now it's solved.

Most problems are more complex than that, of course, but any challenge that has a solution, no matter how difficult to find, is a problem. A *dilemma*, on the other hand, has no solution. A dilemma is an ongoing challenge with two interdependent sides, neither of which can stand alone as the correct and permanent answer. Instead, there are positive and negative aspects to each side, and if you seek to adopt one side as the "solution" to your "problem," you'll get the positive aspects of that side but sooner or later will get the negative ones, too. In order to manage a dilemma, therefore, a leader must work constantly to maximize the benefits and minimize the drawbacks of both sides. In other words, the answer to a dilemma is always both/and, never either/or (see "On tall shoulders: Barry Johnson on the breathing organization").

Among the dilemmas leaders encounter regularly are individual vs. team, cost vs. quality, and planning vs. action. See "Team tool: Managing a dilemma" for a list of 16 common dilemmas for business leaders.

on tall shoulders

BARRY JOHNSON *on* THE BREATHING ORGANIZATION

"I have some bad news and some good news," says Barry Johnson. "The bad news is that there are a large number of unsolvable problems in your life ... The good news is that you can stop trying to solve them."[2] We could call these unsolvable problems dilemmas, paradoxes, or interdependent opposites; Johnson calls them *polarities*. The concepts in this chapter are largely drawn from his definitive book on the topic, *Polarity Management*.

Think about breathing, Johnson says. You would never try to solve a "low oxygen problem" by inhaling and only inhaling, and you'd never try to solve an "excess carbon dioxide problem" by exhaling and only exhaling. To maintain proper levels of oxygen and carbon dioxide, you must inhale and exhale, continuously, without end. Breathing "is not a static situation. It is a process—an ongoing flow of shifting emphasis from one to the other and back again."[3]

And for leaders, he says, the principle remains the same: Stop trying to stamp out problems. Instead, strive to create a breathing organization.

To grasp the structure of dilemmas, let's look at a big one faced by the Constitutional Convention delegates and familiar to business leaders today: *centralized vs. decentralized*. Figure 10.1 shows this dilemma's two sides and their pluses and minuses.[4] The advantages of centralization (upper left quadrant) include common standards, high efficiency, and access to a broad set of resources; the downsides (lower left) include unresponsiveness to local needs, slower decisions, and a tendency to pass the buck. When people live under a centralized regime and suffer its disadvantages, some of them will yearn for the pluses of decentralization, such as responsiveness, speed, and freedom (upper right). What they usually aren't seeing clearly are the minuses of that other side, such as inconsistency, inefficiency, and scarce resources (lower right).

For US citizens in 1787, one of the big drawbacks of life under the Articles of Confederation was the country's lack of credibility with

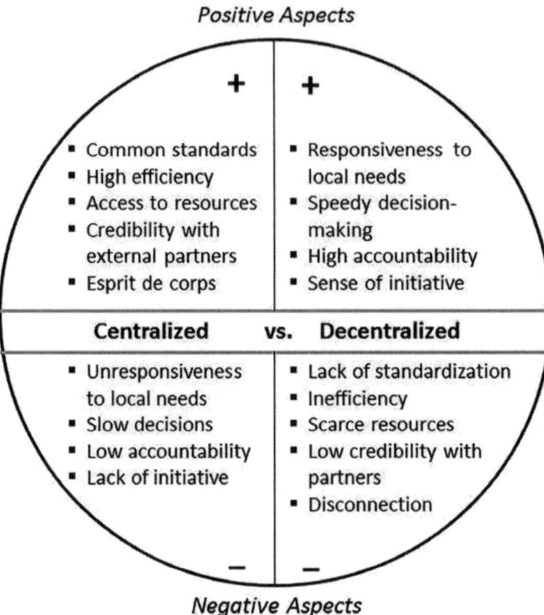

Figure 10.1 Structure of a dilemma

foreign regimes (fourth bullet, lower right). Eager to "solve the credibility problem," some politicians argued for the establishment of a much stronger national government, even a monarchy, which could bolster the United States' claim to be a genuine world power. They were, figuratively speaking, standing in the lower right quadrant of the dilemma and looking over the fence to the upper left quadrant, wishing for one of the benefits of a centralized regime: credibility with outsiders. Others insisted that such a government would set the country on a path back to tyranny. Better stick with decentralization, they said, even if our credibility isn't as high as we'd like. Many found it hard to see anything but the positives of their own side and the negatives of the other side, and most found it hard to envision a structure that wasn't either a monarchy or a loose confederation of independent states.

Fortunately, the delegates gathered in Philadelphia that summer were able to see past the either/or to a both/and. Wittingly or not, they treated the fundamental challenge before them as a dilemma to be managed, not a problem to be solved, and the outcome was federalism: a system that did not plant a flag on one side or the other, but instead struck a balance between the two and paved the way for ongoing navigation of the dilemma.

THE KEY TO MANAGING DILEMMAS

In *Polarity Management*, Johnson talks about the "infinity loop" inherent to dilemmas.[5] Poor navigation of this loop results in poor dilemma management, as we see in the following business situation.

Denise was vice-president of a division of Westmont, a manufacturing firm known for producing high-quality automotive accessories. For most of the past year the company had been struggling to control costs. Under direction from senior management, Denise and her team had worked since January to lower expenses for labor, materials, maintenance, and training. At first, the benefits of their efforts were obvious: the division forecasts looked great, management was happy, and the team received a larger than usual bonus for Quarters 1 and 2. As the year wore on, however, a number of quality issues arose. Cut-rate maintenance on some equipment resulted in defective batches of product, reductions in the training budget led to serious design errors by some new hires in Engineering, and understaffing in Customer Service was causing long response times and declining customer satisfaction scores. As the fourth quarter opened, the division's biggest customer, a large auto-supply retail chain, informed Denise that it was moving its business to one of Westmont's competitors. "We just can't count on your quality any more," she was told. Suddenly, the Q4 forecast looked terrible.

Minutes after the news broke about the lost customer, Westmont's CEO was on the phone to Denise telling her to "get these quality problems under control." After promising to do so, Denise fired off an email to her senior team instructing them to clear their calendars for an all-day "problem-solving meeting" starting tomorrow, 7 a.m.

In this example, let's say *cost* is on the left side of the dilemma circle and *quality* on the right side. Denise's division starts out in the upper left quadrant, enjoying the benefits of a focus on cost control: higher profits and the bonuses that come with them. But soon the negatives of that side begin to assert themselves and the situation sinks down to the lower left quadrant, tracing the left side of an infinity loop (∞). Eventually the negatives overwhelm the positives, and the so-called problem is named: "Poor quality!" Next, as Denise's team members strive to "fix quality," they'll move diagonally up to the top right quadrant, where they'll enjoy—for a while—the benefits of a focus on quality control. If they stop paying attention to costs, however, they'll soon find themselves sinking to the lower right, where the negatives of that side, such as lower profits and lower bonuses, will make themselves felt. Management will complain that costs are out of line, and the team will feel pressure to make a diagonal move back to the upper left, where they started. And on they'll go, around and around the loop.

Now, this isn't to say that the infinity loop is a bad thing. When you're dealing with dilemmas, it's inevitable. What is bad is when leaders fail to understand and work with the loop as a natural and necessary pattern; when they "solve their problem" by jumping to the other side and attempting to stay there permanently, as if holding their breath in order to solve a low-oxygen problem.

We can avoid this mistake. First, we must *recognize* dilemmas when we see them; second, we must *manage* them better by moving around the infinity loop more fluidly. When we put on blinders and lurch from one side to the other, we spend more time experiencing the negative aspects of that particular dilemma. When we strive to see the positives and negatives of each side and encourage our people to move easily and confidently around the loop, we're better able to maximize the positives on both sides (see "Team tool: Managing a dilemma").

At the heart of every successful project you'll find at least one well-managed dilemma. The project known as the United States of America is a case in point. The 1787 Constitutional Convention remains history's finest example of a group of leaders navigating a dilemma's infinity loop—sometimes amicably, often contentiously, but always persistently. And the result was indeed something of a miracle (in Philadelphia): a new system of government that would preserve and uphold a union for centuries to come.

team tool

MANAGING A DILEMMA

Consider an intractable problem your team has been facing, an ongoing challenge or frustration that seems to resist solutions. Consider that this "problem" might not be a problem, but rather a dilemma.

Review the 16 common dilemmas below. Which is most like yours? (If several are applicable, choose the one that seems to fit best. Or, come up with a new label for yours.)

Centralized – decentralized	Structured – unstructured
Long term – short term	Market driven – product driven
Individual – team	Efficiency – engagement
Adaptability – stability	Global – local
Cost – quality	Planning – action
Security – liberty	Theory – practice
Tradition – innovation	Speed – deliberation
Employee centric – customer centric	Profit – growth

With your team, analyze the dilemma using the format shown in Figure 10.1 and the following process.

1. Ask each team member to prepare by reading this chapter and reflecting on his or her experiences with the dilemma you've named.

2. With the team gathered, draw the dilemma circle on a whiteboard, placing Side A on the left and Side B on the right. Restate that this is about analyzing and managing a dilemma, not solving a problem.

3. Ask the team for phrases to put in each quadrant of the circle. Do the positives of Side A, then its negatives; then the positives of Side B, then its negatives. After that round, loop back and ask the team to add more phrases to any quadrant.

4. Lead a discussion on insights gained and implications for action, using the following questions:

- What must we do in order to get more of the benefits of both the upper quadrants?
- How do we know when it's time to shift focus from one side of the dilemma to the other side? In other words, how do we know when we're spending too much time in one of the lower quadrants and therefore need to make adjustments?
- What team behaviors help us move smoothly and rapidly around the infinity loop? Which behaviors create obstacles?
- What new structures or processes might help us better balance the two sides of this dilemma? What current structures or processes are counterproductive?
- How can we open our own and others' eyes to the full picture of this dilemma: to the negatives and positives of each side?

Next, two of the greatest speeches of all time show us how to be better communicators.

great authors

SPEECHES OF PERICLES AND ABRAHAM LINCOLN

It was an annual tradition in the ancient city-state of Athens to hold a public funeral for fallen heroes. In 431 BCE, the first year of the 17-year war between Athens and Sparta, the funeral organizers asked Pericles, the city's most eminent general and statesman, to deliver the ceremony's closing address. Pericles' speech was recorded by Thucydides in his *History of the Peloponnesian War*, although "recorded" may be the wrong word, as Thucydides did not write down speeches verbatim but rather captured their main points. No matter how exact or loose a copy it is, Thucydides' version of Pericles' funeral oration is acknowledged as one of the great speeches of history.

A typical Athenian funeral oration was all about eulogizing the war dead. Pericles' speech departs from this formula. He begins by wondering aloud why a speech is even necessary, since he "should have thought that the worth which had displayed itself in deeds would be sufficiently rewarded by honors also shown by deeds" (in other words, by this very expensive three-day funeral).[1] He also notes that effusive praise for individuals, living or dead, tends to engender not admiration but resentment, for the listener first thinks "*I* couldn't be that good," and then begins to think "*Nobody* could be that good." Still, says Pericles, it is his duty to make a speech, so he will do his best. After a nod to the audience's ancestors and the gratitude owed them, he moves on to his main idea: the greatness of Athens.

That greatness, he says, is rooted in three quintessentially Athenian values: equality, openness, and love of knowledge. He cites examples to show how these values play out in the life of the community and set Athens apart from all other city-states. Moreover, these values set Athenians apart from all other *people*: "In short, I say that as a city we are the school of Hellas; while I doubt if the world can produce a man [who is] equal to so many emergencies, and graced by so happy a versatility, as the Athenian." With praise of Athens as the backdrop, praise of the citizens of Athens comes across not as specious flattery but as a call to excel. Rather than butter up his listeners, Pericles asks them to live up to the high standards of their nation and the high ideals it represents.

Twenty-three centuries later, at Gettysburg, Abraham Lincoln did the same. (He had certainly studied Pericles' oration; he may even have used it for inspiration.) The Gettysburg Address, famously short, was roundly disparaged by some commentators of the day: the *Chicago Times*, for example, decried the "silly flat dishwatery utterances," while the Harrisburg *Daily Patriot and Union* said the speech deserved "the veil of oblivion."[2] Others, however, saw it for the jewel it is: the *Springfield Republican*, for example, predicted it would "repay further study as the model speech." In years to come, the address would be judged to have played a part in restoring a nation's faith in justice, liberty, and unity in the midst of an agonizing Civil War.

chapter 11

COMMUNICATION

There are few more useful objects of study for present-day leaders than the great speeches of the past, not just because they demonstrate what effective communication looks and sounds like, but also because they throw our own errors into sharp relief.

On the afternoon of November 19, 1863, some 75 years after "Publius" presented his defense of the United States Constitution in *The Federalist*, Edward Everett, former president of Harvard University and renowned orator, stepped up to a podium that looked out over a new cemetery for the nation's war dead in Gettysburg, Pennsylvania. He opened his address by citing "the Athenian example," likely a reference to a speech by the ancient Greek statesman Pericles; it was an example he seemingly didn't take to heart, given that Pericles' address lasted about 20 minutes and his more than 2 hours. The day was cold and blustery, and the audience members were huddling deeper into their coats long before Everett finished. But they applauded politely, and as he retook his seat he felt satisfied with his eloquently detailed description of the great battle that had been fought on that same field four months before.

The next speaker was a tall, gangly politician who had been asked to offer "a few appropriate remarks."[3] His speech took less than 3 minutes. Here is what he said:

> Fourscore and seven years ago our fathers brought forth on this continent, a new nation, conceived in Liberty, and dedicated to the proposition that all men are created equal.
>
> Now we are engaged in a great civil war, testing whether that nation, or any nation so conceived and so dedicated, can long endure. We are met on a great battle-field of that war. We have come to dedicate a portion of that field, as a final resting place for those who here gave their lives that that nation might live. It is altogether fitting and proper that we should do this.

> But, in a larger sense, we can not dedicate—we can not consecrate—we can not hallow—this ground. The brave men, living and dead, who struggled here, have consecrated it, far above our poor power to add or detract. The world will little note, nor long remember what we say here, but it can never forget what they did here. It is for us the living, rather, to be dedicated here to the unfinished work which they who fought here have thus far so nobly advanced. It is rather for us to be here dedicated to the great task remaining before us—that from these honored dead we take increased devotion to that cause for which they gave the last full measure of devotion—that we here highly resolve that these dead shall not have died in vain—that this nation, under God, shall have a new birth of freedom—and that government of the people, by the people, for the people shall not perish from the earth.

What makes one speech gripping and another forgettable? Clearly, brevity is important: a 3-minute talk is likely to be a lot more memorable than a 2-hour one. But more than that, a great communication is one that makes its listeners feel part of a lasting, worthwhile, and special enterprise, and then challenges them to live up to the ideals of that enterprise. Abraham Lincoln's amazing feat was to do all that in just 270 words.

Let's start by reviewing the four mistakes great communicators avoid but average ones often commit. Then we'll look to Pericles, the "Athenian example," to show us how it's done.

FOUR COMMUNICATION MISTAKES

Mistake 1: Refusing to tap into people's desire to be part of something special You may recall Pinecone, the California-based public relations firm I introduced in Chapter 2. Among the reasons for Pinecone's strong customer loyalty since its inception were its reputation for quality, its innovative spirit, and, most of all, its exceptional people: fun to work with, collaborative, business savvy. The culture was what you might call celebratory, with employees who took great pride in their work and managers who never hesitated to hand out praise.

Rona, the firm's new chief executive, had led other divisions within parent company Hanover and was familiar with the PR industry. She had long been unimpressed by Pinecone's mediocre financial results and what she saw as its employees' unwarranted arrogance, given those results. We saw earlier how, in an effort to splash a bit of cold water on the firm's collective face, Rona began her first all-company speech with a slide that read: "Pinecone's mission is to deliver profit to Hanover." Later that week, in her first meeting with the management team, she continued in the same vein.

"I see one of my main jobs as getting you all to stop patting yourselves on the back," she began, looking around the conference table with unsmiling eyes. "Pinecone may have a fine reputation with clients, but the truth is, you're at rock bottom of the group in profitability. Now, I don't believe you're any less skilled than the managers of the other Hanover companies, so there's no reason you can't do as well as them. In fact, I'm sure you can. But we have to start by agreeing on one thing: Pinecone isn't all that special."

Mistake 2: Portraying individuals or subgroups as elite Six months later, the winners of Hanover's corporate-wide sales contest flew off to Maui on an all-expenses-paid trip, a reward for exceeding their annual targets. Participation in the contest was new for Pinecone, and on hearing about the trip some employees wondered what was going on. Pinecone's sales process, like everything else it did, was highly collaborative: media specialists, writers, and graphic designers habitually took part in client calls and helped account executives write proposals. So there was some mild grousing when it transpired that several members of the sales team—but no one from any sales-supporting role—were at that moment lounging on a Hawaiian beach.

When the muttering reached his ears, Pinecone's head of sales decided he'd better send out a communication; after all, the contest was something new, so it was no wonder some people were confused. Seeking to cast the trip in a positive light and use it as a motivation opportunity, he sent the following email to all employees:

> Dear Colleagues: I want to congratulate Matt Cohen, Keesha Martin, and Dana O'Donnell, all of whom are at this moment enjoying one last sun-filled day at the Grand Hyatt Wailea Beach. They and the other winners of Hanover's annual sales contest have been having a week of fun complete with margaritas, karaoke, and snorkeling. This trip was a reward for the elite among our account executives; each of the winners exceeded some very challenging targets and made an outstanding contribution to our business this past year. So, if you see a few sunburned coworkers in the office next week, be sure to tell them congratulations and thanks for helping Pinecone succeed!

Needless to say, this note didn't help. The grumblings among non-sales staff grew louder and continued for several months. One wag had T-shirts printed that read: "Some Salespeople Went to Maui and All I Got Was This Stupid Shirt."

Mistake 3: Emphasizing facts and data rather than emotion and story One of Pinecone's clients was TriMark, a midsized pharmaceutical company specializing in medications for autoimmune disorders. Its top product was a drug for rheumatoid arthritis, a progressive inflammatory disease that strikes mostly younger and middle-aged women. One September morning, the Pinecone account team attended a speech being delivered by TriMark's CEO on the occasion of the company's 25th anniversary. The purpose of the talk was to underscore TriMark's proud history of providing treatments for devastating diseases that affect young families. All TriMark employees, as well as a number of media outlets, were in the audience.

The CEO opened the speech by talking about his sister Marcia, a rheumatoid arthritis sufferer; he described her struggles with such daily tasks as getting her kids dressed and using her phone. The audience was leaning forward, eager to hear more. But after a minute or two, he dropped the story and launched into a series of slides filled with statistics: 2 million rheumatoid arthritis sufferers in the United States alone; 25 percent of them currently taking biologic response modifiers; 12 percent of those patients taking TriMark's own biologic; 82 percent of 5,400 US rheumatologists who report being "very aware" or "aware" of TriMark's medications.

As the slides rolled on, the audience began to fidget. Thirty minutes in, Tom, account executive for the Pinecone team, leaned over to Stacy, lead copywriter, and whispered: "What happened to Marcia?"

Mistake 4: Failing to challenge your audience to live up to an ideal A few more months went by. With Pinecone's annual financial results now in hand, Rona was planning an all-company conference call to report the numbers and kick off the upcoming year. Overall, she couldn't have been more pleased: the firm's profit margin had nearly doubled versus the year before. Of course, this was partly a result of the layoffs she'd implemented back in March, which had cut staff by 10 percent and helped reduce the company's cost base. She felt, however, that the gains were due also to the new sense of focus and efficiency she had worked so hard to instill. "Most of these folks are a lot clearer now on why they're being paid," she thought, "and they know it isn't to give themselves trophies."

She decided that, in the conference call, she wouldn't stint on praise for the good financial performance. But since she didn't want anyone resting on their laurels, she would follow the praise quickly with a challenge—one she felt would be inspiring. These were the notes she wrote in preparation for her remarks:

> So again, congratulations on an outstanding finish to last year, and thank you, everyone, for all your hard work. Now I want to talk about our goals for *this* year. Obviously, it would make no sense to set our sights lower than what we've proved we can achieve. I want to challenge us to aim higher. That's why our target for this year's profit margin is set at 15 percent, which as you can see is 5 percentage points higher than what we did last year. It's a stretch, I know, but I'm confident we can do it. After all, we've already shown that we can! Personally, I'm very excited by the idea of tripling our profits in just two years. You can imagine how happy our parent Hanover will be with results like that.

LASTING, WORTHWHILE, AND SPECIAL

Here, again, are the four communication mistakes:

1. Refusing to tap into people's desire to be part of something special
2. Portraying individuals or subgroups as elite
3. Emphasizing facts and data rather than emotion and story
4. Failing to challenge your audience to live up to an ideal

How important is it to avoid these errors? Clearly, our success as leaders depends heavily on how well we communicate. But if you don't happen to be President of the United States, you may think you don't need to aim for, let alone attain, the lofty heights of a Gettysburg Address. Like Rona, you may feel your job is to keep your team informed and tell them what to do to earn their bonus—forget about telling them how special they are. Or, you may want to be motivating and think the way to do it is by touting the achievements of the "elite," as Pinecone's head of sales did; or by presenting a slew of statistics, as the CEO of TriMark did; or by stressing financial targets, as Rona did in her end-of-year remarks. But as our featured classics keep telling us (and contemporary gurus, too; see "On tall shoulders: Stephen Denning on springboard stories"), human beings crave something more from their leaders, and we'd better try to provide that "more," if only in a modest way or on occasion. If we do try, we'll find that even our stumbling efforts are appreciated. If we don't, our team members will simply look for other leaders to follow.

To be inspiring, a communication must meet three criteria. First, it must make the audience feel part of an entity larger than themselves, and that entity must have three attributes: *lasting*, *worthwhile*, and *special*. Second, it must challenge the audience to live up to the ideals described. And third, it should be brief (see "Assessment tool: How inspiring are you?").

on tall shoulders

STEPHEN DENNING *on* SPRINGBOARD STORIES

When I first read Stephen Denning's *The Springboard*,[4] I toyed with the idea of ditching my PowerPoint slides and white papers and instead embracing "springboard stories": brief, memorable anecdotes that, as they spread through an organization, transform thinking and ignite action. As a management consultant, I knew that (to paraphrase Denning) charts leave listeners bemused, prose remains unread, and dialogue is just too slow. When you need people on board with a big change or a big challenge, storytelling is often the only thing that works.[5]

But corporate customs are hard-wearing, and slide decks are the quintessential corporate custom. I found I couldn't ditch the slides entirely. Today I try to buck the trend in a small way by framing presentations with a story at the beginning and one at the end. Though my eloquence certainly doesn't equate to that of a Lincoln or a Pericles, I know the stories will be remembered long after the slides are forgotten.

Although it can't match the Gettysburg Address for brevity, Pericles' funeral oration is only about six pages—around 18 minutes, like a TED talk—and deserves a close read by any leader who wants to understand what makes for a speech with impact. Pericles delivered his address at the annual public funeral for Athenian war dead. His focus in the speech, however, is not the deceased heroes (for, he notes, people can endure to hear others praised only when they can "persuade themselves of their own ability to equal the actions recounted"[6]), but rather the entire city-state of Athens and the qualities that make it special. Among the many things he finds to praise are the city's laws, which offer equal justice to all citizens; its high levels of freedom and tolerance, which reduce nosiness and jealousy; its year-round public games and cultural events, which offer refreshment for the mind; and the unique combination of "daring and deliberation" that infuses all public enterprises. The address is essentially a panegyric to the Athenian character. If we were to look for the leadership character traits we explored in Chapter 7—courage, integrity, resilience, generosity, and concern—we would find all five included here, along with comparisons to other cities whose character, according to Pericles, fails to measure up to the Athenian standard.

Many leaders today don't see the point of waxing on, as Pericles does, about how great the organization is. Like Rona, they worry that such praise will only make employees self-satisfied and lazy; or, while they don't mind holding up certain individuals as examples of excellence, they think it's a bad idea to talk about the excellence of the place overall. They also may be skeptical of the value of "visions," and I have to agree with them there. In Chapter 3, you may recall, Machiavelli told us that vague promises of a glorious future do little to keep people moving along a long road to change.

Pericles' address, however, isn't vague. His picture of Athens emerges in solid detail, and we can feel the effect his words must have had on his listeners: they would have swelled with pride, not in themselves, but rather in their community and all it represented. They would have felt inspired to do almost anything, pay any price, to keep their great city protected and thriving. Far from feeling arrogant, they would have felt humble: perhaps a bit uncertain about whether they as individuals could live up to such high standards, but badly wanting to. And, near the end of his address, Pericles challenges them to do just that:

> So died these men as became Athenians. You, their survivors, must determine to have as unfaltering a resolution in the field ... you must yourselves realize the power of Athens, and feed your eyes upon her from day to day ... and then when all her greatness shall break upon you, you must reflect that it was by courage, sense of duty, and a keen feeling of honor in action that men were enabled to win all this, and that no personal failure in an enterprise could make them consent to deprive their country of their valor, but they laid it at her feet as the most glorious contribution they could offer.[7]

assessment tool

HOW INSPIRING ARE YOU?

Not every leadership communication has to be inspiring, but some of them should be. Use the checklist below to assess the inspiration level of your and other leaders' communications. Rate each item on a scale of 1–5 (1 = "to a very small extent"; 5 = "to a very great extent"). Total the score, and use the key underneath to interpret it.

This communication, speech, or message:

A. Says why the entire organization or endeavor is lasting, worthwhile, and special: ___
B. Challenges the audience to live up to the organization's high standards or ideals: ___
C. Refrains from singling out specific individuals or subgroups as "elite": ___
D. Uses stories and examples, rather than statistics and data, to make the key points: ___
E. Is brief (less than 5 minutes = 5; less than 20 minutes = 4; around 30 minutes = 3; around 45 minutes = 2; more than an hour = 1): ___

Total: ___

Key

20–25 Very inspiring
15–19 Fairly inspiring
10–14 Not that inspiring
5–9 Very uninspiring

The working world is hard. While we don't usually ask people to lay down their lives in the course of duty, we do ask them to slog through tedious tasks, bear harsh disappointments with a smile, and stretch to reach ever-tougher goals. The best leaders know that a paycheck alone does not inspire anyone to slog and bear and stretch—not to the extent required. What does inspire is an image in your mind of something lasting, worthwhile, and special of which you are a part. Something, says Lincoln, that's worth a "full measure of devotion"; something, says Pericles, to "feed your eyes upon" from day to day.

Next, the Greek historian Plutarch shows us how to develop leadership character with the help of philosophy.

great author
PLUTARCH'S *MORALIA*

Plutarch (circa 46–120 CE), the ancient Greek historian, biographer, and essayist, is known today primarily for two of his works: *Parallel Lives* and *Moralia*. The former, sometimes called "Lives of the Noble Greeks and Romans" or simply "Plutarch's Lives," is a study of some 50 ancient leaders: princes, statesmen, generals, philosophers, and scholars. Plutarch arranged them in pairs, one Roman and one Greek—Romulus and Theseus, for instance—and compared each pair's character, education, and achievements. He also included some single biographies, including lives of Alexander the Great and Julius Caesar. (The latter was Shakespeare's primary source for the play of that name.) Because these works are in some cases the main or only source of information still extant on a particular leader of those times, modern-day biographers of classical figures draw heavily on Plutarch.

The *Lives* are consistently entertaining but somewhat lengthy. Readers who want a distillation of Plutarch's wisdom can turn instead to the *Moralia* (loose English translation "Customs and Mores"), a collection of 78 essays. They include practical advice on such topics as friendship, marriage, anger, and curiosity; philosophical and religious treatises such as "That Virtue May Be Taught" and "On the Decline of the Oracles"; and humorous pieces such as "Odysseus and Gryllus," an imagined dialogue between Greek adventurer Odysseus and one of his sailors, unhappily transformed into a pig by the evil enchantress Circe.

Read this in Moralia: "On Education," "How One May Be Aware of One's Progress in Virtue," "How a Man May Be Benefited by His Enemies," "On Restraining Anger," "That Virtue May Be Taught," "How One May Discern Flattery from a Friend," and "On Shyness."

chapter 12
CHARACTER, DEVELOPED

Those of us whose teenage years antedate the internet know what it's like to pour out our rage at a parent or boy/girlfriend onto multiple sheets of paper, only to find that after all that scribbling our emotions had cooled and that delivering the missive—which back then meant finding an envelope, a stamp, and a mailbox—seemed like too much bother. It was a system that, I'm convinced, built self-control and prevented many needless blowups. Today's technologies make it much harder to keep our anger under wraps. It's so easy to click Send.

So we admire Abraham Lincoln for his eloquence, but perhaps we should admire him even more for the words he kept to himself. He had a habit of writing letters that he never sent; he called them "hot letters," because they contained all the anger he felt it unwise to express openly. Thanks to this practice, Civil War general George G. Meade, for example, would never know that at one point his commander in chief blamed him for letting Robert E. Lee escape after the battle of Gettysburg.[1]

In Chapter 7, we examined the five leadership character traits (courage, integrity, resilience, generosity, and concern) and saw how each represents the mean on a continuum that runs between two extremes, from extreme deficiency on the one hand to extreme excess on the other. Strength of character, we saw, is the ability to stick to the mean in our habits and actions, rather than sliding off to one side or wobbling back and forth; the ability, for instance, to stick to courage, avoiding both timidity and rashness. We looked at three types of leader, the Loose Cannon, the Sociopath, and the Lightweight, who fail to hit the mean, and a fourth type, the Champion, who hits it most of the time. The next questions to explore are: How do we develop that strength of character? And how do we know whether we're making progress?

HOW PHILOSOPHY DEVELOPS LEADERSHIP CHARACTER

In the nature vs. nurture debate, the ancient Greeks came down squarely on the side of nurture. While they saw natural ability as important, they believed it was education that formed character. In his essay "On Education," Plutarch tells the story of the Spartan legislator Lycurgus, who took two puppies from one litter and raised them in different ways: one he spoiled and cosseted, while the other he trained to be a good retriever. Some months later in the state assembly he gave a demonstration, saying, "Mighty is the influence on moral excellence of habit, and education, and training ... as I will prove to you at once."[2] He then brought out the two puppies and set out a dish of food and a hare. The first puppy made straight for the dish, while the other rushed after the hare. Turning to the mystified audience, Lycurgus explained the moral: "These puppies are of the same parents, but by virtue of a different bringing up, the one is pampered and the other a good hound."[3] Humans are the same, says Plutarch; education is, and should be, the main shaper of our character.

Today, this view is making something of a comeback. Many US and European primary schools have adopted so-called character-based curricula, designed to instill in children qualities such as self-restraint, kindness, and perseverance. But while the aims may be similar to those of an ancient education, the method is quite different. A present-day reader of Plutarch's *Moralia* will be struck by his assumption that a youth's education should be focused on—in fact, is almost the same as—studying philosophy. That sounds strange to modern ears. Surely, we think, character can't be developed through something as bloodless as philosophy; surely character is a matter of emotions, values, and aspirations. But by *philosophy* Plutarch means something much livelier and broader than the dry, narrow subject it can be today. He means *philosophia*: love of wisdom.

To study philosophy, Plutarch says, is to learn to think clearly and act wisely, free from the confusion created by destructive passions. It is to strive to put reason in charge so that, eventually, those passions don't control you. To use the terminology from Chapter 2, philosophy enables us to perceive leadership traps and avoid them.

Modern-day character-building curricula are similar in that they aim to teach children to think before they act and resist being jerked around by their emotions. For Plutarch and his contemporaries, however, something far more thoroughgoing than a weekly conversation about "values" was required if a youth was to learn to live by reason rather than urges. Above all, he or she had to be taught to seek, recognize, and act in accordance with truth, and that meant both scientific-mathematical and political-moral truth; "ethics" wasn't a separate curriculum from biology or political science. A philosophical education pursued answers to these interrelated questions: What is true? What is good? What is right?

But it wasn't just about pondering abstractions. The idea of centeredness helps us grasp the point: philosophical study allowed one to perceive the mean, the center, and to orient one's thoughts and actions toward it; not to avoid all passion, but rather to keep passion under reason's rule and avoid being knocked off balance by churning needs. Leaders so educated are like navigators with a North Star, always with something to steer by. As Plutarch explains:

> With [philosophy] as ruler and guide we can know what is honorable, what is disgraceful, what is just, what unjust; generally speaking, what is to be sought after, what to be avoided; how we ought to behave to the gods, to parents, to elders, to the laws, to foreigners, to friends ... and, what is of the greatest importance, to be neither over elated in prosperity nor over depressed in adversity, nor to be dissolute in pleasures, nor fierce and brutish in anger.[4]

That last point about anger is so important to Plutarch that he devotes an entire essay, "On Restraining Anger," to it. The essay is presented as a dialogue between two friends, Fundanus and Sylla, in which the former asks the latter how he has managed to grow so much milder than he used to be. After a discussion of anger, its dangers, and how to mitigate it, Sylla explains that his method was to abstain from anger for a few days, then for a month or two, and so on, until finally he was able to give it up almost completely (see "Planning tool: An anger hiatus").

planning tool
AN ANGER HIATUS

Follow Sylla's example (in Plutarch's "On Restraining Anger") and take a break from anger for one day.

Whenever you feel yourself becoming angry, take a breath and repeat a phrase such as "It's not a big deal" or "I have better things to think about"; then turn your attention to those other things. Make an effort to keep your voice, face, and body language calm and pleasant.

At the end of the day, note how you feel, mentally and physically. If you like the effect, take another anger hiatus. See if you can work up to a week, a month, or more.

Today's leaders may find talk of "giving up anger" strange. For Plutarch, though, anger is the quintessential immoderate passion, a "universal seed from all the passions" and a fatal temptation to leaders. "For it is drawn from pain and pleasure and haughtiness," he says, "... and the most unlovely kind of desire is innate in it, namely the appetite for injuring another."[5] And indeed, if we consider the extremes of each of the character continuums (Figure 7.1), we can see how anger is an all-purpose intensifier of those extremes: it heats up rashness and offensiveness, adds frenzy to vacillation, fuels mania, solidifies obstinacy, renders severity even more implacable, and gives indifference a greater chill. Plutarch describes vividly the causes and effects of anger, showing how it stems from weakness and leads to even profounder weakness; as we read the essay, we may be reminded of Creon, in *Antigone* (see Chapter 5), whose anger and resulting actions reduce him to a "vain, silly man" totally lacking influence.

Many of today's psychologists and pundits (though not all; see "On tall shoulders: David Brooks on the road to character") would have it that angry thoughts and feelings aren't bad, only how one acts on them. Plutarch makes no such distinction. He insists that we temper our thoughts as well as our actions, warning that angry thoughts give rise to angry words, which are the spark for angry deeds. He again recommends philosophy, with its calming, centering effects, as the antidote. Had Plutarch been around in the nineteenth century, I suspect he would have endorsed Lincoln's unsent-letter trick. He might also have seconded the advice of Charles Dodgson (aka *Alice in Wonderland* author Lewis Carroll) in the pamphlet "Eight or Nine Wise Words about Letter-Writing":

> When you have written a letter that you feel may possibly irritate your friend, however necessary you may have felt it to so express yourself, *put it aside till the next day*. Then read it over again, and fancy it addressed to yourself. This will often lead to your writing it all over again, taking out a lot of the vinegar and pepper ... thus making a much more palatable dish of it![6]

on tall shoulders

DAVID BROOKS on THE ROAD TO CHARACTER

David Brooks's *The Road to Character* hearkens back to classical ideas about moral depth. Though he never speaks about philosophy per se as the North Star guiding us along the road, he follows the ancients in seeing character development as a long and difficult forging of the self rather than a quick and easy matter of selecting a set of personal values and refraining from hurting others. Here is Brooks in one positively Plutarchian passage:

> Character is a set of dispositions, desires, and habits that are slowly engraved during the struggle against your own weakness ... If you make disciplined, caring choices, you are slowly engraving certain tendencies into your mind. You are making it more likely that you will desire the right things and execute the right actions. If you make selfish, cruel, or disorganized choices, then you are slowly turning this core thing inside yourself into something that is degraded, inconstant, or fragmented. You can do harm to this core thing with nothing more than ignoble thoughts, even if you are not harming anyone else.[7]

THE SCHOOL OF HARD KNOCKS AND ENEMIES

"OK," you say. "Education is obviously important, and I'll even grant you that studying philosophy, in the ancient sense, helps keep one balanced. But if you ask me how I developed character as a leader, I wouldn't talk about formal education. I'd say I learned from the School of Hard Knocks."

Most experienced leaders would agree: it's not the schooling but the struggles with turnaround assignments, failing projects, and dysfunctional teams that really teach one to lead with strength and serenity. Actually, Plutarch would agree, too—with the important caveat that Hard Knocks Academy is a finishing school, not a primary school. Its buffetings will polish the character of leaders already possessed of a philosophical education, but mangle the character of those who lack such a foundation. Not everyone is the Little Engine That Could, digging deeper and pulling harder when faced with a tough challenge. Some people just go off the rails. Assuming that you have the philosophical perspective necessary to turn hardships into character-building experiences, however, hardships can teach you a great deal.

And it's the hardships presented by your enemies, says Plutarch, that teach you the most. His essay "How a Man May Be Benefited by His Enemies" is useful reading for anyone who feels that they have been unfairly abused or done a bad turn by a boss or colleague. (Is there anyone who doesn't feel that way?) It tells exactly how to reframe such attacks as gifts, incorporating them into our education so that, in the end, our attacker has been of service to us. Just as it's the animals with the strongest and healthiest stomachs that can "eat and digest serpents and scorpions," so it is the leaders with the strongest character who can derive benefit even from the attacks of their enemies.[8] Weak leaders, in contrast, have delicate digestions: the smallest insults sicken them.

Enemies, as it turns out, have many lessons to offer. Plutarch's essay names seven ways in which enemies improve our character. First, by scrutinizing us and our affairs, enemies encourage us to be on our best behavior. Second, enemies make us want to "vex them by living virtuously." Third, enemies make us examine our own character: when in their company, we're more likely to wonder, "Am I like that?" and "How can I *not* be like that?" Fourth, by remaining silent when enemies revile us, we gain practice in self-control. Fifth, treating enemies graciously and giving them credit where credit is due makes us look generous. Sixth, a common enemy strengthens bonds among friends. Seventh and last, enemies are a spur to achievement, because they make us want to outdo them.

Leaders with a character tempered by philosophy are able to absorb these "enemy lessons" and, like a skilled standup comic, turn their hecklers into part of the act.

MEASURING PROGRESS: ON THE ROAD TO ORDINARY

Is your character improving or deteriorating, and how do you know for sure?

If you've ever attended a management training course or applied for a supervisory position, you've likely taken a leadership assessment. Maybe it was a series of questions about your preferences and habits, or maybe you were asked to select a handful of colleagues to give you input on your performance. Such tools are called skills inventories, 360 feedback, or personality indicators. While they all have slightly different purposes, they all function basically as a way to measure character and are often useful in giving us a better understanding of our strengths and weaknesses (or "opportunities for improvement," in the jargon).

The trouble with these assessments is that they only provide a snapshot of character at one point in time. Sometimes you're given a chance to receive "Time 1" and "Time 2" feedback so you can see how you've progressed, but even then, it can be difficult to interpret the "Time 2" feedback. Say your rating went up 0.2 points on "Conducting team meetings that generate new ideas" but down 0.3 points on "Encouraging innovative practices." What on earth does that mean, and what should you do about it? Unless personal coaching accompanies the feedback report, it's hard to adjust your behavior, let alone improve your character, based on that sort of data.

The ancient philosophers thought it more useful to offer a picture of what good and bad character looks like and, even more important, a sense of how it *feels* to be moving toward good or bad. These days, we tend to think of a person's character as relatively fixed: "He's a jerk," we say, or "she's a great person." He's shy, she's outgoing; he's a hard worker, she's lazy. We tell our friends, "This is how I am." We may believe that people can change, but we don't typically think of each individual as traveling along a road toward better or worse character, *becoming* better or worse. Yet if we want to improve as leaders and help our team members improve in their roles, we would do well to consider the idea. Just as it's easier to steer a car when it's moving, it's easier to steer thoughts and habits when you see each person, including yourself, not as a bundle of fixed characteristics but as a traveler who can choose to speed up or slow down and turn this way or that.

In "How One May Be Aware of One's Progress in Virtue," Plutarch explains the signs that tell us where we are on that road. At the heart of the essay is a joking remark of Menedemus, an obscure Greek philosopher, whom Plutarch quotes as saying that those who had an Athenian education "became first wise, and then philosophers, after that orators, and as time went on became ordinary kinds of people; the more they had to do with learning, so much the more laying aside their pride and high estimate of themselves."[9] It's a surprising thought: the more advanced a leader is, the more ordinary he or she appears.

One might counter that leaders relying on intrinsic authority (rather than legal or traditional authority; see Chapter 6) sometimes need to make big gestures in order to inspire their followers. That is true. Nevertheless, if you were asked to pick a word to describe the best leader you know, I bet *humble* would come to mind rather than *flashy*. Think of Aung San Suu Kyi, the soft-spoken Burmese opposition leader who spent 15 years under house arrest in her home country, or Pope Francis I, admired partly for eschewing the fancy trappings of the papacy. It's the weak leader who struts around making thundering speeches and issuing loud orders, making sure everyone knows he's the smartest in the room. Leaders far advanced in virtue, in contrast, are quiet, steady, quick to laugh at themselves, and altogether less in the foreground. As a friend of mine once said about a fine manager we both knew: "She's not all look-at-me."

In his book *Good to Great*, business guru Jim Collins tells the story of "a seemingly ordinary man named Darwin E. Smith" who in

1971 became chief executive of Kimberly-Clark and over the next 20 years transformed the underperforming paper manufacturer into one of the world's leading consumer products companies.[10] When his promotion to the top spot was announced, Smith said he wasn't sure the board had made the right choice. As Collins reports:

> A man who carried no airs of self-importance, Smith found his favorite companionship among plumbers and electricians and spent his vacations rumbling around his Wisconsin farm in the cab of a backhoe, digging holes and moving rocks. He never cultivated hero status ... The *Wall Street Journal* did not write a splashy feature on Darwin Smith.[11]

Yet mild-mannered Smith went on to make one of the boldest moves in business history. He sold Kimberly-Clark's paper mills, at the time considered the core of the company, and directed all resources into the consumer products side: paper towels, diapers, and so on. In the face of competitors' jeers, media scorn, and stock analysts' downgrades, he stood firm. And by the end of his tenure as CEO, the company was at the top of the industry, beating Procter & Gamble in three-fourths of its product categories. In retirement, Smith would explain his outstanding performance in these terms: "I never stopped trying to become qualified for the job."[12]

Darwin Smith sounds like one of those strong-stomached animals who, according to Plutarch, digest serpents and scorpions without a wince. I don't know if he became that way through a philosophical education or simply by contemplating life as he trundled around his farm in his backhoe, but I'm certain he followed Lincoln's lead and Charles Dodgson's advice when it came to dealing with anger. Any irate letters he wrote as CEO of Kimberly-Clark were no doubt neatly filed away in drawer or box, unsent.

Next we turn from philosophy to psychology, and look at motivation through the eyes of a psychiatrist and concentration-camp survivor.

part IV

MINDS

Psychology, from the Greek *psukhe*, means "study of the soul." Although the word has been in use for more than 300 years,[1] it wasn't until the late 1800s that German physician Wilhelm Wundt defined psychology as a field of study separate from philosophy or biology. William James, author of *Principles of Psychology*, was the first to argue that the discipline should provide practical benefits to individuals. And Sigmund Freud, developer of psychoanalysis in the early 1900s, is why we associate psychology with couches and taciturn therapists.

In the 1960s, psychology began to infiltrate the business world. Today, it seems that every other bestselling leadership book is really a psychology book—which perhaps shouldn't surprise us, because nothing could be more useful for leaders than an understanding of what makes human beings behave and think the way they do. There are dozens of psychology-related topics that leaders might profitably explore. We'll focus on five: motivation, personality types, decision-making, culture, and courage.

The first great book we'll take up is *Man's Search for Meaning*, an Austrian psychiatrist's account of his time in concentration camps and one of the ten most influential books in America, according to a Library of Congress survey that asked respondents to name a book that had made a difference in their life. Next we'll tackle C.G. Jung's *Psychological Types*, the foundation for today's most widely used personality assessment, the Myers-Briggs Type Indicator.

The remaining three chapters feature classics that wouldn't appear in a bookstore's psychology section but nevertheless shed light on the workings of the human mind: Roald Dahl's short stories, which hinge on cognitive bias, aka "blind spots"; Ruth Benedict's *The Chrysanthemum and the Sword*, a seminal work of anthropology that helps us understand cultural perspectives; and Mary Shelley's *Frankenstein*, a classic horror story that offers unexpected lessons about courage and cowardice.

great author
VIKTOR FRANKL'S *MAN'S SEARCH FOR MEANING*

Psychiatrist Viktor Frankl was one of millions of German and East European Jews deported to a Nazi death camp during World War II. His two-part book based on his experiences was published some 14 years after his release. Part I tells of his time in the camps; in Part II he explains logotherapy (derived from the Greek *logos*, or "meaning"), the doctrine he developed based on his observations of what sustained certain prisoners through their ordeal and enabled them to survive.

A big part of the answer, he acknowledges, is luck; he describes the many twists of fate that allowed his own survival, including one on the very last day before the Allied liberation, when he and a comrade were inadvertently left off a convoy of trucks that, the inmates were told, would take them to freedom, but that instead took them to another camp, where they were herded into huts and burned to death. Yet, despite the undeniable role of chance, there was something else that kept some people going while others succumbed to starvation or disease: the will to live. And, says Frankl, the will to live came from the simple belief that one's life had meaning.

Frankl's account shows glimmers of hope forcing their way through the black despair born of intense physical and mental suffering. The prisoners find solace in small things: a place in a work group with a less vicious guard, a morsel of bread found in a pocket, a running joke shared with a comrade. But even more, they cling to ideas and images they find meaningful: their families, children, work, or faith. And in extremis, when all other hopes are gone, they cling to the possibility of meeting death with dignity; of walking into the gas chamber upright, with a prayer on their lips. The survivor's experience is summarized, Frankl says, by the words of Nietzsche: "He who has a Why to live for can bear almost any How."

❀ Read this in *Man's Search for Meaning*: Part I, Frankl's memoir of his time in the death camps.

chapter 13

MOTIVATION

Sigmund Freud, father of psychoanalysis, said we are motivated by two things: the pursuit of pleasure—mostly sexual—and the avoidance of pain. B.F. Skinner, father of behaviorism, said we act based on expectations of external rewards or non-rewards. The ideas of these two scholars, both of whom set out to overturn long-held views of human nature, have shaped the leadership practices of the past 100 years far more than most of us realize. True, today's managers don't usually try to motivate employees with full-body massages or electric shocks; nevertheless, when the members of an executive team talk about "designing our compensation plan to drive desired behaviors," they are following in Freud's and Skinner's footsteps. Before proceeding, they might want to read the work of an Austrian psychiatrist who spent four years in Hitler's concentration camps and, as a result, developed a very different theory of motivation.

WHEN A FINE DOESN'T DETER

If you're a parent, you know what it's like to speed through a yellow light in a desperate attempt to be on time to pick up your child at daycare or preschool. Late pickups are such a problem for child-care facilities that many of them impose fines on the tardy, and in 2000, economists Uri Gneezy and Aldo Rustichini designed a study to find out whether such fines work.[1] They selected ten Israeli day-care centers, all of which closed at 4 p.m. and none of which charged for late pickup. They had six of the centers start imposing a late fee of ten shekels (about US $3) and kept the other centers as controls.

Almost immediately, the number of late parents at the fine-charging centers went *up*. And, after steadily increasing for a few months, the late pickup rate at those centers settled at a level nearly twice as high as the original one.

The outcome of this experiment seemed to turn decades of motivational theory on its head. Painful consequences are supposed to deter behavior, not encourage it. People would obviously prefer not to pay a fine, so why on earth would more parents come late in response to one? The researchers suggest an answer in the title of their paper: "A fine is a price." When there was no fine, parents understood that the teachers who stayed late to watch their children were doing so out of kindness, and they didn't want to impose on that kindness; it's a not-nice person, after all, who takes advantage of an overworked teacher. But when the fine was imposed, the center seemed to be offering extra time for a price. What was meant as a punishment quickly began to look more like a good deal. "Ten shekels," thought the parents. "Not bad for being able to spend an extra half-hour at work, worry free, when I need to." The fine turned good-hearted community members into shrewd cost–benefit calculators.

Until the 1980s, the "economic man" who seeks to maximize monetary gain and minimize monetary cost was an idea widely accepted by social scientists. But in recent decades, partly as a result of studies such as the one above, more sophisticated views of human motivation have emerged. In *Drive: The Surprising Truth about What Motivates Us*,[2] Daniel Pink divides human motivators into two types: intrinsic and extrinsic. If money (the big extrinsic motivator) isn't made the focus of a task or enterprise, he says, we are driven primarily by intrinsic motivators, such as the desire to master a skill or contribute to group success. And if those inner drives are allowed to flourish, motivation will be high. But if money is made the focus, intrinsic drives wither and overall motivation declines.[3] Pink cites three primary intrinsic motivators: autonomy, mastery, and purpose. Other researchers have proposed different lists.[4] What these theorists all have in common is the belief that Freud and Skinner were wrong: that carrots and sticks are not the only things, nor even the main things, that drive us.[5]

Psychologist Abraham Maslow was one of the first to propose a non-Skinnerian theory of motivators. His "hierarchy of needs," presented in a 1943 paper, is a five-level pyramid with basic human needs at the bottom and more complex ones at the top.[6] Level 1 contains physiological needs, such as breathing, food, and sleep. Level 2 contains security needs, such as safety of body and property. Next come needs for love and belonging (Level 3) and for achievement and respect (Level 4). At the peak, Level 5, are "self-actualization" needs such as morality, creativity, and problem-solving. From the 1950s on, other psychologists have applied Maslow's hierarchy to the workplace, noting that employee motivation is a multi-layered phenomenon (see "On tall shoulders: Frederick Herzberg on workplace hygiene").

The theories of Maslow and his followers improve on the old carrot-and-stick ideas of motivation. Yet they fail to capture a still deeper truth: *Even when we are thrown to the absolute bottom of the needs pyramid, we pursue more than physiological necessities.*

Let's look at a stark example.

THE DRIVE FOR MEANING

Viktor Frankl, a Viennese psychiatrist born in 1905, was sent to Auschwitz and three other Nazi concentration camps during World War II. He survived; his parents, brother, and pregnant wife did not. His experiences in the camps later served as the foundation for his theory of logotherapy, which holds that our primary drive, no matter the circumstances, is to pursue what is meaningful to us.

Frankl's descriptions of life in the death camps are, as one would expect, horrifying. The "lucky" prisoners—those who weren't sent to the gas chambers immediately but kept alive to work—received rations of 10½ ounces of bread and 1¾ pints of thin soup, often less. They did hard labor in the snow with no coat and sometimes no shoes. They received savage beatings, not to mention constant verbal abuse, from the guards. Starvation, sores, edema, typhus, frostbite, gangrene, and lice were their daily concerns. Early in his account, Frankl seems to concur with Maslow's view that higher-order needs become irrelevant when a person is faced with such conditions. "Reality dimmed," he says, "and all efforts and all emotions were centered on one task: preserving one's own life and that of the other fellow." The overriding need simply to stay alive "forced the prisoner's inner life down to a primitive level."[7]

on tall shoulders
FREDERICK HERZBERG on WORKPLACE HYGIENE

According to Maslow, only when needs at one level are met do we become concerned with the next level. A hungry person isn't focused on increasing his Twitter followers. But a person who is well-fed, with a nice house and a steady job—he might well be concerned with his follower count. If this is true, what are the implications for the workplace?

Frederick Herzberg's "One More Time, How Do You Motivate Employees?"[8] has remained among the most-requested *Harvard Business Review* articles since it came out in 1968. In it, Herzberg sorts job elements into "hygiene factors"—things like salary, working conditions, and security—and "motivators"—things like achievement, recognition, and fulfilling work. Hygiene factors meet needs at the lower levels of Maslow's pyramid; motivators sit at the higher levels.

Hygiene factors do not motivate, says Herzberg, but they can demotivate if absent: if you cut Sally's pay by 50 percent, Sally will likely lose her desire to do a good job or even stick around. So, if your employees seem unmotivated, you might want to check your hygiene.

As Frankl's memoir proceeds, a different picture emerges. To be sure, the camp inmates were preoccupied most of the time with brutally basic problems, such as how to get a spot at the center of a cluster of ditch-diggers in order to be out of the freezing wind. And useless sentiment was absent: when an inmate died in the night, men too weak to lift a cat had no choice but to drag the corpse up the barracks stairs by the feet. Yet, despite the grim focus on survival, the prisoners also engaged in activities inexplicable under a "hierarchy of needs" theory of motivation. Frankl tells of six practices that weren't about physical self-preservation.

Religion It's perhaps not surprising that the prisoners prayed. What is surprising is the effort they put into improvised religious services, which they set up in the corners of their barracks or in the dark, locked cattle trucks that transported them back from work sites. According to Frankl, those who continued their spiritual lives in this way survived longer than those who did not.

Being of service While many in the camps would not or could not help anyone but themselves, there were, says Frankl, some who performed extraordinary acts of altruism, whether it was giving a sick comrade their own food ration or staying with their friends rather than taking a chance at escape. Also, people still valued meaningful work. Frankl describes a time when he was asked to volunteer to go to another camp and look after typhus patients. He knew that doing so would increase his chances of death, typhus being highly contagious; he decided to go anyway, figuring that "it would doubtless be more to the purpose to try and help my comrades as a doctor than to vegetate ... as the unproductive laborer I was then."[9]

Contemplation of the beautiful One frigid dawn, during a forced march, a remark by a comrade started Frankl thinking about his wife, Tilly, who was imprisoned (as far as he knew) in another camp. As he envisioned her face, a thought transfixed him: "I understood how a man who has nothing left in this world still may know bliss ... in the contemplation of his beloved."[10] It wouldn't have mattered right then, he says, whether she was alive or dead, for in that moment he understood the meaning of the biblical words "The angels are lost in perpetual contemplation of an infinite glory."[11] The prisoners were absorbed also by beauty of a more trivial sort; in the evening, someone would often draw attention to "a nice view of the setting sun shining through the tall trees of the Bavarian woods."[12]

Culture and entertainment Perhaps most at odds with Maslow's view of motivation were the shows arranged by inmates. Of course this wasn't *Hogan's Heroes*, with funny performances by Sergeant Schultz. But entertainment there was. A kind of cabaret would be got up, with songs, poems, and satire about camp life. Those who didn't have to go to distant worksites would attend, and "the gatherings were so effective," says Frankl, "that a few ordinary prisoners went to see the cabaret in spite of their fatigue even though they missed their daily portion of food by going."[13]

Solitude Here's another improbable desire for people bereft of warmth and safety: Frankl describes an "irresistible urge to get away" for short periods. Prisoners yearned for privacy, to be alone with their thoughts. Humans may be the only social animal who, even when hungry and shivering, will sometimes choose to be by themselves.

The noble bearing of suffering Last and most striking is the motivation that the prisoners found in suffering itself, or rather, in their ability to bear suffering with dignity. Many came to believe that meaning lay not in what they expected of life but rather in what life expected of them. "Someone looks down on each of us in difficult hours—a friend, a wife ... or a God," said Frankl to his hut-mates after a particularly bad day, "and he would not expect us to disappoint him."[14] These words moved his listeners to tears.

If people continue to seek meaning even when starving to death—if they'll forgo food in order to hear a song, or volunteer to nurse typhus patients in order to exercise their medical skills—then it looks as if intrinsic motivators can overpower extrinsic ones even at the lowest level of Maslow's pyramid. And if that's true, then intrinsic will certainly trump extrinsic for people sitting higher on the pyramid: comfortable people laboring in comfortable workplaces for comfortable wages (that is, nearly everyone we know). People in this position just aren't moved much by carrots and sticks. It would be much easier for leaders if they were, but that won't change the facts. If I were CEO of a large company today, I would arrange to send every newly promoted supervisor a poster reading: "Much as you might wish that money and yelling worked, they don't."

Suppose, then, that we as leaders decide to focus on intrinsic motivators. We put down the carrots; we put down the sticks. What do we pick up in their place?

planning tool

A MOTIVATING CLIMATE

Think of a time when you were working with a highly motivated group of people. It might have been something work related or a sports team, artistic endeavor, or volunteer project.

How would you describe the climate of that group? Write how people felt about each climate dimension, what the group leader(s) did to promote it, and what you could do to promote a similarly positive climate in your team.

DIMENSION	HOW PEOPLE FELT	WHAT THE LEADER(S) DID	WHAT I COULD DO
Clarity			
Standards			
Commitment			
Responsibility			
Support			
Recognition			

CLIMATE: THE BEST MOTIVATIONAL TOOL

The best motivational tool to pick up is one of the most thoroughly researched yet least understood concepts in the business world: *workplace climate*. A brief overview follows; see the Notes for a list of books and articles that address the topic in depth.[15]

A well-managed workplace climate creates conditions that support employees' quest for meaning, thereby causing them to feel connected to the enterprise and its goals. This doesn't mean your organization has to be saving the world; you can create a positive climate in a stock brokerage just as well as in a charity. Life, as Viktor Frankl reminds us, is a BYOM (bring your own meaning) affair. In order to motivate, leaders simply need to harness people's natural tendency to find intrinsic satisfaction in their work.

Climate is people's perceptions of the workplace, or *what it feels like* to work in a team or organization. While quantifying "what it feels like" may seem tricky, researchers have done it and have shown climate to have a strong effect on motivation, performance, and financial results. One study, for example, found that different climates accounted for 33 percent of the difference in earnings among a company's business units.[16] Climate is not the same as culture; climate is malleable and can change rapidly, while culture (the underlying values and unwritten rules of an organization; see Chapter 16) is durable and slow to change. Moreover, climate is shaped mostly by the daily actions of people's managers and not by anonymous forces such as systems, strategy, and history. That is to say: You as a leader have enormous power to affect your team's climate and, hence, your team's level of motivation (see Figure 13.1).

While different researchers describe climate using different terms, there is general agreement on its six dimensions:

- ***Clarity*** How well people understand goals, policies, and job requirements
- ***Standards*** The perceived emphasis placed on high standards of performance
- ***Commitment*** How strongly people are dedicated to achieving goals

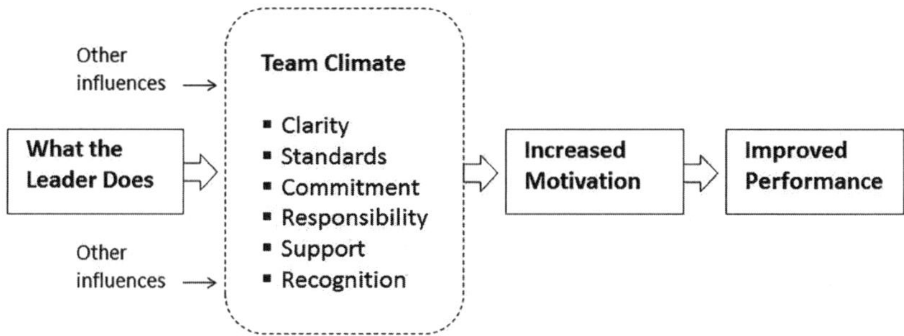

Figure 13.1 Workplace climate

- ***Responsibility*** The degree to which people feel accountable for solving problems and making decisions
- ***Support*** The level of cohesion, teamwork, mutual pride, and trust
- ***Recognition*** How much people feel they are recognized and rewarded for good work

With an awareness of these dimensions, leaders can intentionally shape a positive team climate, boosting team motivation (see “Planning tool: A motivating climate”).

Research on workplace climate shows that factors often dismissed as fluffy can produce solid financial results. Similarly, in Frankl’s account of the concentration camps we see how intangibles—art, dignity, friendship, laughter, love—preserved the will to live in human beings rendered skeletal by starvation. Leaders do badly to ignore the so-called soft stuff. The soft stuff is hard as money ... hard as bone.

Next, we explore personality types via the most popular psychological assessment tool and its inspiration, C.G. Jung.

great author

C.G. JUNG'S *PSYCHOLOGICAL TYPES*

Carl Gustav Jung—the Swiss psychiatrist who gave us the collective unconscious, the inferiority complex, and the archetype—thought, like Frankl, that Freud focused too much on the libido and that psychology's aim should be to help us live a meaningful, productive life. In *Psychological Types*, the best known of his many works, Jung said that the key to such a life was psychological integration, aka individuation: "the process by which human beings are formed and differentiated ... the development of the individual as a being distinct from the general, collective psychology" (par. 757).[1] Although individuation is fundamentally healthy, it has a downside, namely: "people are virtually incapable of understanding and accepting any point of view other than their own" (par. 847). Jung wrote the book, he says, partly in order to build a bridge across the psychological chasms that separate us.

According to Jung's theory, individuals aren't utterly unique; if they were, there would be no hope for mutual understanding. There are, fortunately, a finite number of human types, or perspectives on the world. While each of us is unique in certain respects, such as our memories and experiences, we can also be categorized—hence, understood—by type.

Jung acknowledges many possible typologies. He bolsters his version with nine chapters devoted to the "type problem" in different arenas, including theology, aesthetics, myth, poetry, and philosophy. In Chapter X he presents his framework, which is a combination of two psychological attitudes (extraversion and introversion) and four psychological functions (thinking and feeling, sensation and intuition). The functions, for Jung, are like the four points of a compass; each individual will have a preference for, or "point toward," just one function. Each individual will also have a preference for one attitude, either extraverted or introverted. Four possible functions times two possible attitudes gives us eight possible types, for example, "Introverted Feeling" or "Extraverted Sensation."

Read this in Psychological Types: *Introduction; Chapters III, IV, and X; Epilogue; and Appendix 4, "Psychological Typology" (a 1936 paper in which Jung summarizes his types theory)*

chapter 14

PERSONALITY

I took a personality test for the first time in 1990, sitting in a Wendy's restaurant after work. My employer, a consulting firm, had employees take the assessment within six months of being hired; afterward, you were supposed to meet with a licensed coach who would help interpret the results. My manager handed me the test (paper and pencil, in those days) and said to bring it back in the morning. It was long, maybe 30 pages, and took me a while to finish. I don't remember ever meeting with the coach, but I do remember finding out my "type": INTJ, which stood for Introverted–iNtuitive–Thinking–Judging.

JUNG POPULARIZED: THE MYERS-BRIGGS TYPE INDICATOR

The Myers-Briggs Type Indicator, or MBTI, was developed by Katharine Cook Briggs and her daughter, Isabel Briggs Myers, during World War II. Seeking a way to help women new to the workforce identify suitable and congenial jobs, they decided to take C.G. Jung's masterwork on personality, *Psychological Types*, and turn its somewhat esoteric theories into a tool that ordinary people could use. (Legend has it that they created the instrument while sitting at their kitchen table, so maybe they wouldn't have minded my filling it out at Wendy's.) The MBTI has since become the most widely used personality assessment in the world, taken by roughly two million people a year.[2] While it receives mostly scorn from trained psychologists—we'll look at a few of their criticisms in a moment—it's an excellent way to grasp the essentials of Jung's theory of types.

Let's begin, therefore, with an overview of the tool, and then we'll be in a position to see how Jung's original work provides even deeper insights for leaders.

The MBTI is based on four pairs of personality traits, all of which are either stated or implicit in Jung's theory:[3]

- ***Extraversion* (E) *or Introversion* (I)** Drawing energy and enjoyment from the outer world *or* from your own inner world (What's your source of energy?)[4]
- ***Sensing* (S) *or Intuition* (N)** Relying on the five senses *or* on interpretation and imagination (How do you process information?)
- ***Thinking* (T) *or Feeling* (F)** Preferring to make judgments based on logic, reason, and rules *or* based on your and others' feelings (How do you decide things?)
- ***Judging* (J) *or Perceiving* (P)** Liking to have things decided *or* liking to remain open to new developments and options (How do you operate in the world?)[5]

The 16 combinations of these 4 dichotomies make up the 16 Myers-Briggs types; for example, an ESFP would be someone who is extraverted, sensing, feeling, and perceiving. There are books and websites that go into detail on each type, providing everything from "type portraits" to career advice to suggestions for personal growth; if you enter "Myers-Briggs" into a search engine, you'll find a slew of them.[6] And other people have come up with their own permutations of the Jungian framework, with various colorful names for the types (see "On tall shoulders: David Keirsey on the four temperaments").

The best way to grasp the 16 Myers-Briggs types is to take a set of fictional characters and imagine where each would fall in the schema. And no characters could be better for the purpose than those well-known denizens of Hogwarts School for Witchcraft and Wizardry, Harry Potter and his associates. See Table 14.1 for my analysis.

Explanation of a couple of these characters may shed more light on the types. First, Hermione: I've seen her labeled INTP, but the mere fact that someone is highly intelligent doesn't mean that he or she is automatically a T for Thinking. The key to Hermione is that she applies her intelligence to causes and people she cares deeply about (Ron, Harry, and house elves, for example), showing that she's an F for Feeling. And she's clearly not a P; if anyone likes to decide things (J for Judging), Hermione does. She is INFJ: the Counselor and Crusader.

on tall shoulders

DAVID KEIRSEY *on* THE FOUR TEMPERAMENTS

David Keirsey took Jung's psychological types, combined them with the ancient idea of temperaments, and came up with the Keirsey Temperament Sorter. His 1978 book *Please Understand Me*[7] presents his version of a Jungian personality assessment, which, like the MBTI, sorts people into extraverts or introverts (E/I), sensing or intuiting (S/N), thinking or feeling (T/F), and perceiving or judging (P/J).

But Keirsey adds another layer. Following the Greeks, he identifies four basic types, or temperaments: Dionysian, Epimethean, Apollonian, and Promethean. In his later books, he renamed them Artisans, Guardians, Idealists, and Rationals; further divided each temperament into two roles (for example, Artisan Operators and Artisan Entertainers); and subdivided each role into two variants (for example, Crafters and Promoters).

Like Myers-Briggs and their corporate disciples, Keirsey uses his types to promote an "I'm OK, you're OK" view of the world. It's worth remembering that Jung was a practicing psychologist who developed his theory of types primarily in order to help people who were feeling decidedly not OK.

Second, Dumbledore: Some say that he's an F, but I disagree. He certainly isn't without feelings, but neither is he led by them. He admires Harry precisely because Harry has an ability to love that he can't match. Moreover, Dumbledore is well able, perhaps *too* able, to shut off empathy and rely on his awesome powers of mind. His ability to conceal his schemes, even when such concealment will cause pain to his friends, reveals a merciless streak. Young Dumbledore was ENTJ: the energetic Field Marshal, eager to map out grand plans and impose them on the world "for the greater good." The older Dumbledore has grown more introverted: a little sadder, a little quieter, a little less eager to engage with the world. He's INTJ: the Mastermind.

Table 14.1 *The Myers-Briggs types of Harry Potter characters*[8]

CHARACTER	TYPE	MONIKER	MOTTO
Severus Snape	ISTJ	examiner, duty-fulfiller	"Doing what should be done"
Neville Longbottom	ISFJ	defender, loyalist	"True to the end"
Hermione Granger	INFJ	counselor, crusader	"A vision for the common good"
The mature Dumbledore	INTJ	mastermind, strategist	"Leading behind the scenes"
Arthur Weasley	ISTP	crafter, mechanic	"Ready to try anything once"
Hagrid	ISFP	artisan, free spirit	"My own take on life"
Luna Lovegood	INFP	idealist, dreamer	"Imagine the world as it should be"
Xenophilius Lovegood	INTP	thinker, architect	"Knowledge for knowledge's sake"
Ginny Weasley	ESTP	doer, promoter	"Let's get real"
Ron Weasley	ESFP	performer, adapter	"Common sense and good fun"
Sirius Black	ENFP	champion, inspirer	"Giving life an extra squeeze"
Fred and George Weasley	ENTP	inventor, visionary	"One cool challenge after another"
Minerva McGonagall	ESTJ	supervisor, guardian	"Keeping an eye on things"
Molly Weasley	ESFJ	provider, caregiver	"Hostess to the world"
Harry Potter	ENFJ	hero, giver, teacher	"Responsive and responsible"
The young Dumbledore	ENTJ	field marshal, executive	"Setting goals and taking charge"

The Myers-Briggs framework has detractors, including many professional psychologists, who point to its flaws as a psychometric instrument. To begin with, it forces respondents into false dichotomies, labeling people extraverted *or* introverted, sensing *or* intuiting, instead of placing them somewhere on a continuum. Also, its results may vary: someone might be labeled an ESTP (say) at one sitting and an ESFJ at the next, suggesting that the test doesn't measure real personality traits, which are stable over time. Finally, like Jung's theories, the framework lacks a basis in scientific evidence.

Nevertheless, the MBTI remains popular, and for good reason: it reduces our puzzlement about other people, providing a nuanced yet simple way to understand our differences. Instead of thinking "He's an opinionated jerk," someone versed in the Myers-Briggs types is more likely to think "He's an ESTJ; that's why he states his opinions firmly." Also, unlike the model most accepted by psychologists—the so-called Big Five, which measures levels of openness, conscientiousness, extraversion, agreeableness, and neuroticism—the MBTI is all positive. It's never going to label you "closed" or "neurotic." There are no bad types among the 16. Directing employees into or away from certain jobs based on their supposed type is a poor idea, given the tool's lack of scientific basis. But when it's used simply as a way to spark conversation about diverse personalities and strengths, the MBTI seems at worst harmless fun, at best an enlightening tool (see "Team tool: Tell me how to work with you").

TWO DEEPER INSIGHTS FROM JUNG

As usual, however, we learn even more when we go to the source. While Jung's *Psychological Types* is no more scientific than the MBTI, it offers a number of insights about personality that go deeper and may even be a bit disturbing. Here are two of them.

First, failure to acknowledge your "other side" leads to trouble. Myers and Briggs don't care whether someone leans way over toward a particular trait (is strongly Perceiving, for example), but Jung certainly does. For him, neurosis is the result of over-reliance on our dominant tendencies and failure to integrate our less dominant ones, driving the latter into the unconscious where they "take on a regressive character according to the degree of repression; the less they are acknowledged, the more infantile and archaic they become" (par. 571). A key role for a therapist is to help individuals integrate their dominant and less dominant traits, allowing the less dominant to be expressed in productive ways instead of repressed.

team tool
TELL ME HOW TO WORK WITH YOU

Use this process to help your team appreciate personality differences. Be clear, in advance, that the purpose of the exercise is not to psychologically analyze or stereotype anyone, but rather to increase mutual understanding and collaboration.

1. If your team members don't already know their Myers-Briggs types, have them go to an online resource, such as humanmetrics.com or personalitypathways.com, and take an assessment. (You'll see disclaimers on the sites stating that these quizzes aren't substitutes for the MBTI, but given that the MBTI also lacks a scientific basis, it's hard to see the problem with unofficial versions used for discussion.)

2. Ask them to find an online description of their type (see, for example, personalitypage.com).

3. Ask each team member to prepare the following: three words or phrases from the online description that seem especially fitting; and three pieces of advice on how best to work with them, given their personality type.

4. In a team meeting, ask each individual to share their type, the three words or phrases, and the three pieces of advice on how to work with them.

5. Discuss how these insights might improve teamwork.

Jung gives the example of a man who worked his way up to become the owner of a successful printing business in which he invested much energy. As the company expanded, it gradually took over the man's life and swallowed up all his other interests. In the end, says Jung:

> This proved his ruin. As an unconscious compensation of his exclusive interest in the business, certain memories of his childhood came to life. As a child he had taken great delight in painting and drawing. But instead of renewing this capacity for its own sake as a compensating hobby, he channeled it into his business and began wondering how he might embellish his products in an "artistic" way. Unfortunately his fantasies materialized: he actually turned out stuff that suited his primitive and infantile taste, with the result that after a very few years his business went to pieces. (572)

Most of us aren't therapists, of course, but we can nevertheless take a few lessons from the story of the Artsy Printer. What tendencies are being pushed down or shunted aside in yourself, your team members, or your organization as a whole? How are these tendencies making themselves felt in destructive (Jung would say "infantile") ways? Instead of repressing them, how might you give them a useful role or voice?

Second, feelings of rapport are often based on false assumptions. We tend to interpret other people's actions in light of our own type, which can lead us to conclude that they are "just like us." Take the example of Gary, a J for Judging, who attends a political rally one Saturday afternoon at a local park and falls into conversation with Rachel, a woman standing next to him. Based on Rachel's friendliness and his enjoyment of their chat, Gary assumes that she shares his political views. He's a J, so for him, opinions are fundamental. He thinks that Rachel supports this candidate just as he does; if she doesn't, why would she be at the rally? Rachel, however, is a P for Perceiving. For her, opinions are fluid, always subject to revision, and certainly not something on which to base friendships. *She* assumes that her rapport with Gary stems from the fact that they're both standing in the crowd, eating Sno-cones, soaking up the sunshine and listening to interesting debates concerning the life of their city. Gary, she thinks, obviously enjoys these events as much as she does.

Jung says (rather depressingly) that this false kind of rapport, arising from what he calls mutual projection, is by far the most frequent kind of rapport. It is also a major cause of misunderstanding.

We don't realize that others are different from us, because we see their behavior through the lens of our own type. I meet someone new, we get along, and I decide he's "nice" (translation: "just like me"). Later, when this imaginary soulmate acts in unexpected ways, I feel betrayed: "Turns out he wasn't so nice after all; I guess all that stuff was just an act."

What do you suppose Gary will think of Rachel on their second date when she suggests that they attend another political rally: same park, opposing candidate?

EXTRAVERSION, INTROVERSION, AND LEADERSHIP CHARACTER

While the MBTI considers all four type pairs equally important, Jung believes that extraversion-introversion is the primary, most basic pair. (He calls these two the psychological *attitudes* and the other pairs the psychological *functions*.) Moreover, while MBTI adherents tend to talk about extraversion vs. introversion as "how you recharge your batteries," Jung presents a less breezy explanation: it's a question, he says, of one's attitude toward "the object." Introverts withdraw from other people, from things, indeed from the whole outside world, as though to prevent that world from gaining power over them. Extraverts, on the other hand, orient and define themselves entirely by what's outside them; the worst thing for an extravert is not to be in others' power, but to be separated from them. You might say that introverts have control issues while extraverts have abandonment issues.

The two attitudes, says Jung, are founded on the two fundamental adaptive strategies found in nature: Strategy 1, a high rate of fertility with low powers of defense and a short life for each individual (extraverted); and Strategy 2, a low fertility rate plus multiple means of self-protection (introverted). The extravert wants "to expend and propagate himself in every way, while the tendency of the introvert is to defend himself against all demands from outside" (559). Jung paints a picture of extreme introversion as anxious, rigid, fastidious, and prudish; extreme extraversion as rash, soft, gluttonous, and debauched.

Yet he doesn't mean that all introverts are cold-hearted snobs and all extraverts are hot-headed sluts. What he does mean is that each of us has a slippery slope down which we are prone to slide. If we lean too far toward our preferred side, we'll end up devaluing the other side's positive aspects, lose our balance, and go tumbling down—just like Jung's printer friend, who defined himself entirely by an external object (his business) and repressed the artistic impulses blooming inside him, to his ultimate ruin. In fact, Jung would probably add "repressing one's non-dominant attitude" to my list of leadership traps (see Chapter 2), and label it the first and most dangerous trap of all.

Revisiting the leadership character continuums (see Figure 14.1) helps us understand this fundamental trap more fully. As we've seen, each leadership character trait is the mean, or balance point, between two extremes: on the left, too little of the trait, on the right, too much. But another way to look at the diagram is to see the left as the Land of Introverts and the right as the Land of Extraverts: introverted leaders are prone to timidity, deceit, obstinacy, severity, and indifference, while extraverted leaders are in danger of being rash, offensive, vacillating, slack, and manic.

In his allegory *The Pilgrim's Regress*, C.S. Lewis, a Jung appreciator, envisions the two sides as two countries stretching to the north and south of a long, narrow road.[9] John, the story's hero, is a friendly sort with a tendency to adopt the views of strangers immediately on meeting them. He travels the road with his friend Vertue, an upstanding but rigid person who dislikes socializing. Their journey takes them deep into the Northlands and Southlands, where they encounter characters such as Mr. Sensible, whom introverted Vertue considers a decent fellow, and Mr. Broad, whom extraverted John finds congenial. In the end, though, they find that the only way to succeed is for each to acquire some of the qualities of his non-preferred country. Vertue must dare to fight a Southern Dragon and absorb some of its fiery energy, while John must confront a Northern Dragon and win some of its icy toughness. Once their dragon quests are complete, the two go on their way, "singing and laughing like schoolboys." Vertue has shed his pomposity and John is never tired. Each has been made whole.

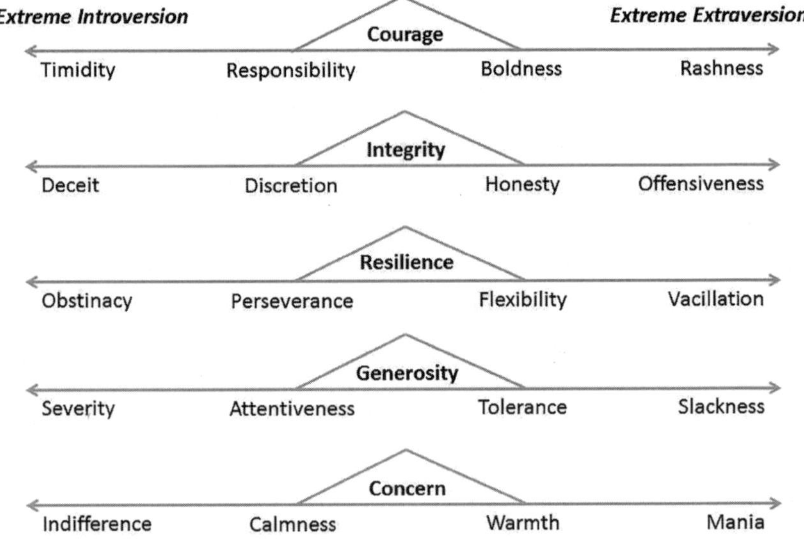

Figure 14.1 *Leadership character and introversion/extraversion*

Woe to the leader who runs from his or her dragon and heads for the extreme North or South. If you're an introvert, says Jung, you'll end up on a cold, lonely island where nothing moves except what you permit to move. If you're an extravert, you'll wind up in a hot, noisy swamp where other people's opinions and desires suffocate all attempts at clear thought or resolute action. And there's little chance that anyone will follow you to either place.

What lies behind poor decisions? In the next chapter, fiction writer Roald Dahl and philosopher Martin Heidegger teach us about blind spots.

great author
ROALD DAHL'S STORIES

Roald Dahl is best known for his children's books (especially *Charlie and the Chocolate Factory*), but he also wrote short stories for adults. By turns macabre and slyly humorous, these stories feature characters who think they are sharp-sighted but who are actually myopic. As a portrayer of the phenomenon of cognitive bias and its effects on decision-making, Dahl has few equals.

In "Lamb to the Slaughter" (the story featured here), a woman takes advantage of blind spots in order to get away with murder. In most of Dahl's tales, however, the hero only dreams he or she is getting away with murder—or at least with a scam—and in the end is rudely awakened. In "Mrs. Bixby and the Colonel's Coat," a wife is thrilled with the plan she has contrived in order to cover up an affair and still keep the stunning mink coat her lover gave her, but she fails to recognize that her husband is not quite the milksop he seems. In "The Landlady," young Billy Weaver dismisses a sweet but rather peculiar old woman as harmless, until all of a sudden he sees she isn't. "Parson's Pleasure" is about a conman who spends years pulling the wool over the eyes of country bumpkins, only to have three of the bumpkins destroy his hopes one summer afternoon by taking his pitch at absolute face value. And in both "The Visitor" and "The Great Switcheroo," a man who sees women as sexual playthings gets an unpleasant surprise when one of his basic assumptions turns out to be wrong.

In each of these tales and many more by Dahl, the main character does what we're all wont to do: regard people through the lens of our intentions and collapse in shock when they turn out to have intentions of their own. It's easy to sit back and laugh at a scoundrel's comeuppance, but in order to learn from a Dahl story we must go a step further. We must imagine ourselves as the scoundrel and think about how we might have opened our eyes to the impending disaster.

✵ Read this in Roald Dahl's stories: "Lamb to the Slaughter," "Taste," "Mrs. Bixby and the Colonel's Coat," "Parson's Pleasure," "The Landlady," "The Visitor," "The Bookseller"—and for a hilariously R-rated look at blind spots, "The Great Switcheroo."

chapter 15
DECISIONS

An experienced cyclist rides across train tracks directly in front of an oncoming train. A group of mountaineers heads for the top of Mount Everest despite clear warnings of an approaching storm. Four police detectives sit around a murderer's kitchen table and, with their sergeant's encouragement, destroy the murder weapon.

These people—some real, some fictional—made terrible decisions. In each case, the reason to make a different and better decision was staring them in the face. Why couldn't they see it?

BLIND SPOTS ARE EVERYWHERE

Behind many poor leadership decisions lies a problem called *cognitive bias*. Cognitive biases are blind spots, and psychologists have uncovered many of them. One example is anchoring, which is our tendency to tie a decision too tightly to a recently presented piece of information. To name just a few more, there's the availability heuristic, the bandwagon effect, confirmation bias, the gambler's fallacy, hyperbolic discounting, loss aversion, and the money illusion. Wikipedia's "Cognitive Biases" page lists more than 75 such errors.[1]

The 2000s saw the rise of a subcategory of business books devoted to explaining cognitive biases and providing advice on how to avoid them.[2] But there's a problem: we can't. Scientific evidence suggests that cognitive biases are hardwired into our brain, and being made aware of them doesn't help. Some researchers claim that blind spots evolved as aids to efficient decision-making, so that when a saber-toothed tiger was headed our way (for example), we didn't need to stop and think about what to do; a mental shortcut helped us make the right choice fast. Unfortunately, the same mental shortcuts that helped us survive tiger encounters now tend to trip us up when we have to make more typically modern decisions involving supply chain management or organizational restructuring. So, what can we do? To become consistently conscious of 75 blind spots and prevent them from influencing our decisions is impossible. Our only hope is to gain insight into the source of them all—the fundamental blind spot, if you will—and try to mitigate it.

This fundamental blind spot is our tendency to regard everything in the world as equipment; that is, as a tool for our purpose rather than as a thing-in-itself unconditioned by any use we might have for it. Psychologists call this tendency *functional fixedness* and consider it as only one among many cognitive biases, but twentieth-century philosopher Martin Heidegger called it *readiness-to-hand* and argued that it is the primary way human beings see (or grasp) the world. I believe that Heidegger's view is the more helpful one for leaders, because it not only provides an account of the über-blind spot that generates all the others but also hints at how we might take off the blinders, or at least peek around them now and then. More on Heidegger in a moment, but first, let's look at a short story by Roald Dahl, an author whose works often hinge on blind spots. Called "Lamb to the Slaughter," it's a good illustration of functional fixedness.[3]

Mary Maloney is a happily (or so she thinks) married woman. One evening her husband, Patrick, comes home from work and informs her with brutal abruptness that he's leaving her. Mrs. Maloney takes this in and says that she'll fix supper. She goes down to the cellar, gets a leg of lamb out of the freezer, comes back upstairs, walks up behind her husband in his armchair, and swings the leg of lamb down hard on his skull. He keels over, dead.

Realizing that she must make this look like an intruder's work, Mrs. Maloney puts the lamb in the oven and sets about playing her part: going out to the store to pick up some peas, coming back and finding her husband on the floor, calling the police in shock and horror. The detectives soon arrive and go about their investigation. They are all very kind to Mrs. Maloney, since her husband was also on the police force and the lead detective, Sergeant Noonan, is an old friend. The men spend hours searching the house for the weapon, which they know is a heavy blunt object, something like a large wrench or a metal vase. Nothing turns up.

Late in the evening, Sergeant Noonan reminds Mrs. Maloney that the oven is still on with the meat for dinner inside. She turns tearful eyes on him and begs him to do her a favor, he and his men who must be so tired and hungry and who were all such good friends of dear Patrick: Won't they please eat up the leg of lamb?

A few minutes later the detectives are sitting around the table, mouths full, discussing the case. They agree that it must have been "a hell of a big club" the guy used; unlikely that he's still carrying it around. No, it's probably right there on the premises—right under their noses.

READY-TO-HAND AND PRESENT-AT-HAND

Functional fixedness means that we have a tendency to see things solely in terms of their accepted use rather than their inherent qualities—qualities that nearly always lend themselves to alternative uses. In the story just outlined, there's a leg of lamb that the detectives can see only as something to eat (which it is) and not as a large club-shaped object (which it also is). In the real world, likewise, there are products, processes, technologies, and people that we see only in terms of the role they currently play and not as what *else* they might be or do.

For Heidegger, our myopic focus on function stems from our fundamental experience of the world as "ready-to-hand." First described in his 1927 book *Being and Time*, the concept of ready-to-hand rocked Western philosophy, which up to then had pretty much assumed that we experience the world as a subject looking at objects and seeing their qualities: big, small, red, yellow, smooth, jagged, what have you.[4] Not so, said Heidegger: humans aren't detached observers but purposeful engagers. We make use of things. We produce, acquire, give up, undertake, look after, intend, and accomplish things. We are constantly engaging with the equipment of the world. And because we constantly engage with it, we are, in a sense, blind to it.

Consider the accelerator pedal in your car. When you're driving you're aware of it, but you don't perceive it as a three-by-six-inch rectangular object with a ridged gray rubber surface approximately four inches from the floor and offering resistance to your foot as you press down. You don't actually perceive it at all. You simply *drive the car*, and the accelerator—along with the steering wheel, the brake, the seats, everything—disappears into the driving. It is all equipment that you are using for its accustomed purpose. Assuming that it keeps functioning smoothly, it remains transparent.

Our normal experience of the world as ready-to-hand is the chief reason that blind spots inevitably arise and engender poor decisions. An infamous 1996 expedition to the peak of Mount Everest, in which five individuals lost their lives, is a case in point (see "On tall shoulders: Michael Roberto and Gina Carioggia on mountain madness"). In brief, one sub-team of climbers and their leader decided to press on to the summit late in the afternoon, despite a prior agreement that they'd turn around if they weren't at the top by two o'clock and despite indications of a storm on the way. Some of them didn't get to the summit until four o'clock, became lost or trapped in the darkness and bad weather on the way down, and perished. While the causes of the disaster were complex, many analysts agree that the main factor was "summit fever," a syndrome whereby mountain climbers are seized by a determination to get to the top and all other considerations fade.

When summit fever gripped the Everest team, the mountain became entirely ready-to-hand: just one more piece of equipment, one more part of their plan. The climbers no longer saw the ice and snow, the signs of approaching storms, and the deepening dark. They were blind to Everest as an objective entity with qualities at odds with their purpose and the power to kill.

Human beings are also capable of a more detached, subject-object view of the world. Heidegger called this mode *presence-at-hand*. The present-at-hand tends to snap into focus, he said, when things break or go wrong in some way.[5] All at once there appears a thing-in-itself, separate from its function for us. For example, imagine your car accelerator were to stick in the raised position; in an instant you'd be bent over, peering at a three-by-six-inch rectangle of ridged gray rubber sitting atop a metal lever that does not yield to pressure. The emergence of an intractable *object* from a world of smoothly functioning equipment is incredibly jarring; it's as if an old and much-loved doll suddenly morphed into Chucky. That's why the present-at-hand draws our attention like nothing else and, like the ready-to-hand, creates blind spots. The breakdown can happen in a matter of seconds and to tragic effect, as in the following true incident.

Suzanne LeBeau of Santa Fe, New Mexico, was 60 years old and an avid cyclist.[6] At 11 a.m. on an April Saturday she was riding west across St. Francis Drive, a busy highway running north to south through the city. Parallel to St. Francis, on its west side, were the train tracks for the Rail Runner Express. At that moment a train was heading south, about 50 yards from the intersection where LeBeau was riding. The railroad crossing gates were down, blocking the east-west road that cut across St. Francis and the tracks; the red lights were flashing and the warning bells were ringing. The train engineer saw LeBeau and sounded the horn, loud. She was not wearing earphones and her hearing was fine. She pedaled across the highway, up onto the bike path, and straight in front of the train. She died instantly.

Readers of the newspaper story were mystified. How could this have happened? Some wrote letters suggesting that LeBeau must have had a minor stroke or been dehydrated. But I don't think so, and here's why: Surveillance video of the accident shows the north-south traffic lights on St. Francis changing to green just as LeBeau reached the median, causing her to hurry across the southbound lanes. In other words, she was in the middle of a six-lane highway when suddenly something "broke": the light turned green against her. At that moment, certain phenomena must have snapped into focus. The oncoming cars, the median, the three southbound traffic lanes, the bike trail up ahead—she would have seen them in vivid detail as potentially dangerous objects that required her whole attention. The oncoming train wasn't in this picture at all. With all her attention fixed on the looming present-at-hand, LeBeau was blind to the rest.

on tall shoulders

MICHAEL ROBERTO *and* GINA CARIOGGIA *on* MOUNTAIN MADNESS

"Incredible achievement and great tragedy unfolded on the treacherous slopes of Mount Everest in the spring of 1996," write Michael Roberto and Gina Carioggia in one of the most popular case studies in Harvard Business School's portfolio, a case used by many a leadership trainer to drive home the principles and perils of decision-making.[7]

On May 10, Rob Hall and Scott Fischer, two of the world's most experienced high-altitude guides, led 23 climbers to the summit. But despite their expertise, both Hall and Fischer, along with three others, lost their lives when a storm hit as they made their descent. Some observers later emphasized Everest's inherent risks and the inevitability of tragedy. Others disagreed, saying that the disaster was no accident, but rather the end result of leaders making faulty decisions.

Natural disaster or human error? Perhaps there's no real difference. Above 26,000 feet, said one survivor, "the line between appropriate zeal and reckless summit fever becomes grievously thin."[8] And summit fever, it seems, is as blinding as any blizzard.

HOW TO MITIGATE BLIND SPOTS

So there are two major ways in which blind spots, and their consequent bad decisions, naturally arise. Most of the time we chug along happily immersed in the *ready-to-hand*, our trusty "equipment," grasping but not seeing it and never considering the alternative roles it might play or the dangers it might pose. Then when things break down, we rivet our attention on the momentarily *present-at-hand* and work frantically to fix whatever's broken; not a bad mode for emergencies, but still not ideal, since it can blind us to oncoming trains. What can we do about these two types of myopia?

Cognitive biases are, as we've seen, unavoidable. Nevertheless, it is possible to mitigate them and make clearer-eyed decisions; in fact, some leaders are known for this ability. Think, for example, of

Nelson Mandela and his championing of the Springboks rugby team shortly after he became president of South Africa (the topic of the film *Invictus*).[9] A lesser leader might have seen the Springboks as nothing other than a hated symbol of racial oppression, which was the role they had played in South African blacks' lives for decades. That was their "function"; for most people, that's what they were. But Mandela saw them simply as a sports team: one with objective qualities that could be adapted to a very different role. They could become, say, a unifying source of national pride for a country desperately in need of one.

Like Mandela, some leaders are able now and then to take off the blinders of functional fixedness and see *what else* something (or someone) could be. They make better decisions as a result. What enables them to remove the blinders?

Heidegger said that the clarity of the present-at-hand only emerges when the autopilot of the ready-to-hand breaks down. We've seen, though, how that sudden over-clarity can create a kind of panicky tunnel vision that's no better than the autopilot. The best leaders, then, don't stay on autopilot, nor do they passively wait for break*downs* to happen; rather, they take ongoing, proactive steps to break *out* of their ordinary way of looking at things. They consistently manage to see entities, people, and situations in a fresh light. To adopt these new perspectives, some leaders might attend innovation workshops or hire creativity consultants. But the best way to go about it is actually much more direct: leaders need to talk—and more importantly, listen—to a diverse set of people.

A 2011 study by MIT professor Alex Pentland backs up this advice neatly and quantitatively.[10] He analyzed the decisions of thousands of stock traders on eToro, an online platform that allows traders to observe and copy one another's moves. He found that the traders fell into three groups: (1) those who made their decisions in a kind of isolation chamber, with zero interest in what anyone else was doing; (2) those who slavishly followed trends, only copying what most of the other traders did; and (3) those who drew ideas from a wide variety of other traders but didn't follow the herd. The third group saw returns 30 percent higher than the others.

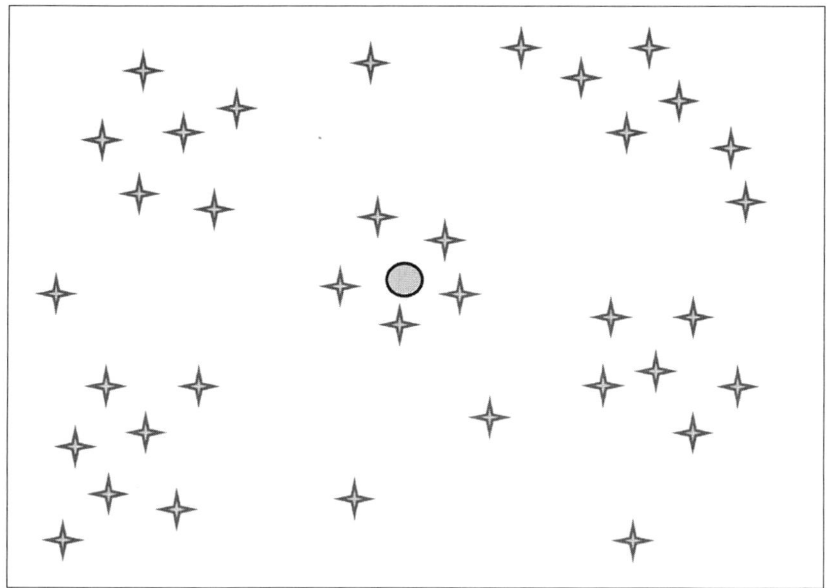

Figure 15.1 The Star Chart—a galaxy of ideas

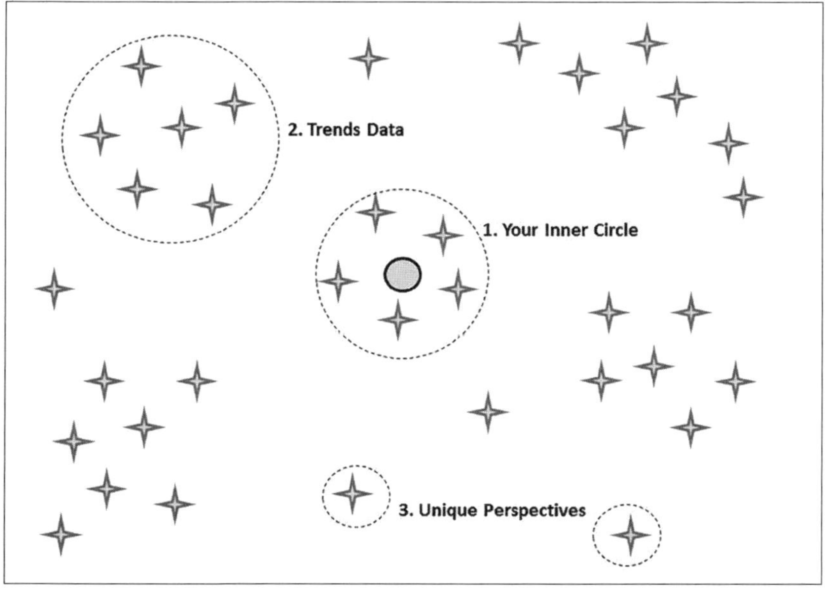

Figure 15.2 The Star Chart—aiming the telescope

The Star Chart makes the same point visually. As leaders, we are surrounded by a vast galaxy of ideas and perspectives (Figure 15.1). When it comes time to make a major decision, the question becomes where to aim the telescope (Figure 15.2). Our first impulse will be to focus on our *inner circle*: our ready-to-hand advisers. Should we seek to cast a wider net, our next step is likely to be *trends data*: what are all those people out there doing and thinking? A trend, however, is simply a mathematical abstraction representing the average of many opinions, and chasing after trends only swaps one kind of myopia for another. In order to lift the blinders, we must explore the *unique perspectives* of diverse individuals. We can't just talk to friends and study data. We must get out there and talk with the oddballs, the mavericks, the lone stars.

All of this may seem obvious. Still, many leaders behave as if good decisions arise mainly in conferences with their executive team, while many others feel confident only when they're flying along a clear trend line. Keeping the Star Chart in mind may help you avoid both traps (see "Communication tool: Consulting the stars").

communication tool

CONSULTING THE STARS

Think of an important and complex decision you need to make, one that will affect at least several other people besides yourself. Use the questions below to help you break out of your current perspective and mitigate blind spots as you make this decision.

1. What is "everyone doing" when it comes to situations such as this? Name two or three trends you might be tempted to follow in making your decision.
2. Who are some individuals likely to have differing opinions or perspectives on the situation? Be sure to consider people who are outside your immediate circle, have no expertise on the issue, or have an unusual point of view (the head of a different business unit, a competitor, your college roommate, your grandmother, your gardener). List five or six of these "stars."

3. Go talk to each star. Ask for their perspective on your decision. Make it clear you are not asking them to tell you what to do, but simply looking for their thoughts on the situation.
4. Once you have concluded all the conversations, answer the following questions:
   - What did you learn?
   - What potential blind spots were revealed as a result of hearing the diverse perspectives?
   - What new possibilities or alternative roles do you now see for some of the individuals, groups, products, or systems involved in this decision?
   - What are some dangers or downsides to the trends you identified?
   - Overall, how are you thinking about this decision differently?

Sometimes, diverse points of view don't prevent a leader from making a poor decision but, rather, save him or her from the consequences of one. Take another Roald Dahl story, this one about Mike, a London stockbroker who wants to acquire a reputation for "taste."[11]

Mike is inordinately proud of his wine cellar, and one evening he bets his dinner guest, a famous gourmet, that the guest can't name the breed and vintage of the claret being served. So blindly confident is Mike in winning the bet that he decides to wager his 18-year-old daughter's hand in marriage. As the gourmet (a repulsive man) tastes and retastes the wine and slowly, gleefully homes in on its district, commune, and vineyard, we share Mike's growing horror at his catastrophic decision.

I won't spoil the rest. Suffice to say, it is an often-overlooked individual's unique perspective that saves Mike, his daughter, and the day.

Next, anthropologist Ruth Benedict's classic study of World War II Japan reveals the dimensions of culture.

great author

RUTH BENEDICT'S *THE CHRYSANTHEMUM AND THE SWORD*

Say "famous anthropologist" and many people still think "Margaret Mead." Mead's book *Coming of Age in Samoa* gained her a level of fame that her teacher, Ruth Benedict, never enjoyed, but Benedict was arguably the more influential thinker. Benedict not only shaped the emerging discipline of anthropology but also wrote a book that shows the depth of understanding we can achieve, even in the midst of violent conflict, by appreciating cultural differences.

National character is an idea that has come in and out of fashion since Benedict was commissioned by the US government, in the middle of World War II, to write a cultural analysis of Japan. Contemporary anthropologists have noted that nationwide labels such as "China is hierarchical" are silly. But as Benedict points out, it's equally silly to think that all countries are the same. Especially when it comes to questions of morality (Where does one's duty lie? What actions are worthy of respect? What makes a life good or bad?), the people of different countries evince different patterns of thought, and these are worthy of study.

Benedict's descriptions of the Japanese patterns are at once vivid and subtle. Her examples range from everyday anecdotes, such as the son who puts aside a beloved wife in deference to his mother's wishes, to popular legends, such as the tale of the 47 *ronin* who show what honor means by plotting, lying, and dying for their liege lord. Much has changed in Japan since 1944, and some aspects of the "national character" described by Benedict may not apply today. Nevertheless, as a demonstration of how to understand a national culture different from one's own, the book remains without equal.

✿ Read this in *The Chrysanthemum and the Sword*: Chapters 1–3, 5–8, and 10.

chapter 16
CULTURE

If cognitive bias is a hot topic in the leadership literature, *cultural* bias is even hotter. Thanks to the rise of multinational organizations and the flowering of technologies that make it easy (logistically, anyway) to communicate with people halfway around the world, leaders often find themselves working with cross-cultural teams—and fielding offers of help from cross-cultural consultants. These consultants, perhaps not surprisingly, emphasize the difficulty of intercultural communication. Some even say that it's impossible to understand another culture's perspectives, so bound are we by our own, and that the best we can do is learn how not to be offensive.

In fact, we can do much better. Fortunately for global leaders, cultural bias is the sort of bias most susceptible to education; that is, to a liberal arts–style education that immerses us in a diversity of ideas and teaches us to question what seems obvious. And while wide travel and facility in several languages are helpful, they aren't essential. What is important is to develop the habit of *attending to what other people think, feel, and believe* and then to expand our attention so that it takes in the thoughts, feelings, and beliefs of various cultures. If we do, we'll find that yes, cultures can be amazingly different; and yes, it is possible to understand one another.

UNDERSTANDING AN ENEMY: THE US AND JAPAN, 1945

In June 1944, the US government commissioned anthropologist Ruth Benedict to conduct a cultural analysis of the Japanese people. The study's purpose was to help Allied leaders predict how the Japanese would behave as World War II drew to a close: Would they surrender without a full-scale invasion? When peace was declared, would there be bitter-enders hiding in the countryside, waiting to attack? How long would martial law need to be imposed? Would a Japanese revolution of the order of the French and Russian revolutions be necessary as a basis for lasting peace?

Much depended on the answers to these questions and more, and arriving at the answers wouldn't be easy, for, as Benedict explains on her book's first page, "The Japanese were the most alien enemy the United States had ever fought in an all-out struggle. In no other war ... had it been necessary to take into account such exceedingly different habits of acting and thinking."[1] Armed with an open mind, she set out to understand that enemy. Her question was how *they* would think and behave—not how *we* would think and behave if we were in their place. It is the question every cross-cultural leader should ask.

The Chrysanthemum and the Sword paints an intricate portrait of Japanese ideas and ways in the mid-twentieth century. One concept that had a particularly profound impact on the events of the time was *gimu*. Often translated as "duty," gimu is actually a much bigger idea: it is a limitless debt that one takes on at birth and can never discharge or repay. Gimu to parents and ancestors is called *ko*; gimu to the Emperor, the law, and Japan is *chu*. It was chu, Benedict says, that led to the extraordinary (to Western eyes) behavior of the Japanese on the nation's surrender to the Allies in 1945.

Chu is something like what Westerners call patriotism, but it is not the same as loyalty to flag and country. It is focused on the Emperor himself and is intensely personal. Westerners, and especially Americans, may find repugnant the idea of patriotic loyalty directed toward an individual, but for the Japanese it was both necessary and wonderful that their supreme symbol was supremely human. "They could love and he could respond," says Benedict. "They were moved to ecstasy that he 'turned his thoughts to them.' They dedicated their lives to 'ease his heart.'"[2] Japanese teachers in training were flunked if they named love of country as the highest duty; the correct answer was repayment to the Emperor. To obey the Emperor or those who spoke for him was to make a minuscule return on an overwhelming debt. It would be unthinkable to do otherwise.

On August 14, 1945, the world saw a demonstration of chu's power. Many Westerners with experience of Asia had thought it naïve to imagine that the Japanese armies would ever surrender, let alone peacefully yield up arms while they were still able to fight. Others thought surrender possible only if a Western-style revolution occurred and the Japanese government was overthrown. But, says Benedict, these observers reckoned without chu. When the Emperor spoke, the war ceased. US troops landed at the airfields and were greeted with courtesy. Foreign correspondents arrived in the morning and by evening were shopping for souvenirs. The Japanese were easing the Emperor's heart by following his desires, which a week ago may have been for war but today were for peace. While revolution or underground resistance might be a Western nation's strength, Japan's strength was:

> the ability to demand of herself as chu the enormous price of unconditional surrender before her fighting power was broken. In her own eyes this enormous payment nevertheless bought something she supremely valued: the right to say it was the Emperor who had given the order even if that order was capitulation. Even in defeat the highest law was still chu.[3]

THREE DIMENSIONS OF NATIONAL CULTURE

There are many frameworks for understanding culture. Most are derived from the "dimensions" model developed in the 1970s by social psychologist Geert Hofstede (see "On tall shoulders: Geert Hofstede on national culture"). Business consultant Fons Trompenaars, for example, proposes these five dimensions: universalistic vs. particularistic, communitarian vs. individual, neutral vs. emotional, diffuse vs. specific, and achievement vs. ascription.[4] Other authors have other models, most with a similar "this vs. that" structure.[5] If we consider these models together with a deep cultural analysis such as *The Chrysanthemum and the Sword*, three dimensions of culture stand out as primary:

- Universalistic vs. particularistic
- Egalitarian vs. hierarchical
- Individualistic vs. communitarian

on tall shoulders

GEERT HOFSTEDE on NATIONAL CULTURE

Between 1965 and 1971, Geert Hofstede, founder of IBM Europe's Personnel Research department, conducted an attitudes and values survey of 117,000 IBM employees around the world.

From that mountain of data emerged Hofstede's four dimensions of national culture: (1) *Large or small power distance*, the extent to which an unequal distribution of power is accepted; (2) *Individualism or collectivism*, the extent to which people are integrated into groups; (3) *Strong or weak uncertainty avoidance*, the extent to which ambiguity is tolerated; (4) *Masculinity or femininity*, the extent to which achievement, heroism, and assertiveness are valued vs. cooperation, modesty, and caring.

Later, Hofstede added a fifth dimension: *Long- or short-term orientation* (extent to which people sacrifice the pleasures of today for the sake of their future).

Why worry about all these nuances? Ruth Benedict no doubt would have approved of Hofstede's answer: "If we inhabitants of the globe do not acquire an awareness of our mutual differences, knowledge of basic cultural variables, the skills to communicate effectively across boundaries and the will to do so, our world will be the worse for it."[6]

The second and third dimensions are easy to grasp; the first requires a little explanation. Universalistic vs. particularistic can be translated as "rules vs. relationships." Which does a culture think is more important: rules that apply to everyone, or particular relationships with their particular circumstances? In his writings, Trompenaars uses this example: You're riding in a car driven by a close friend. He hits a pedestrian. You know he was going 15 miles per hour above the speed limit. There are no witnesses. If you testify under oath that he was going no faster than the speed limit, it may save him from serious consequences. Trompenaars then poses a question: How much right has your friend to expect you to testify in his favor?[7]

As it turns out, people from different cultures have very different views on this. Most North Americans and many northern Europeans tend to take a strongly universalistic approach: This is about upholding the law, they say. No one has a right to expect even a close friend to break the law, so you should tell the truth. But many Latin Americans, southern Europeans, and Asians are particularistic: they would lie in court to save their friend.

Even more interesting, says Trompenaars, are people's reactions when they're told that the pedestrian died. The universalists feel even less of an obligation to help their friend, for the pedestrian's death underscores the matter's severity and makes upholding the law still more important. The particularists, on the other hand, think their friend needs their help more than ever now that he's in serious trouble. People from each type of culture tend to be amazed at the others' reaction. "How could you be so immoral as to lie under oath in a grave situation such as this?" the universalists say. "How could you be so immoral as to refuse to help a dear friend in grave need?" the particularists counter.

Japanese culture, as a whole, leans toward particularistic, hierarchical, and communitarian.[8] In the idea of gimu (which, remember, comprises ko and chu), all three qualities are crystallized. Gimu is *particularistic*: it is a debt owed to benefactors to whom you are bound in a personal relationship—your parents, your ancestors, the Emperor. Gimu is *hierarchical*: these people are your superiors, enshrined for ever above you. And gimu is *communitarian*: virtue lies not in being self-made or in repaying debts you chose to incur, but in the never-ending attempt to repay your benefactors, whom you did not choose. Of course matters are seen very differently in the United States, which is strongly universalistic, egalitarian, and individualistic. No wonder that in World War II, each culture found the other mystifying.

It's important to recognize that culture isn't either/or. Like the four dimensions of psychological type (see Chapter 14), the three dimensions of national culture are sliding scales; a culture might be, say, strongly universalistic, fairly hierarchical, and halfway between communitarian and individualistic. Where your culture sits will determine your view of other cultures. Mexico, for example, falls somewhere in the middle of egalitarian and hierarchical: more hierarchical than the Netherlands, but more egalitarian than China.[9] A Mexican leader transferred to a Dutch company might be surprised by how readily her employees question her instructions, but that same leader transferred to a Chinese company might find those employees unpleasantly deferential. It's a matter of perspective (see "Communication tool: Cross-cultural interview").

"MORNING, CHAPS!"

A story will show what can happen when cultures collide within an organization.[10] A London-based conglomerate sent one of its British executives, Mr. Greene, to Tokyo to serve as managing director for its Japanese operations. Mr. Greene was eager to establish trust and credibility with his Japanese employees. He knew that Japanese companies often held a Monday-morning meeting with group calisthenics and discussion of the week ahead, so he asked his second in command, Mr. Akita, whether establishing such a meeting might be a good idea. Mr. Akita said yes, indeed, it was an excellent idea and the employees would appreciate it. So Mr. Greene set it up, and every Monday at 9 a.m. he would hurry down to the auditorium and greet his assembled employees with a cheery "Good morning, chaps!"

Six months went by, and Mr. Greene couldn't understand why he was making no headway at all. The employees remained distant. In meetings, especially the Monday-morning ones, they were coldly silent. He couldn't seem to build relationships with anyone, at any level. Finally, he called Mr. Akita into his office and asked him flat out: What was the problem? Mr. Akita looked pained and said he didn't know. But Mr. Greene kept pressing until finally Mr. Akita, averting his eyes with embarrassment, asked Mr. Greene to please forgive him for being so blunt, but he suspected the employees didn't like it when Mr. Greene began each Monday meeting by saying, "Good morning, Japs."

No doubt Mr. Greene's first thought was, "Where's the rock I can crawl under?" After all, he'd been mortally offending his entire staff every week for half a year. But his second thought was probably, "Why didn't anyone tell me? And why didn't it occur to them that I might be stupidly using an English word that merely sounded like 'Japs'?"

communication tool

CROSS-CULTURAL INTERVIEW

Make a concerted effort to learn about one or more national cultures different from your own. Start by identifying someone (colleague or friend) who has lived and worked both in your country and in another country for extended periods. Conduct a 45-minute interview with that person to learn about the other culture and how it contrasts with your own.

Ask questions such as these:

- What do people from this country find surprising when they go to live or work in that one?
- What do people from that country find surprising about this one?
- What is it like to do business in that culture? What does one need to keep in mind?
- Can you share an anecdote or two illustrating the cultural differences?
- What advice would you give a leader sent to work in that country?

Consider writing up the interview for your organization's newsletter or blog.

If we think about the culture dimensions, however, it makes sense that no one said anything to Mr. Greene. For Japanese employees in a particularistic, hierarchical, communitarian culture, the boss is always right. Like a parent, he is your personal benefactor and is owed unquestioning respect and obedience. To criticize his choice of words would be deeply shameful, along the lines of slapping your father in the face. Moreover, such criticism would bring shame not only on you, but also on all your colleagues. It clearly cost Mr. Akita a lot to be honest about the difficulty, even though he'd worked closely with Mr. Greene for some time.

The same dynamic could have played out with the situation reversed: with a Japanese senior manager sent to New York, say, to run a US division of a Japanese company, and making a terrible faux pas of which he was unaware. In that case, the egalitarian, individualistic culture of the American employees might have led them to reason as follows: "This guy is clearly an idiot. But it's none of my business; I'm just here to do my job. Eventually HR will find out, and he'll be toast. In the meantime, I'll go on keeping my head down." Just like Mr. Greene, the Japanese executive could have been left in the dark for ages.

From either scenario, the lesson to draw is that as leaders we must often "go first" (see Chapter 1) not only in the obvious ways—setting strategy, launching new projects, and so on—but also in some less obvious ways: We must be the first to check our assumptions. The first to admit ignorance. The first to ask forgiveness, even when we don't know why it's needed.

CORPORATE CULTURE IS JUST AS IMPORTANT

National culture is clearly important. In my experience, however, more leaders are felled by the unfamiliar ways of an organization than by those of a nation. A corporate culture is sometimes strong enough to overwhelm the diverse customs of a global workforce, imposing a uniformity that cuts across national boundaries and rejects people who don't fit the mold, no matter where they were born. Moreover, unlike workplace climate (see Chapter 13), workplace culture is not malleable. Culture is like a concrete slab poured and set in the first few years of an organization's life; the handprints that decorate it are the founders' beliefs, goals, and values. Typically, it will repel all efforts to reshape it or remove those handprints. A leader who tries will have no more luck than if he or she tried to reshape the culture of a nation.

Corporate cultures can be arrayed along the same three dimensions as national cultures: universalistic–particularistic, egalitarian–hierarchical, and individualistic–communitarian. Once again, the first dimension translates roughly to "Rules or relationships?" A universalistic organization emphasizes rules, roles, and results; people are there to follow the rules, fill the roles, and get results. Not much is left to chance and little allowance made for personal idiosyncrasies. A particularistic organization, on the other hand, sees building personal relationships and serving customers as ends in themselves. If you ask someone how the place works, you'll likely hear all about who's who, who's close to whom, and who thinks what; hardly anything about the rules.

A manager who moves from one geographic region to another may have difficulty understanding the behaviors and mindsets of the people there, but a manager who moves from one organization to another can often experience a bigger jolt; if, that is, the new organization has a very different culture from the old.

Take Rona, the leader we met in Chapters 2 and 11; she was the new chief executive of public relations firm Pinecone, a recent acquisition of media conglomerate Hanover. She had spent the past 20 years working her way up through several other Hanover-owned companies. Hanover's headquarters were in Sydney, and Pinecone was California based; nevertheless, the geographic origins of the two companies, which one might expect would make them compatible (Australia and America have fairly similar national cultures), didn't matter nearly as much as their corporate cultures, which were radically different. Pinecone was strongly particularistic, moderately egalitarian, and extremely communitarian, while owner Hanover was strongly universalistic, extremely hierarchical, and moderately individualistic (see Figure 16.1).

When Rona arrived at Pinecone, she felt as if she'd parachuted into an alien land. The emphasis on personal relationships, the desire to put a team on every little task, the easy questioning of authority—it all flew in the face of the values she had absorbed in her years at other Hanover companies. To her, the Pinecone culture seemed unprofessional and unproductive, verging on insubordinate. From a Hanover perspective, it probably was all those things. But that didn't mean it could be changed by a leader's edict.

Consider what happened when Rona tried to quash one small Pinecone tradition. Since Pinecone's early days, any employee leaving the firm would send a farewell email to the entire company distribution list saying thank-you, wishing everyone the best, perhaps sharing a fond memory. At rule-oriented, hierarchical Hanover, this sort of thing was considered highly inappropriate; the

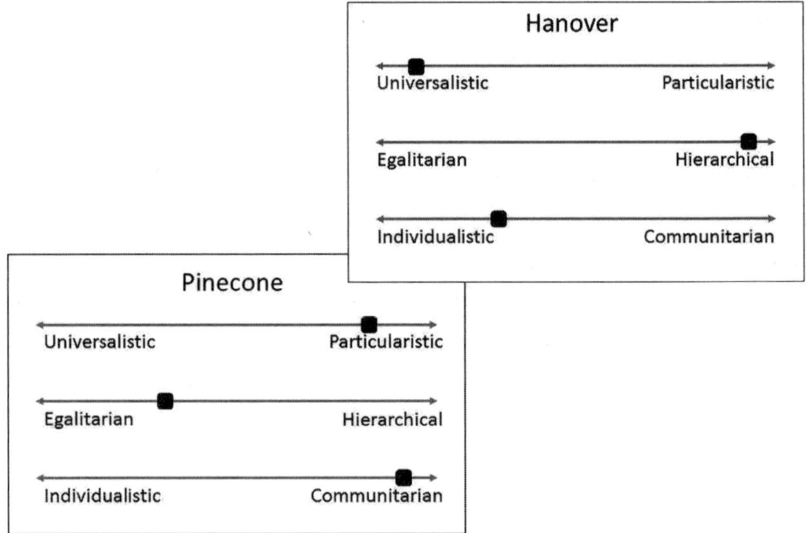

Figure 16.1 *Two company cultures*

company was seen as owning all communication about personnel matters and such emails were fraught with legal risk. Rona, taking the Hanover view, told her senior team to put a stop to the practice. They dutifully did so: from then on, they instructed any departing employee to send his or her farewell message not to the global distribution list but to individual email addresses—and to be absolutely sure that Rona's address was not among them.

Management sage Peter Drucker famously said, "Culture eats strategy for breakfast." I would go further and say that it eats strategy, policy, flowcharts, organizational charts, and managerial directives for breakfast and munches on PowerPoint presentations the rest of the day.

If approached with humility, however, culture can be both fascinating and kind. Case in point: once he adjusted his morning "hello," Mr. Greene was forgiven.

In the next chapter, the world's best-known horror story reveals the one character trait a leader cannot do without.

great author

MARY SHELLEY'S *FRANKENSTEIN*

Mary Godwin wrote *Frankenstein* when she was barely 19 years old. Vacationing near Lake Como in the summer of 1816, she and the poet Percy Shelley, whom she was to marry in December that year, took a neighboring property to British aristocrat Lord Byron (also a poet) and his physician, John William Polidori. The weather was wet, so the group, with Mary's stepsister Claire Clairmont, sought ways to amuse themselves indoors. "We will each write a ghost story," Byron announced one evening at his Villa Diodati. Only Mary finished her tale.[1] The first edition of *Frankenstein* was published anonymously; when the author's identity was revealed, some readers and critics were shocked that a story so macabre could have been written by a young woman.

Today, *Frankenstein* comes saddled with two common misconceptions. First, many people assume that the title of the book refers to the monster; in fact, it refers to the monster's creator, Victor Frankenstein, like Mary Shelley a youth of about 19. Second, Hollywood provides our stock image of the monster as a grunting brute with bolts in his neck, but Shelley's monster is sensitive and benevolent. By the second year of his existence, thanks to his own efforts, he is also educated and articulate. Despite his outward ugliness, he has a beauty of soul; that beauty, however, cannot flourish without the care of his creator, who rejects him utterly.

Victor Frankenstein is another example of a leader caught in Trap No. 8: *Dominating and abdicating*. As long as his creature is inanimate, feeding his ambitions and being shaped by his hands, Frankenstein couldn't be more dedicated to its success. As soon as the creature comes to life, however, he flees in terror. The heartbreaking result of this abdication is revealed only later, in the creature's story. Here's how the "monster" describes his first night on earth after stumbling blindly from Frankenstein's laboratory:

> It was dark when I awoke; I felt cold also, and half frightened, as it were, instinctively, finding myself so desolate ... I was a poor, miserable, helpless wretch; I knew, and could distinguish, nothing; but feeling pain invade me on all sides, I sat down and wept.[2]

✯ Read this in *Frankenstein*: The first two-thirds of the book take us through the monster's story (Chapters 11–16), a compelling section for leaders. The final chapter, containing the last speeches of creator and creature, is also extraordinary.

chapter 17
CHARACTER, ANCHORED

This chapter looks at the first and foundational character trait: *courage*. "Courage is not simply one of the virtues," said C.S. Lewis, "but the form of every virtue at its testing point." Poet Maya Angelou said, "Without courage, we cannot practice any other virtue with consistency." And enlightenment philosopher John Locke praised fortitude as "the guard and support of the other virtues."

COURAGE AND COWARDICE

The five leadership character traits, as we've seen, are courage, integrity, resilience, generosity, and concern, and each represents the midpoint, or mean, of a continuum. Churchill's essays (Chapter 7) showed us that effective leaders stick to the mean while less effective leaders slide off to one side or wobble around. Plutarch (Chapter 12) argued that strength of character is developed by an education in philosophy, which keeps one centered on the mean. And Jung's treatise on personality (Chapter 14) helped us parse character in terms of two psychological types: introversion and extraversion. But courage is the backbone of a leader's character, bracing each virtue, holding it straight and true (see Figure 17.1). Cowardice is the opposite: the enfeebler of character, the vice that makes every virtue flabby and unreliable. Since courage and cowardice sit at the heart (or spine) of character, leaders need an especially good understanding of both.

Note that timidity, the trait at the far left of the courage continuum, is not the same as cowardice. Timidity is a reluctance to engage; as we saw in Chapter 14, it's a trait to which introverts, with their tendency to turn inward and away from the world, are especially prone. Timidity isn't desirable in a leader, but it isn't the same as cowardice, which is a much farther-reaching vice with much worse effects. Cowardice is the absolute determination to protect the self: from fear, pain, ridicule, rejection, failure, uncertainty, and any other injury, physical or emotional. Depending on the leader and the situation, cowardice can manifest as any one of the extremes

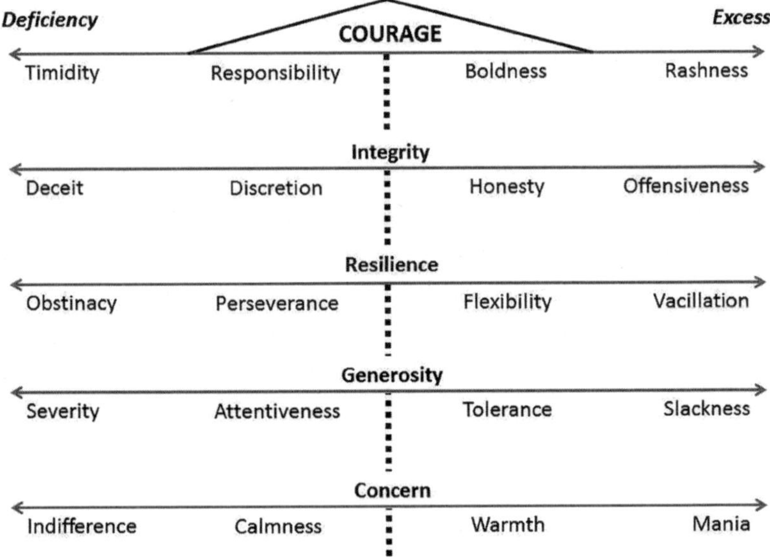

Figure 17.1 The backbone of leadership character

on the character continuums. For example, an extraverted leader subjected to ridicule might seek to protect his ego by loudly belittling his antagonist (offensiveness). An introverted leader facing a professional failure might adopt a "don't care" attitude (indifference). Cowardice takes many forms, not all of them timid.

Courage, on the other hand, is doing what must or should be done even at the risk of injury to the self. That's hard enough for anyone, but leaders face a particular difficulty in that their role demands that they lay themselves open to fear, pain, ridicule, and the rest. When a person goes first or stands in front, that's what happens. The lead cyclist bears the brunt of the wind, the first soldier over the wall draws the enemy's fire, the actor in the leading role gets splattered with rotten tomatoes, and the manager who makes the big decision is the one blamed when things go wrong. To be any kind of leader means to risk death—perhaps not actual, physical death, but the little death of the soul that comes with sneers and jeers. When we lead, we are necessarily vulnerable.

Yet, as leaders, we often feel that we should be the opposite. People are depending on us, holding us accountable for the mission's success and the team's performance, therefore we must be invulnerable. We must put on armor and carry a sword, so that if we're attacked, we can either hit the other guy first or deflect the blows. It would be terrible, we think, to leave our team bereft of a leader.

But here's the paradox: courage, because it means forgoing self-protection in favor of doing the right thing, usually requires that we put down the sword and take off the armor. As former US Navy Captain L. David Marquet says in his book *Turn the Ship Around!* (a tale of leadership on a nuclear submarine), courage in a leader is a matter of "caring and not caring": caring about the success of your subordinates and the mission, and not caring about the consequences to yourself or your career.[3] Cowardly leaders have it the other way around: they care a great deal about their own success and safety and not much about anyone else's. They want to enjoy the perks of leadership without bearing the risks, so they keep tight hold of the sword and stay wrapped inside the armor.

And when something threatening presents itself—*even something they had a hand in creating*—they either run away or, because they know that running away is not leaderly, deny responsibility. They call the threat a bad thing, an evil thing; a monster to be shunned.

English literature's most famous horror story centers on a leader of just this sort.

THE LEADER WHO CRIED "MONSTER"

> I had worked hard for nearly two years, for the sole purpose of infusing life into an inanimate body ... but now that I had finished, the beauty of the dream vanished, and breathless horror and disgust filled my heart. Unable to endure the aspect of the being I had created, I rushed out of the room.[4]

Victor Frankenstein, a brilliant student of natural philosophy from a well-to-do Swiss family, plans to create a living being from inanimate materials. If he succeeds, and he knows he will, he'll be hailed as a thought leader, an innovator, perhaps the greatest man in the world. Most gratifying of all will be his swarms of devoted followers: "Many happy and excellent natures would owe their being to me," he muses. "No father could claim the gratitude of his child so completely as I should deserve theirs."[5] He works furiously on his plan, neglecting his university studies. He designs his creature bigger than normal so that he doesn't have to fuss with details. He selects each physical element for impressiveness: flowing black locks, smooth white skin, good teeth, large muscles. Every hour of every day is devoted to the project. He brushes aside worries that he might be growing obsessed (after all, no great thing is achieved without dedication) and presses on until he discovers the final secret necessary to impart life to dead matter. At long last, on a November night, he accomplishes his goal.

Immediately, his hopes are dashed. The live creature doesn't look or act as he imagined it would. It doesn't threaten him in any serious way, but it simply isn't what he'd pictured. With hindsight, he admits that the creature *was* unattractive when it was lying inert on the table, but when it started to move—that's when it became horrifying. He knows that it will horrify others, as well. He can't bear the sight of his hideous failure.

Take away the supernatural trappings, and we have a familiar situation. Think about a time when you (or another leader) made a bold move: a controversial hiring choice, or a bet on an innovative product or technology. You had high hopes, but soon after rollout you realized all was not well. The new hire wasn't cutting it. Customers weren't buying the product. The technology didn't work as advertised. It was a nightmare! Worst of all, you felt sure that everyone was going to blame *you*. Given such a mess, what's a leader to do?

Victor Frankenstein knows what to do: he runs to his bedroom and hides. Terror isn't what's driving him, however, because he doesn't call for help, doesn't warn the neighbors, doesn't even barricade the door. His focus is, rather, on his spoiled hopes: "I felt the bitterness of disappointment; dreams that had been my food and pleasant rest ... were now become a hell to me; and the change was so rapid, the overthrow so complete!"[6] At once he begins referring to his creation as "wretch," "monster," and "fiend," and after a bit of anxious pacing he gets into bed and falls asleep, unconcerned about where the creature is or what it might be doing. A few hours later, the beast enters the bedroom and reaches out a hand, "seemingly to detain me," says Frankenstein, although we learn later that the bewildered being was, quite understandably, seeking help. Appalled by the "inarticulate sounds" (did he expect French or German?) and unattractive grin, Frankenstein dashes out into the courtyard, where he passes the rest of the night. Next day he heads home to Geneva, where he occupies his time wandering despondently around the countryside. He neither reports the situation nor takes any other kind of constructive action. He simply broods on the dreadful existence of the wretch ... monster ... fiend.

A year later, the two meet again. About a month earlier Frankenstein's younger brother, a child of 7, was brutally murdered. Frankenstein suspects, correctly as it turns out, that it was his own creature who committed the deed and that the creature is still somewhere in the neighborhood. While hiking in the mountains one day, he comes face to face with it. He tries an attack, but his blows are deflected easily by his eight-foot opponent (remember, Frankenstein worked large because he found details tiresome). The creature, who we later learn has devoted the year to educating himself, now delivers the book's central speech:

> Oh, Frankenstein, be not equitable to every other and trample upon me alone, to whom thy justice, and even thy clemency and affection, is most due. Remember that I am thy creature; I ought to be thy Adam, but I am rather the fallen angel, whom thou drivest from joy for no misdeed ... I was benevolent and good; misery made me a fiend. Make me happy, and I shall again be virtuous.[7]

For the first time, Frankenstein is confronted with his cowardice. He created a living being and then, when it failed to turn out as expected, refused to care for it; indeed, abandoned it. That being, now articulate, has reappeared and is making demands.

The creature's major demand is to be heard. The words *listen* or *hear me* appear seven times in his ensuing speech. He admits to killing Frankenstein's brother, but says, "I ask you not to spare me; listen to me, and then ... if you will, destroy the work of your hands."[8] He covers Frankenstein's eyes, saying he doesn't have to look at him, but he must listen. "Hear my tale," he says; "it is long and strange." From the tale we learn that he started out inclined to see humans as his protectors and to revere them. Over the past year he has demonstrated amazing patience and ingenuity, hiding himself in a lean-to next to a cottage and learning to speak by listening to the inhabitants. He is perceptive and kind: at first he stole food from the cottagers, but when he noticed that this rendered their poverty more extreme, he reverted to gathering nuts and berries to survive. At night, he chopped firewood for his "family" and cleared snow from their paths. Moreover, he educated himself by listening to them as they read aloud and eventually by studying their cast-off books and papers. All in all, he seems to have a far better character than Frankenstein.

Eventually, the creature says, he turned murderous. He did so, however, only after suffering severe injuries. His carefully planned attempt to befriend humans was violently rejected, and his gallant rescue of a child from drowning earned him a bullet in the shoulder. It was then that he vowed to seek out his creator and have his revenge.

ENCOUNTERING MONSTERS

Had Victor Frankenstein been more courageous, how might he have behaved? A reasonably brave man would at least have tried to mitigate his mistakes and the danger to others, either by confining the "monster" or, if it escaped, by reporting its existence to the authorities. But a truly brave man would have *cared* for his creation. Realizing that he stood in relation to it as father to child, he would have sought to understand its needs and feelings and to help it thrive. The same is true in the real world: leaders show courage when they face down their adversaries, but they show more courage when they face up to their responsibilities. A good leader listens to and looks after the people, pleasant or not, who are in his or her charge. In the words of Pope Francis, "Peacemaking calls for courage, much more so than warfare. It calls for the courage to say yes to encounter and no to conflict"[9] (see "On tall shoulders: M. Night Shyamalan on encountering monsters").

on tall shoulders

M. NIGHT SHYAMALAN *on* ENCOUNTERING MONSTERS

Horror-film writer and director M. Night Shyamalan, like Mary Shelley, is probably among the last people you'd include in a list of leadership gurus.

But consider *The Sixth Sense*, Shyamalan's film about a small boy named Cole who is able to see and speak with dead people.[10] A shy and isolated child, Cole is terrified by the ghosts that confront him daily. His psychologist, however, suspects that the ghosts don't want to harm him; he advises Cole to try listening to them. Cole eventually gathers his courage and faces one of them, a little girl with a gruesome aspect who invades his bedroom one night. "Do you want to tell me something?" he asks her. It turns out that she does, and that he can help her. Once Cole starts listening to the ghosts, he discovers they're not so terrifying. They simply want to be heard.

While we tend to associate courage with grand deeds in history books, Cole's story suggests that a leader's most courageous moments are apt to be small and quiet. No sword, no armor, no fanfare; just someone standing in front of a monster and asking what it has to say.

If we as leaders make a courageous effort to "encounter"—if, as the hideous beast rises from the table, we step forward with concern rather than recoil in fear—we will find that, in most cases, the monsters aren't really monsters at all. While that's not to say that they'll always turn out to be angels, neither are they likely to be the fiends we initially took them for. We can begin by simply acknowledging their point of view and encouraging them to speak on, for nothing is more disarming than an empathetic ear (see "Communication tool: The courage of a soft answer").

communication tool
THE COURAGE OF A SOFT ANSWER

The next time someone accuses or attacks you, avoid lashing back with an angry or sarcastic reply. Instead, gather your courage and use the "ASSET" approach:

Acknowledge their point of view
Seek to understand more
Solicit their advice on how to move forward
Enlist their help with a solution
Thank them for engaging

Examples

- *A neighbor with a complaint*: "I see your point, and I'm sorry you've been inconvenienced. Can you say more about the problem? What do you think would work as a solution, here? Could you help me out by ...? I appreciate that, and thanks for bringing the issue to my attention."
- *A team member with an attitude*: "I can tell you're frustrated; I'm sure I would be, too, in your shoes. Can you describe what led up to this situation? What do you think we should do? OK, I will do x, and it would be very helpful if you would do y. Thank you for coming to me; this has been a good conversation."

The quiet moment of leadership courage I remember best happened in an orientation class for new hires at a company where I worked in the late 1990s. It was mid-afternoon on the first day, and the upcoming segment was a presentation by the CEO, whom I'll call Sam. Sam was running late, and since the facilitator didn't want to send the class on break and risk missing the CEO's window, everyone sat waiting for about 15 minutes. Sam eventually showed up and gave his talk about the company's code of behavior, a code that emphasized treating others with respect. At the end he asked if there were any questions or comments, whereupon a young man raised his hand

and said a little too loudly, "Yes, I have a comment. You've just told us this company values respect, but you showed up late. I don't think that was respectful."

Sam listened attentively to the employee's remarks. He paused for a moment, and then said: "You're right. It wasn't respectful to keep you all waiting. I'm sorry, and I thank you for calling me on it. You just gave us a great example of applying the code."

The young man subsided. He faced no negative consequences for being rude to the CEO in his very first week, and he went on to spent many productive years with the company.

Who was the most courageous person in the room that day? Some would say it was the new employee, but I say it was Sam. He may have been the CEO, but he was also a sixtyish man standing before a group of smart young things, one of whom had just made him look bad. The temptation to give a self-protective response—a coward's response—must have been great. One kind of coward would have retorted that he'd been late because he was busy running the company that provided everyone's paychecks, so shut the hell up. Another kind of coward would have said "Next question," and later dropped a hint to the kid's manager to make things difficult for him.

Sam did neither of those things. Instead, he listened, acknowledged his error, and made the snarky little monster—who was, after all, one of *his* monsters—look good. No Victor Frankenstein was he.

Who are your friends? More important: Who are your allies? Smart leaders know who's really who in their network, as we shall see next.

part V

JUDGMENTS

In Part V, the theme is judgment: leaders judging others, being judged themselves, and (often) misjudging the situation. The main characters in these stories are confident they understand something they don't really understand at all; or perhaps, like the proverbial blind men describing the elephant, they grasp just one piece of the picture and assume it to be the whole. These books teach us to question our certainties as leaders: to question whether we truly know, for instance, who is a friend, who is immoral, or where responsibility lies for a failure. They ask us not to put judgment aside, but to think and think again before we judge.

The chapter topics are relationships, accountability, talent, vision, and, once again, character. In each case we'll begin with a simplistic view and then explore a more nuanced one suggested by a great work of literature. First there's a story by Maupassant and a play by Shakespeare, each featuring relationships more complex and fluid than might initially be supposed. Next is Melville's *Billy Budd*, a tale of a shipboard murder that asks whether the perpetrator of a crime should always be the person held accountable; and *Emma*, Jane Austen's novel about a young woman who overestimates her abilities as a mentor, but gradually gains a humbler perspective on her talents and a clearer perspective on the talents of others. *Saint Joan*, by G.B. Shaw, is a play about a teenager who leads an army and saves a nation, but eventually pays the price for her vision. Finally, James Joyce's novella *The Dead* presents Gabriel Conroy, pillar of the community, man of sound judgment and good character, whose self-understanding is transformed by a New Year's party and its aftermath.

great author

GUY DE MAUPASSANT'S "BOULE DE SUIF"

"Boule de Suif" was short-story writer Guy de Maupassant's first big success and continues to be regarded as a masterpiece. The opening sentence—"For days on end, the tatters of the routed army had been passing through the city"—begins a tale that, although focused closely on the occupants of a stagecoach and their travel delays, conveys as much about strategic alliances as might be found in a sweeping military history. Maupassant was known for using keenly observed details to reveal hidden aspects of human relationships; in this story, for example, a few picnic baskets and the looks and remarks they engender are windows into the characters' innermost emotions.

The setup for the story is as follows: We are in the midst of the Franco-Prussian War of the 1870s, and ten French residents of the occupied city of Rouen have hired a coach to take them to free French territory in Le Havre. The group consists of a wealthy factory owner and his wife; a count and countess; a political agitator; two nuns; shopkeepers M. and Mme. Loiseau; and Boule de Suif, or "Butterball," a prostitute. Their journey is slowed by snow, and the first nine travelers, not having thought to bring supplies, grow hungrier as the day wears on. Butterball, in contrast, has brought a hamper of delicious food, which she graciously shares, causing the others' attitudes toward her to thaw a little. Later the party find themselves delayed at a wayside inn under the control of a Prussian officer. He won't allow them to leave, and after a day of puzzlement, they learn from Butterball that he plans to detain them there until she goes to bed with him.

"Boule de Suif" has been interpreted as a commentary on social snobbery. It is surely that, but simply to label the characters snobs for their poor treatment of a fellow traveler is to miss a larger point about relationships based on common interests, and what happens when those interests diverge.

chapter 18

RELATIONSHIPS

The ability to manage relationships is often what differentiates successful from unsuccessful leaders, according to Laurence Stybel and Maryanne Peabody, authors of the *Sloan Management Review* article "Friend, Foe, Ally, Adversary … Or Something Else?"[1]

We all know the importance of cultivating relationships. What many of us don't know is how to be strategic about it, and by "strategic" I don't mean polishing a LinkedIn profile or working the crowd at an industry event. Techniques of that sort are useful, of course, but they're easy to acquire from the many available books and websites about networking. Stybel and Peabody—along with Maupassant and Shakespeare, our two classic authors for this chapter—are talking about something deeper: knowing what each of our relationships is and could be, and adjusting our actions accordingly.

FRIENDS, FOES, ALLIES, AND ADVERSARIES

After the Iranian revolution of 1979, which ousted the US-backed Shah and installed the first of the ayatollahs, relations between the United States and Iran turned bitterly hostile. Iran's quarrels with its neighbor Iraq date back much further, beginning in the sixteenth century and continuing through the Iran–Iraq War of the 1980s. In the spring of 2014, as tensions rose again in the Middle East, one could say with certainty that Iran saw the United States and Iraq as its worst enemies and that they saw Iran in the same light.

That June, however, some surprising shifts occurred. They were triggered when the al-Qaida offshoot Islamic State (aka ISIS or ISIL), announcing as its aim the formation of a new caliphate, defeated the much larger Iraqi army and seized control of three cities in Iraq's north. The group's success was partly due to the aid of some local Sunni tribes who, despite rejecting fundamentalist Islamic ideologies, saw in ISIS a useful partner in their struggles against the Shiite-led Iraqi government. Their dislike of that government was apparently strong enough to outweigh their mistrust of the militants, and it led to an alliance of Islamic moderates and extremists in the region. "We are [eventually] going to fight ISIS," said Sheikh Bashar al-Faidhi, leader of one Sunni group, "but not now."[2]

Another shift followed. With the corrupt Iraqi army collapsing, the task of fighting the insurgents and defending the Iraqi capital fell to Shiite militias. Ill-equipped and struggling, they turned for assistance to their Shiite neighbor and longtime adversary Iran, which was quick to offer arms, money, and advice. "All Shiite factions have pushed their disagreements away ... to protect Baghdad," said one militia leader.[3]

Then, US President Barack Obama decided to target ISIS with airstrikes. This decision was greeted with silence by Iranian leaders, and given Iran's status as the United States' fiercest critic, that silence, to quote Middle East expert Alex Vatanka, "was tantamount to a roaring approval of Washington's intervention."[4] The roar grew even louder when, on the Monday following the start of airstrikes, a deputy to Iran's foreign minister told the press that Iranian–American cooperation against ISIS was "possible and achievable."[5]

To summarize: Over the course of a few days in June 2014, several of the world's worst enemies morphed into friends. Or did they?

We tend to think of relationships as falling along a single dimension from *friend* to *enemy*. We apply this view not only to nations and organizations ("the United States and Iran are enemies") but also to our individual relationships, personal or professional. For example: You and Julianne from Marketing get along great. She always supports you in meetings, and the two of you go out for drinks once a month. You consider Julianne a friend. But Bridget, the head of R&D, constantly shoots down your ideas and blocks your proposals. While you hesitate to call anyone an enemy, Bridget is certainly not your friend.

This view is inadequate. Relationships should in fact be arrayed along not one but two dimensions: whether the person is *with* you or *against* you; and whether that stance is *conditional* or *unconditional*. Combined, these two dimensions give rise to four main relationship types: friends, foes, allies, and adversaries (see Figure 18.1).[6]

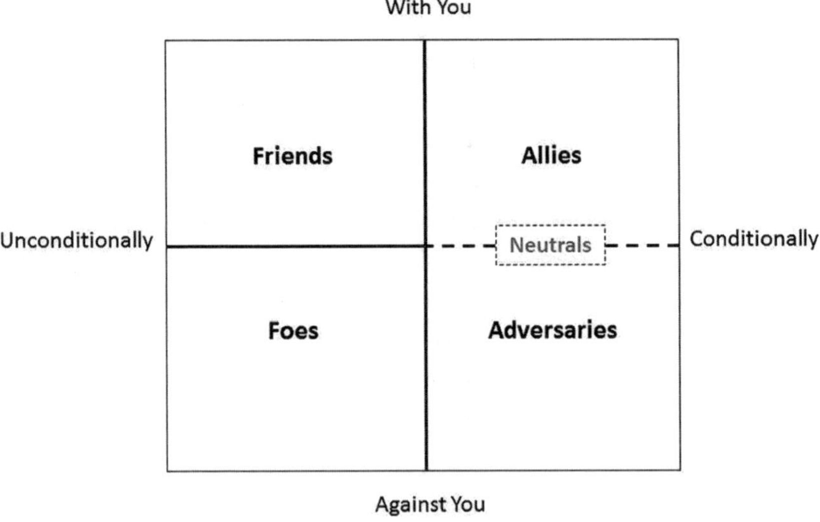

Figure 18-1 Relationship types

Friends are unconditionally with you, foes unconditionally against you. Allies and adversaries, on the other hand, support or oppose you when and because it suits their interests. Given that their stance is conditional, allies and adversaries may convert to the opposite state depending on whether they see their interests as aligned with yours. In other words, the line between ally and adversary is permeable, while the line between friend and foe is impermeable. The remark of Sheikh Bashar al-Faidhi—"We are going to fight ISIS, but not now"—sums up the contingent, temporary nature of allies and adversaries.

Relationship management, then, is first of all a matter of correct classification. Know what people are—friends, foes, allies, or adversaries—and you'll know how to relate to them (see "Planning tool: The relationship map").

planning tool
THE RELATIONSHIP MAP

Make a list of 10–20 people you know professionally or personally. Next, copy Figure 18.1 onto a sheet of paper, and map the names into the boxes: friends, foes, allies, adversaries, and neutrals. Reflect before categorizing each relationship, using the following guidelines and bearing in mind that how much you like someone tells you little about where he or she falls in the framework.

- A *friend* is someone with whom you share a close bond based on love and/or duty; someone who will always support you, no matter what.
- A *foe* is someone who regards you with a personal, deep-rooted antagonism; someone who will never support you, no matter what.
- An *ally* is someone who supports you based on currently shared interests.
- An *adversary* is someone who works against you based on currently conflicting interests.
- A *neutral* is someone whose interests, for now, neither align nor conflict with yours.

Then, select one of the people whom you categorized as an adversary. Ask yourself:

- What would need to change in order for this person to become an ally?
- What questions might you ask in order to understand his or her interests better?
- How you might you bring your two sets of interests into closer alignment?

MISTAKING ALLIES FOR FRIENDS

In an episode of the television series *Downton Abbey*, there's a scene in which Cora, Countess of Grantham, tries to enlist her mother-in-law, the Dowager Countess, in an effort to protect a particular family interest. The two women haven't always seen eye to eye. When the Dowager indicates her willingness to help, Cora sighs with relief and says, "So we're friends?" The Dowager replies, "*Allies*, my dear, which are far more useful."

When people in your life are friendly toward you, it's tempting to think of them as friends. And, very likely, some of them are. The question to ask, though, is not "How friendly is this person?" but rather, "*Why* is he or she being friendly?" If the answer is "because we have a bond based on love or duty," you have a friend. If the answer is "because we want the same things" or "because we have the same goals," you have an ally. Of course it's not always as neat as that; someone could be both a friend and an ally, or an ally on the way to becoming a friend. Nevertheless, striving to make the distinction helps you avoid a trap into which less perspicacious leaders tend to fall: taking an ally's support for granted and consequently neglecting to keep your interests aligned. When interests fall out of sync, an ally may transform into an adversary—an unpleasant surprise, if you thought you had a friend.

In Maupassant's "Boule de Suif," we see the ease of mistaking allies for friends and the painful consequences of doing so. The stagecoach occupants, having partaken of Butterball's picnic basket, arrive at the inn in an affable mood. It's wartime, after all; why insist on social distinctions? When they are detained by the Prussian officer and learn of his designs on Butterball, the others support her, prostitute though she is, in her refusal to have anything to do with an enemy of France. After a tedious two days, however, they start to grow desperate and decide she must comply. The men plan tactics to persuade her; at lunch, the ladies share bible stories of self-sacrificing heroines. Butterball, at first adamant, is eventually swayed. She resolves to help her "friends," and submits to the officer's demands.

You can guess how the story ends. The party is permitted to leave, and as they gather in the inn courtyard in the gray dawn to await the coach, no one addresses or even looks at Butterball. Later we find that the nine "respectable" travelers have brought plenty of food this time, while Butterball, rushed and upset after a disagreeable night, has not thought to prepare anything. Nobody shares with her. As tears of rage appear on the girl's cheeks, Mme. Loiseau gives "a triumphant soundless chuckle" and whispers to M. Loiseau: "She's crying from shame."[7]

Butterball's coach-mates start out as her adversaries, become her allies thanks to some shared interests, and then, when those shared interests evaporate, revert to adversaries. Are they hateful, hypocritical snobs, and is Butterball's situation heartbreaking? Yes—but, given that era's rules regarding association with prostitutes, their behavior is also unsurprising. Mme. Loiseau's interest in maintaining her social position is as strong as your or my interest in hanging on to a job. Imagine a work colleague who supports you staunchly, until there comes a day when supporting you means he'll be fired. If he turns his back on you then, can you blame him?

Perhaps you can, but it's pointless to do so. We as leaders cannot afford to blame our allies for not being our friends. Instead, we should appreciate our allies as the supports they are and strive, whenever possible, to keep our interests aligned with theirs; for friends are wonderful things, but allies (to quote the Dowager Countess of Grantham) are far more useful.

CONVERTING ADVERSARIES TO ALLIES

If you're feeling a little downhearted after realizing that some of your supposed friendships are only alliances, you can find solace in the converse: many of your imagined enemies are only adversaries, and adversaries don't have to stay that way. Another common error leaders make when it comes to managing relationships is failing to recognize adversaries as allies-in-waiting.[8] Unlike foes, adversaries will change their stance and support you when it is in their interest to do so. Figure out how to align your interests and theirs, and you've got a new ally. Change the circumstances, change the relationship (see "On tall shoulders: Doris Kearns Goodwin on allies-in-waiting").

on tall shoulders

DORIS KEARNS GOODWIN *on* ALLIES-IN-WAITING

Abraham Lincoln, the master communicator, was also a master of relationships. In this scene from her Lincoln biography *Team of Rivals*, Doris Kearns Goodwin describes the reaction of Benjamin Butler, a Democrat from Massachusetts, when Lincoln made him a brigadier general in the Union army:

> "I will accept the commission," Butler gratefully told Lincoln, but "there is one thing I must say to you ... That as a Democrat I opposed your election, and did all I could for your opponent; but I shall ... loyally support your administration as long as I hold your commission, and when I find any act that I cannot support I shall bring the commission back at once."
>
> Lincoln replied, "That is frank, that is fair. But I want to add one thing: When you see me doing anything that for the good of the country ought not to be done, come and tell me so ... and then perhaps you won't have any chance to resign your commission."[9]

In a moment, two sets of interests are aligned, and two former adversaries become allies.

An extreme but instructive example of an adversary-to-ally conversion can be found in Shakespeare's *Richard III*. The adversary in the case is Lady Anne, daughter-in-law of the dead King Henry VI and widow of Henry's son. King Richard killed both men, and Anne knows it. When the scene opens (Act I, Scene ii), she is weeping over Henry's coffin and calling for vengeance on the murderer of her husband and father-in-law. Here are just a few of the names she calls Richard: "dreadful minister of hell," "lump of foul deformity," "diffused infection of a man." Ninety-nine percent of us, in Richard's shoes, would assume that Anne is an implacable enemy and steer clear of her. Richard, undaunted, sets about winning her over.[10]

One way to read the scene is as a simple contest of wills. After goading Anne with banter and confusing her with flattery, Richard hands her his sword and dares her to kill him; when she can't do it, all the fight goes out of her, leaving her open to any suggestion he might make, including marriage. That interpretation is fine as far as it goes, but it doesn't take into account the many subtle ways in which Richard aligns himself with Anne's interests. Consider the following lines, which lie at the heart of the scene:

ANNE It is a quarrel just and reasonable
To be revenged on him that killed my husband.

RICHARD He that bereft thee, lady, of thy husband,
Did it to help thee to a better husband. (I.ii.136-139)

Despite our doubts about Richard's sincerity (not to mention his overall character), we can see the brilliance of his strategy. In one brief sentence, he reframes all his actions—everything for which Anne has been cursing him—as actions aimed at *helping her*. "I did it all for you," he says, thereby placing the two of them, however improbably, on the same side. Anne isn't immediately mollified; when he tells her "a better husband" means himself, she hurls a few more insults. Nevertheless, the dynamic between them has changed, and in response to his subsequent professions of love she can manage only a scornful look. This subtle realignment places Richard's dare in a different light: his kneeling and begging Anne to kill him in revenge for the murders ("But 'twas thy heavenly face that set me on") now come across as a physical demonstration of his desire to further her interests. She wants to kill him? Very well, he'll make it easy for her. She still can't do it? If she gives the word, he'll do it himself. See, he's ready to drive the sword in! But she must give the word, and she must know that he'll be doing it *for her*. Richard waits for instructions, the sword's point on his naked breast.

Anne hesitates, and then, with the soft remark "I would I knew thy heart," shifts from attacking a longtime adversary to assessing an unlikely ally. From then on, all Richard has to do is reassure her of his good intentions.

Shakespeare's Richard is clearly no leadership role model. Nevertheless, leaders can take a lesson from his refusal to be daunted by Anne's invective and from his bold approach to aligning interests. "She's against me now," we can hear him thinking, "but that doesn't mean she'll be against me always." Richard knows that even someone who spits at him and calls him a minister of hell *could* be an ally-in-waiting. His success with Anne should also remind us that attempting to win over an adversary, even if it's a long shot, is generally preferable to treating that adversary as an enemy and thereby guaranteeing that he or she becomes one.

That leads me to one final point about relationships: Enemy-making is a tempting activity for leaders. Whereas creating an ally takes hard work and self-control, creating an enemy is easy. Moreover, enemies yield emotional payoffs; defining ourselves in opposition to them can make us feel powerful. That sort of power, however, is often illusory and always dangerous, because a foe is forever. King Richard's taste for making enemies results in a slew of former allies and adversaries working tirelessly to destroy him. In the end, it is his downfall.

No doubt you know the adage about keeping friends close and enemies closer, but here's some better relationship advice:

Keep friends close.
Keep allies closer.
Keep an open mind about adversaries.
Keep foes to a minimum—and far away.

Next, how can leaders increase accountability while driving out fear? A famous sea story offers some insights.

great author
HERMAN MELVILLE'S *BILLY BUDD*

The plot of *Billy Budd* is as straightforward as the character of its protagonist. A handsome young sailor is taken off a merchant ship and pressed into service aboard a British man-of-war in 1797. Billy Budd's sunny temper makes him an immediate favorite with the ship's crew. Completely without guile, he is unable to conceive of guile in others, so he takes the friendly remarks of master-at-arms John Claggart at face value and brushes aside warnings that Claggart is, in reality, "down" on him. When Claggart tells Captain Vere that Billy is plotting mutiny—a complete falsehood—Billy is required to defend himself against the accusations. His congenital stutter, exacerbated by his inexperience with lies, renders him mute, and after a few minutes of strangled silence he lets fly a fist, striking Claggart on the forehead and accidentally killing him.

The rest of the story concerns the deliberations of Vere and the hastily convened drumhead court as to Billy's guilt or innocence. Though all are sympathetic to Billy and suspicious of Claggart's role in the incident, they decide to follow the letter of naval law and deliver a sentence of death. Billy is hanged from the yardarm the next morning with the entire crew looking on. His last words are: "God bless Captain Vere!"

Melville expresses the central dilemma of *Billy Budd* as follows: "[The event] was close on the heel of the suppressed insurrections, an after-time very critical to naval authority, demanding from every English sea commander two qualities not readily interfusable—prudence and rigour."[1] But there is more than a mismanaged dilemma here; there is a tragedy in which, says Melville, "the jugglery of circumstances" causes innocence and guilt, personified in Billy and Claggart, to change places.

Read this in Billy Budd: Captain Vere's speeches and reflections hold the most interest for leaders. His argument for Billy's conviction appears in Chapter 21.

chapter 19

ACCOUNTABILITY

Jacob Farr, global account director at GuestTech, pressed the Volume Up button on his desk phone. "Say that again, Tensia? I couldn't hear you."[1]

The soft-spoken account manager repeated herself: "I said, I just got my third complaint from Stacy about our customer service reps being unavailable. Her people can't reach anybody in Gurgaon after 11 a.m. London time, is what she says."

GuestTech, a provider of software and tech services to the hospitality industry, had recently created dedicated teams to serve its global clients. Each account team was led by an account director and included account managers and consultants, who in turn were supported by CSRs, software developers, and project managers. The latter were all located at GuestTech's office in Gurgaon, India. Support staff assigned to a global account team reported on a dotted line to the team and on a solid line to the head of the Gurgaon facility, Nikhil Chopra.

Jacob's team's client was Summers Inn, an international hotel chain where Stacy Rouse was the head of IT. They had been working on upgrades to Summers' tech infrastructure.

"That's been my experience, too." Philip, the team's lead consultant, had a big voice that was shattering on speakerphone. "The people in Gurgaon are never there!"

Jacob hit Volume Down a few times. "You're talking about the CSRs?" he asked.

"No, I don't know about the CSRs," said Philip. "I'm talking about the people I work with, the developers. You know how Summers wants that upgrade to their reservations module? They asked for it months ago. So, I'm going back and forth with Anuja and her team, and every cycle takes two days because by the time I have the revisions ready, they're all packing up to go home. When they're back in the morning it's the middle of the night for me here in Boston, so I can't chase them. It's frustrating. There's an incredible lack of ownership."

"Alexandra, are you finding the same thing?" asked Jacob.

There was silence on the line. Jacob tapped the Volume Up button and leaned forward. "Alexandra, are you there?"

"Sorry, sorry, I was on mute!" Jacob lurched back as the senior project manager's voice blasted out. "Yeah, same story here. I mean, the project managers are great, but Philip's right. Late afternoon, they're all gone. Maybe there's mandatory happy hour."

A few chuckles wafted from the speaker. Jacob massaged his eyebrows.

"All right, I'm glad you all brought this to my attention," he said. "Bottom line, it's not OK. I'll have a talk with Nikhil. He's got to start holding his people accountable."

ACCOUNTABILITY PROBLEMS

Accountability is a word you hear often once you take on a leadership role, and the higher you go, the more you hear it. In one company where I worked, the external consultants who were brought in each year to figure out why we weren't making more money would consistently name low accountability as the issue. The prescriptions for improvement apparently never took, because when the next group of consultants arrived, their diagnosis would be, you've guessed it, low accountability. It's the same in many organizations: "accountability" is something leaders are forever chasing and never quite catching. Granted, it's a worthy pursuit, for no one wants poor performance to be tolerated, and we all want to be able to count on our colleagues. Even our featured author from Chapter 13, concentration-camp survivor Viktor Frankl, showed himself a fan of accountability when he recommended that "the Statue of Liberty on the East Coast be supplemented by a Statue of Responsibility on the West Coast."[3]

If we're all in favor of accountability, why is fostering it so hard? There are three main reasons: the problem of unknown intentions, the problem of many hands, and the problem of blame avoidance.

The problem of unknown intentions The first reason it's hard to hold people accountable is that we never know exactly what's going on in their head. "What does that matter," you might ask, "when we can see what they do?" Yes, but the problem is that what they do is often defined by what they intend. Suppose it's 8 a.m. at the office and you observe an anxious-looking man walk quickly into the kitchen and over to a jar of money marked *Bagels*. He sticks his hand in the jar, removes the bills, stuffs them in his pocket, and runs out the door. What did the man do? One possible answer is "stole the money." Another is "forgot it was his turn to buy the bagels for the morning meeting and rushed off to get them." His actions alone won't tell you which answer is correct. To know the deed, you must know the intent.

The story of Billy Budd offers a weightier example. The central incident of the book occurs when master-at-arms Claggart falsely accuses Billy—young, handsome, and naïve—of plotting mutiny. Billy, called on by the captain to defend himself, is tongue-tied by his stutter, and in an agony of frustration he punches Claggart, killing him. It's obvious to Captain Vere and the ship's officers who must judge the case that Billy didn't mean to do it; moreover, they sense that Billy is being truthful when he asserts his loyalty and they suspect Claggart, on the other hand, of being an inveterate liar whose depravity "folds itself in the mantle of respectability."[4] The naval laws passed in response to recent mutinies, however, state that killing a man of superior rank is a capital offense and allow for no adjustments based on the presumed intentions of those involved; or at any rate, Captain Vere interprets the law that way. "Struck dead by an angel of God! Yet the angel must hang!"[5] he exclaims, and later in the proceedings he insists that Billy and Claggart's motives in the case are "hardly material"; a martial court must "confine its attention to the blow's consequence, which consequence justly is to be deemed not otherwise than as the striker's deed."[6]

Vere's attitude is shared by many leaders when they strive to raise accountability. Perhaps they worry, as he does, that making exceptions based on a transgressor's presumed intent will be seen as permissive and set a bad precedent. But whether or not that worry is valid, punishment meted out with blindness to intentions can sometimes be obviously, hideously unjust, making a mockery of accountability.[7]

The problem of many hands If the first problem with accountability is the difficulty of knowing just *what* was done and *why*, the second is the difficulty of knowing just *who* did it. For any organizational outcome there is more than one person—usually, many more—who contributed to it, and this "problem of many hands" (so named by Dennis F. Thompson, professor of political philosophy at Harvard University) creates a puzzle with respect to accountability.[8] If individuals are held accountable for a poor result, each person can with justification say, "It's not my fault. I did my part, but I couldn't control what those other people did." If, on the other hand, the organization as a whole is held accountable, everyone can hide behind "the system," and responsibility again has no place to rest.

In *Billy Budd*, Melville presents a complex web of accountability for the events aboard HMS *Bellipotent*. At the center of the web is the trio of Billy, Claggart, and Vere, each of whom bears some direct responsibility for the outcome. A little farther out we have the drumhead court officers, who passively accept Vere's arguments for Billy's execution; old navy veteran "the Dansker," who warns Billy about Claggart but seems to enjoy making his warnings too cryptic to be of any use; and Lieutenant Ratcliffe, the officer who, at the beginning of the story, selects Billy as the sailor to be taken off the merchant ship *Rights of Man*, his pick based on nothing more than Billy's good looks. And Melville pulls our perspective back still farther to show us the web itself, the context for events: there are the recent mutinies, which have every navy captain on edge; the draconian laws that were passed because of those mutinies; and finally and most influential of all, the system of impressment, whereby the Navy could grab sailors off any commercial vessel and force them into military service—a practice that, as you might imagine, created morale problems aboard British warships.

Out of this vast web of individuals and institutions, Captain Vere chooses one man, Billy Budd, to hold accountable. Perhaps it is what he must do, given that the institutions aren't subject to his authority; it's telling, however, that in the process of making the case for Billy's punishment he absolves *himself* of all responsibility by invoking martial law. "For that law and the rigor of it," he says, "we are not responsible."[9] In other words: none of this is his fault.

The problem of blame avoidance The last and largest problem of accountability is this: Emphasizing accountability tends to heighten fear, and fear tends to lower accountable behavior. This paradox may be hard to accept, especially if you believe that accountability is simply about setting and upholding standards, and what's scary about that? Nothing, if that's really all you're doing; high standards and clear expectations are strong motivators and climate enhancers, as we saw in Chapter 13. But when "accountability" becomes the headline, people get anxious, and when people get anxious, they devote a great deal of their time and energy to avoiding blame. Consultants Roger Connors and Tom Smith have noted that most people view accountability as something that happens to them when things go wrong—with good reason, because when things go right nobody ever asks, "Who is accountable for this success?"[10] The fact is, the more a leader talks about accountability, the more people will step back and cover their rear as opposed to doing what the leader wants them to do: step forward and raise their hand.

By framing the crime on the *Bellipotent* as he does, Captain Vere feeds his own fear, the officers' fear, and, ultimately, the climate of fear on the ship. His speech to the drumhead court conjures up an alarming picture of what will happen if they give Billy a lesser punishment: the sailors, he says, will think that a flagrant act of mutiny has been winked at and that their officers are afraid of them. "What shame to us such a conjecture on their part, and how deadly to discipline," he says.[11] The court members, who earlier were posing questions about the motives in the case, retreat into uneasy silence as they imagine the blame they might incur. But the honor and discipline they seek to uphold only grow shakier. The next day dawns on the shameful spectacle of ship's officers trying to hide their fear of crew members who, mustered to witness an execution for which they've received next to no explanation, show signs for the first time of becoming a mutinous mob.

planning tool
MANAGING TWO DILEMMAS

Accountability problems 1 and 2 can be reframed as dilemmas of actions vs. intentions and behaviors vs. processes. In their zeal to build accountability, leaders may pay a lot of attention to one side of each dilemma (actions and behaviors) and less attention to the other side (intentions and processes). A more balanced focus is often warranted.

Think about a past situation in which you were held accountable for a poor outcome.

- What questions do you wish your manager(s) had asked about your intentions?
- What questions do you wish they had asked about relevant organizational processes?

Next, consider: What does this exercise suggest about the range of questions you should ask when you're looking to hold someone accountable?

BUILDING A CULTURE OF ACCOUNTABILITY

How do we sidestep these difficulties with accountability? The key to problems 1 and 2—unknown intentions and many hands—is recognizing that they're not actually problems, but dilemmas: ongoing challenges with two sides, neither of which can stand alone as the correct and permanent answer (see "Planning tool: Managing two dilemmas"). As we saw in Chapter 10, we manage a dilemma not by picking a side but by seeking constantly to maximize the benefits and minimize the drawbacks of *both* sides. The problem of unknown intentions can be reframed as a dilemma of actions vs. intentions. In a culture of accountability, if something goes wrong, leaders do their best to learn what the people involved did *and* what they meant to do or thought they were doing. Unlike Captain Vere, they encourage questions about motives; and when in doubt, they assume good intent.

The problem of many hands can be reframed as a dilemma of behaviors vs. processes. In a culture of accountability, leaders seek to understand how individual behaviors and organizational processes contributed to a negative outcome. The phrase "Blame the process, not the person," coined during the total quality management movement of the 1990s, is apropos; I would, however, rephrase it as "Fix the process, coach the people." Both undoubtedly need attention, and assigning blame, whether to a process or a person, is simply not a useful business activity.

And speaking of blame, the third problem, blame avoidance, is not a dilemma but an actual problem with a straightforward answer. W. Edwards Deming, the father of TQM, provided the answer in number 8 of his 14 points for management: *Drive out fear.*[12] He wasn't saying that employees should be kept ignorant of real dangers, but rather that leaders should do all they can to make employees feel safe: safe to identify problems, safe to try and fail, safe to tell the truth (see "On tall shoulders: W. Edwards Deming on human systems").

Tyrants do the opposite: they make people afraid to identify problems, afraid to try and fail, afraid to tell the truth. Josef Stalin, for example, sent a telegram in January 1940 to a plant manager telling him his entire management team would be shot if they failed to meet a deadline.[13] That's a threat most petty tyrants can't match, but they do their best. I recall one who, frustrated with his regional managers' failure to hit their forecasted revenue, hammered his fist on the conference table as he snarled: "This is either incompetence or cowardice: either you don't know how to forecast or you're scared to report the real numbers. *Which is it?*" The managers chose incompetence. There was no subsequent improvement in forecast accuracy.

Note that overcoming these three accountability problems (or dilemmas) comes down to the leader's behavior. If we must blame someone for a poor result, it is ourselves, as stewards of the processes and leaders of the people, to whom we should look first. It is our own acceptance or rejection of accountability that sets the tone for everyone else.

on tall shoulders

W. EDWARDS DEMING *on* HUMAN SYSTEMS

In 1986 when he wrote *Out of the Crisis*, W. Edwards Deming was revered in Japan as the guru behind that country's post-war rise to economic power. It took another decade before he gained a similar level of fame in the United States and Europe.

For Deming, the "crisis" was bigger than poor quality. It was nothing less than the decline of Western industry, and his mission was to halt that decline. "There must be an awakening to the crisis," he wrote, "followed by action, management's job."[14] Though he writes in an engineer's dry style, Deming clearly isn't talking about blueprints and spreadsheets. He's talking about conceiving of organizations as systems: not of machines, but of people. Management's job is to create a system in which the natural intelligence, energy, and ingenuity of employees can flourish, leading to sustained success.

Deming's famous 14 Points (from the book's preface) are one long plea to managers to stop crushing the human spirit in the name of productivity. Consider the second half of Point 10:

> Eliminate management by objective. Eliminate management by numbers and numerical goals. Instead substitute with leadership.

None of this is to say that genuine crimes should be excused or that people should never be fired for poor performance or malfeasance. Sometimes a leader needs to be clear that certain things are not OK. But be careful: the story of Billy Budd tells us that even in apparently clear-cut criminal cases, the culprit may not be so clear and our judgment may be wrong. In the penultimate chapter of Melville's book, a newspaper account of the *Bellipotent* incident paints the evil Claggart as the soul of respectability and fidelity. When we see an angel hanged for murder and a snake praised to the skies, our zeal to "hold people accountable" should wane a little. At the very least, we should be open to hearing the other side of the story.

THE GUESTTECH TEAM: ANOTHER PERSPECTIVE

Nikhil Chopra pressed the End key on his mobile phone and sighed.

Jacob Farr's call had been the fourth this month from an account director regarding the supposed non-availability of support staff in Gurgaon. And only yesterday Nikhil had sent his second company-wide email regarding hours in the Gurgaon facility: 7 a.m. to 4 p.m., with no late shift. The trouble was, the account directors thought the staff dedicated to their teams ought to be more flexible when a big project called for it. "Please understand, Nikhil, it's OK with us if your people come in late if they need to," Jacob had said. "In the US and Europe, we're asleep at 7 a.m. your time, anyway. It's just odd that everyone bails out of there right at 4. The hourly workers, I get it, but most of the folks on the global teams are salaried, so I'd expect a bit more professionalism. Especially for a huge client like Summers."

Just then three sharp buzzes emanated from the intercom speaker: the 10-minute warning for the minivans' departure. In Gurgaon, a satellite city to Delhi, public transportation was minimal. There were a few public buses, but I wouldn't take them myself, thought Nikhil, let alone allow my sister or daughter to take one. The private GuestTech vans pulled up outside the facility at 4 and left precisely at 4:10. If you missed them, you found your own way home. There were just enough seats for everyone—usually.

Packing up his things, Nikhil wondered for the umpteenth time whether there was a way to shift some of the vans to an hour later, and for the umpteenth time rejected the idea. Without more vans (his boss had already said no to that), there would be no way to match the number of seats to the varying number of people needing flextime each day.

Leaving his office, he nearly slammed into Anuja, the senior software developer on Jacob Farr's team. "Oh, Nikhil, sorry," she said, not breaking stride. As they joined the stream of workers headed for the door, she continued, rapid fire: "Hey, I need to tell you. You know Philip, from the Summers team? So, he emailed me at 3:45 with more changes to the reservations module. He said he wants to go over them by phone before I leave today. I said please enter them as change requests in the system—you know he's had the training on that. Give me a chance to review the changes, I said, and we can talk tomorrow if need be. He says, 'I want to cover them now.' I'm like, sorry, no!"

The crowd picked up pace as Anuja continued. "Nikhil, I am honestly doing my best, but I'm having a hard time with how this team ignores our processes. Can't we hold them accountable?"

In the next chapter, characters in Jane Austen's *Emma* demonstrate the right and wrong way to develop talent.

great author
JANE AUSTEN'S *EMMA*

Emma, the second to last of Jane Austen's six novels, rivals *Pride and Prejudice* for popularity. Austen said of the book that she decided to create a heroine "whom no one but myself will much like,"[1] yet the plethora of film, television, and stage adaptations suggest that the heroine is, if not completely likeable, at least highly interesting.

Twenty-year-old Emma Woodhouse, "handsome, clever, and rich," is the undisputed social leader of the town of Highbury. With a comfortable home of which she has been mistress since her mother's long-ago death, an indulgent father, and a set of admiring friends, she is rarely given cause to doubt her superiority or her right to guide and direct the people around her. The one person who seems immune to her charms and presumes to guide *her* from time to time is Mr. Knightley, friend of the family and owner of the neighboring estate. Emma has a protégé, 17-year-old Harriet Smith, a boarder at the local girls' school. Harriet is "the natural daughter of somebody" (i.e., illegitimate), none too bright and lacking connections, but Emma is nevertheless delighted with her beauty and warm-heartedness. She decides to take Harriet on as a project. Complications ensue.

Like Austen's other works, *Emma* is often called a comedy of manners, meaning a satire on the behavior and affectations of a leisured class of society. The book has plenty of humor, much of which stems from sharp takes on the conversations of people who, it must be admitted, have very little to occupy them. But Austen hasn't remained a steady seller for the past 200 years and a focus of academic study simply because she's amusing about the British upper classes. Her books are also deep studies of the processes by which individuals develop, or fail to develop, intellectually and morally.

Great managers are both realistic and optimistic when it comes to talent, and so is Austen. She is clear-eyed about her characters' strengths and weaknesses and undeceived about the difficulty of personal growth, yet she is confident that people can grow—if, like Emma, they have a good heart, a reasonable amount of self-awareness, and someone who cares for them enough to reach out and release their potential.

chapter 20

TALENT

Twice in my career, a business unit I worked for was in financial straits and a new leader was brought in from outside to turn things around. The leaders in those two cases—I'll call them Dmitri and Caitlin—wasted no time getting to work. Dmitri, a newly appointed CEO to whom I reported as head of a function, began by asking each of his direct reports to prepare a business plan with an emphasis on improvement opportunities, and a few days later called us one by one into his corner office and silently took notes as we presented our plans. Caitlin, the new managing director of a small region, took a different approach: she scheduled a meeting at her house for her team of ten and asked each of us to come prepared to tell our biggest client success story of the past year, including what we personally had contributed to that success. We sat on the floor of her living room and took turns telling our stories.

Both these requests seemed sensible to me at the time, and both leaders went on to take many other actions. Caitlin ended up doing better with her turnaround: she retained her whole team and the region's profits rose steadily, while Dmitri's organization enjoyed a brief financial uptick, due almost entirely to a wave of downsizings and resignations, and then sank back into a trough. Most of those events, however, have faded in my mind. What remains clear is how I felt—how we all felt—in that first meeting with our new leader. With Dmitri: tense, inadequate, fearful. With Caitlin: excited, confident, hopeful.

"I'M THE EXPERT"

Certain types of leaders are susceptible to certain pitfalls (see Chapter 2). For turnaround leaders like Dmitri and Caitlin, the big one is Trap No. 7, *devaluing others' strengths*. Newly promoted supervisors also tend to fall into this trap, because like turnaround leaders they tend to think the main reason they've been put in charge is their superior skill in the area. Their promotion, they think, means a chance to display their strengths on a larger scale: to move from low dive to high dive, from chorus to star. And in a sense, they're right. They *have* proved themselves stronger than others, so why wouldn't they be the guiding light for the team?

In the research for her book *Becoming a Manager*, Harvard Business School professor Linda Hill studied a group of salespeople as they received a promotion to sales manager and gradually adapted to the role (see "On tall shoulders: Linda Hill on a manager's identity"). Here's how one of them, in his first week, described the view from the leather chair: "[My reps] come to me because they are having difficulty with deciding what the next step should be, to strategize and see if I can use my expertise or clout to help them follow through."[2] Another person put it this way: "I've got to know the products and help my people build an approach to sales. I have to give them specific ideas and suggestions on how to sell and I've got to run effective meetings that impart the necessary information."[3]

In other words, "I'm the expert."

According to this all too common managerial perspective, the talents of subordinates are irrelevant. Sure, they need the basic skills for the job, but any ability beyond that is superfluous, because they have a leader to tell them what to do. Should a subordinate happen to stand out, she too will eventually be promoted to a management position, where she too can call the shots. In the meantime, talent development—or "personnel issues," as one of Hill's interviewees labeled the entire matter—is not the leader's concern.

Most of Hill's research subjects dropped that stance after a few months in their new role. They came to understand that management is largely about delegation, which means team capabilities must be a manager's chief concern. They also realized that since a team is the transmitter and executor of a leader's ideas, a leader can't maximize his or her impact unless team members work to their full potential. As we saw in Chapter 5, a leader with an unimpressive team will accomplish unimpressive things.

But suppose you've been a leader for some time and you understand all this. You want to develop your team members. You want to help them grow. How should you go about it?

on tall shoulders
LINDA HILL on A MANAGER'S IDENTITY

Linda Hill's interviews with 19 new managers over the course of a year formed the first research study of what it feels like to adopt a manager's identity. *Becoming a Manager* documents in detail the transformation from someone who does the work to someone who gets work done through others. For all Hill's subjects, it's a painful journey.

Here's one manager being confronted by a subordinate who wanted more independence:

> He shouted at me, "If you really want to be the rep for this account, you make the phone call. Just take the account; now that you've told me exactly what to do." I [said], "You don't have to be so nasty about it," but deep down inside I knew he was right.[4]

"The common opinion," says Hill, "is that managers are reluctant to delegate because they do not want to share or reduce their power. For many ... reluctance came from a more fundamental insecurity: delegation was a threat to their self-identity and self-esteem."[5] In the end, Hill suggests, managers' biggest talent development challenge is developing themselves into people who enjoy helping others shine.

A NOTE ON TALENT AND ITS SISTERS

Before we look at talent development, a note on what *talent* is. Psychologists and business researchers have identified at least seven qualities that could fall under that heading: *skills*, *knowledge*, *attitudes*, *intelligences*, *character*, *drives*, and *personality*. (Another is *competencies*, an HR term that's a catchall for the first six items and therefore doesn't add much clarity to the discussion.) The definitions of these qualities vary depending on whom you ask, and there are overlaps, but some examples will help bring them into focus:

- *Skills*: arithmetic, horseback riding, Microsoft Excel
- *Knowledge*: customer buying patterns, safety regulations, laws of physics
- *Attitudes*: competitive, team oriented, positive, customer focused
- *Intelligences*: verbal intelligence, creativity, strategic thinking
- *Character traits*: courage, integrity, generosity, rashness, obstinacy
- *Drives*: need for achievement, need to be liked, need to serve
- *Personality traits*: extraversion, neuroticism, conscientiousness

The seven qualities fall on a continuum from *very malleable* to *not malleable*. Skills and knowledge are very malleable; people can acquire them readily through study or training. Attitudes, intelligences, and character traits are somewhat malleable; while they cannot be picked up in a training class, they can (as we saw in Chapter 12) be cultivated over time by good teachers or distorted over time by bad ones. And drives and personality traits are not malleable; we are born with them, and while it would be an exaggeration to say they never change, trying to change them, whether our own or other people's, is effort better placed elsewhere.

Talent—the Greek philosophers called it *arete*, which translates as "excellence" or "strength"—encompasses the three semi-malleables of attitudes, intelligences, and character. And it's these three things that should be our focus if we want our people to flourish. Of course skills and knowledge are important, too, but they are straightforward: if an employee needs to learn how to work in Excel or understand customer segments, we can send him or her to a class. As for drives and personality traits, we should be aware of them if only so that we don't waste time trying to turn, say, introverts into extraverts (see Chapter 14). Talent, however, is at once the most productive and the trickiest avenue for realizing team potential. The attitudes, intelligences, and character traits that make up talent can be developed—in fact, must be developed if an organization is to thrive—but that won't happen in a one-day training workshop. Oil executives seeking to improve their company's safety record will tell you that a "safety-first attitude" counts a lot more than an exact knowledge of safety regulations, but the attitude is much harder to teach. In short, talent development is both necessary and hard.

IMPROVEMENT PROJECTS

Jane Austen's *Emma* centers on a heroine who loves to develop talent, takes the wrong approach, and learns from her mistakes. The book begins with "handsome, clever, and rich" Emma Woodhouse deciding to mentor the pretty but gauche Harriet Smith. Emma's excitement about the project is reminiscent of the attitude of the newly promoted sales managers in Linda Hill's study:

> She [Emma] would notice her [Harriet]; she would improve her; she would detach her from her bad acquaintances, and introduce her into good society; she would form her opinions and her manners. It would be an interesting, and certainly a very kind undertaking; highly becoming her own situation in life, her leisure, and powers.[6]

When Harriet receives an offer of marriage from young farmer Robert Martin, the brother of two of her schoolmates, Emma persuades her to turn him down, first hinting and then stating frankly that he is not a gentleman and therefore not worthy of her. The man Emma has picked out for Harriet is the town's vicar, Mr. Elton. He, however, has grander aspirations than a bride with unknown parents and no fortune, so Emma is disappointed in her initial goal. She vows to give up matchmaking but persists in her efforts to groom Harriet for a high station in life—a higher station, says Woodhouse family friend Mr. Knightley, than Harriet has any right to expect or indeed wants.

Emma's cluelessness about matters of the heart causes some embarrassment to herself and her friends, but the real damage arises from her determination to "improve" people in ways that don't match their nature. Mr. Knightley describes the harm Emma's schemes have done to Harriet:

> "Till you chose to turn her into a friend, her mind had no distaste for her own set, no ambition beyond it. She was as happy as possible

> with the Martins in the summer. She had no sense of superiority then. If she has it now, you have given it. You have been no friend to Harriet Smith, Emma."[7]

While Austen was writing about the social maneuverings of leisured men and women of two centuries past, Emma's mistake with Harriet is the same as that of the business leader today who writes employee development plans citing numerous "opportunities for improvement," or the supervisor who conducts "coaching sessions" telling you exactly how to do your job. It's the same mistake my onetime boss Dmitri made when his first action as a turnaround leader was to have his direct reports present their improvement plans while he stroked his chin and took notes. And it's the same mistake I once made when I sent a team member a two-page email about how he could build his executive presence. Like those other leaders and Emma, I meant well. But like them, I was taking the wrong approach: I was pushing to improve, rather than cultivating potential.

PUSH TO IMPROVE VS. CULTIVATE POTENTIAL

When leaders push someone to improve, they are trying to add talents that aren't there. It's as if they're looking at a circle and thinking, "This circle would be way better if it had a triangle in the middle—and what about a square on the outside?" (see Figure 20.1). What they should be thinking instead is, "How might I help this particular circle, with all its unique charms, grow?"

In Chapter 4, we saw how the research presented by Gallup's Marcus Buckingham and Curt Coffman in *First, Break All the Rules* can be applied to questions of justice. That research is also applicable to questions of talent. Great managers, the authors say, don't waste time trying to inject talents that are absent; instead, they try to draw out or cultivate the talents that are present.[8] (The most famous educational theorist of the twentieth century, John Dewey, would agree. In his 1910 treatise *How We Think*, he says, "Training must fall back upon the prior and independent existence of natural powers; it is concerned with their proper direction, not with creating them.") The publication of *First, Break All the Rules* launched a slew of "strengths-based" management training programs, the worst of which advised managers to give only praise and ignore their team members' weaknesses. That's a distortion of the Gallup research, which actually suggests that effective talent development rests on three attitudes—or talents—in a leader:

1. Interest in what makes people tick, their strengths and weaknesses
2. Desire to see them become their best self
3. Willingness to say and do what's necessary to help them become that best self

The third point means that a leader must sometimes be a critic. The criticism, however, ought to stem not from an urge to "fix" people, but rather from an appreciation of their unique potential and a sincere wish that they realize that potential.

Take Mr. Knightley. He, not Emma, is the real talent cultivator of Highbury, and the focus of his mentoring efforts is Emma. He's in love with her, though we don't know that for sure until the end. What we do know is that while everyone else is singing her praises, he is the one telling her she can do better. In the book's pivotal scene, he chides Emma for a sarcastic comment she has aimed at Miss Bates, an annoying but good-hearted neighbor, during a picnic:

> "Emma, I must once more speak to you as I have been used to do; a privilege rather endured than allowed, perhaps, but I must still use it. I cannot see you acting wrong, without a remonstrance. How could you be so unfeeling to Miss Bates? How could you be so insolent in your wit to a woman of her character, age, and situation? Emma, I had not thought it possible."[9]

When Emma tries to brush off the incident, Mr. Knightley does not relent. He explains why her remark was not only cruel to Miss Bates but unworthy of herself. "I will tell you truths while I can," he says, "satisfied with proving myself your friend by very faithful counsel and trusting that you will some time or other do me greater justice than you can do now."

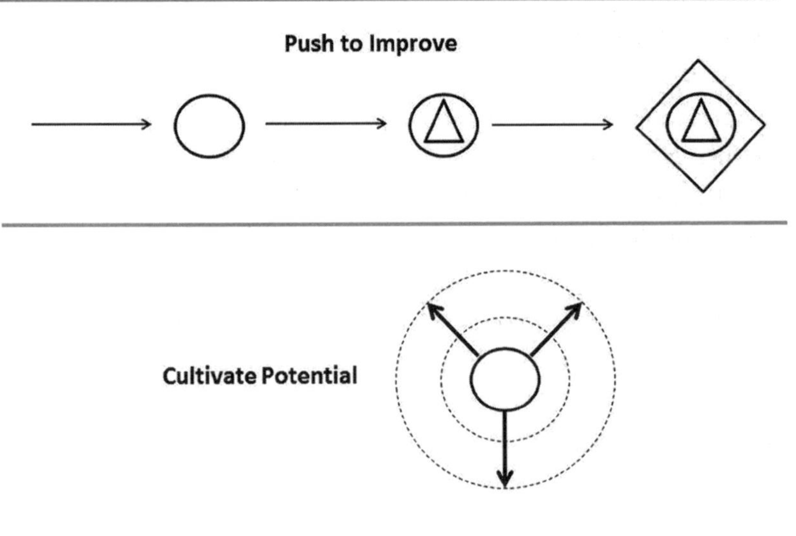

Figure 20.1 *Two views of talent*

The others of the party, who see Emma simply as Miss Woodhouse, star of their social set, laughed at her unkind joke, but Mr. Knightley won't let it pass. He knows that Emma is something more; knows that she is, underneath a somewhat flighty exterior, a kind, sensitive, intelligent woman who may be trusted to understand what he means, regret her error, and make amends (all of which she does, and quickly). When in the end the two are engaged to be married, it is clear that their type of love bodes well for the ongoing happiness and improvement of both. Mr. Knightley calls Emma "this sweetest and best of all creatures, faultless in spite of all her faults."[10] We get the sense she feels the same way about him.

What, then, should leaders do to cultivate potential? This is one topic on which you can find good guidance in the Management section of any bookstore, not to mention online. Type "how to coach employees" into a search engine and you'll find oceans of advice, including step-by-step processes and detailed tactics. Most of that *communication tool*

TEN QUESTIONS FOR TALENT DEVELOPMENT

Incorporate a talent development discussion into your regular one-on-one meetings with your team members. (Or schedule separate talent development discussions every three to six months.) Depending on time available, use some or all of these questions:

1. What do you see as your strengths? Your weaknesses?
2. What do you find energizing about your work? Which part of your job do you enjoy most?
3. What are some of your goals for the future—work related or personal?
4. Tell me about your greatest success from the past three [six, twelve] months. What did you do, specifically, to make it happen?
5. What makes you unique in this organization?
6. With what sorts of people do you work best? Who are your best partners?
7. What is getting in the way of your success? Which parts of your job are you struggling with? What might we try as solutions to these problems?
8. What things related to your current role would you like to learn or do better?
9. What is the most meaningful praise you have ever received?
10. What would be the perfect role for you here, and why?

advice, however, boils down to three points corresponding to the three leadership attitudes mentioned earlier:

1. Learn about your people: their interests, goals, and talents
2. Encourage them to talk about what they know, what they do well, and what they're proud of
3. If they go astray, provide brief, direct guidance on how to return to a better path

For how to talk with your team members about these issues, see "Communication tool: Ten questions for talent development."

Consider, once again, turnaround leaders Dmitri and Caitlin. How did they do as talent developers? Dmitri had the right idea, at least, when he held off on presenting his improvement plans until after his direct reports had presented theirs. But Caitlin did much better when, in her first action as regional manager, she had us all sit on her living-room rug and share success stories. She sparked our enthusiasm, confidence, and desire for improvement, setting the team on an upward trajectory that led, ultimately, to excellent performance and results.

Joan of Arc achieved her vision but paid for it with her death. The next chapter considers whether leaders can realize a bold vision without endangering themselves.

great author

GEORGE BERNARD SHAW'S *SAINT JOAN*

It is a fine spring morning in the year 1429, at the castle of Vaucouleurs. The English hold half of France, but Robert de Baudricourt, captain of Vaucouleurs, is in a rage over the castle hens' failure to lay eggs. His steward tells him there are no eggs and will be none, "not if you were to kill me for it—as long as The Maid is at the door."[1]

The Maid is Joan, a farm girl from Lorraine who has been hanging about Vaucouleurs for a week, talking with the soldiers, praying, and demanding to see the captain. Attempts to make her leave have been unsuccessful, for "she is so positive," says the steward. Incredulous, Baudricourt says to send the slut up and *he'll* make her leave.

When Joan appears, her manner is unabashed and hopeful. She says good morning and without further ado tells the captain he is to give her a horse, a suit of armor, and some soldiers to go with her to see the Dauphin of France. Those, she says, are her orders from her Lord. On learning that "her Lord" is "the King of Heaven," Baudricourt declares her mad and threatens to send her back to her father with orders to thrash the madness out of her. Joan, unperturbed, says he may *think* that's what he'll do, but it will all happen quite differently. And indeed it does.

Shaw's play adheres in outline to the historical facts. In the spring of 1429, an 18-year-old peasant girl who wrote her name as Jehanne claimed to hear voices of angels and saints telling her to lead the French army against the English, raise the siege of Orleans, and place the Dauphin (later Charles VII) on the throne. Somehow she convinced the authorities to let her try, and over the course of a year she achieved all she had promised. In 1430, she was captured by the English-sympathizing Burgundians and handed over to the Earl of Warwick. An ecclesiastical court declared her an unrepentant heretic and sentenced her to be burned at the stake.

Twenty-five years later, Pope Callixtus III authorized a new trial: Joan was pronounced innocent, and her original judges were posthumously excommunicated. Five centuries after that, in 1920, the Catholic Church made her a saint. She is today one of nine patron saints of France.

chapter 21

VISION

Suppose one of your junior employees walked into your office and announced she had orders from God to lead a new company strategy guaranteed to crush the competition. What would you think: "genius" or "nuts"? Surely you'd settle on the latter and place a quick call to HR.

George Bernard Shaw's *Saint Joan* is a play about a teenage girl who announces that God wants her to take charge of the French army, expel the country's English invaders, and crown the king of France with her own hands. The wonder is not that she is initially regarded as mad, nor that she is finally executed for heresy, but that in between she realizes her vision.

VISION IS A HIGH-STAKES GAME

Vision is often discussed as if it were simply a matter of happy plans for the future. When leadership gurus tell us to create a vision, usually all they mean is that we should articulate our goals clearly and enthusiastically; good advice, of course. Real vision, however, is not the same as setting goals or (to use current management jargon) "creating catalysts for action." The true visionary has a plan that stretches way beyond happy to touch crazy. His or her radical ideas pose a threat to an organization's entrenched interests, and those interests, inevitably, push back. Remember Niccolò Machiavelli's famous comment about change: "Nothing is more difficult to handle, more doubtful of success, nor more dangerous to manage, than to put oneself at the head of introducing new orders."[2] Vision is a high-stakes game, probably the most dangerous a leader can play.

Change leadership and visionary leadership are related but different. Driving change is a captain's problem: once a ship has been assigned a new course, how does its captain ensure it steers that course, avoids reefs and shoals, and arrives in port? That task is hard enough (see Chapter 3), but even harder is convincing the ship's owners and shareholders to agree to the new course in the first place—getting them to say, for example, "Although we've been taking an eastern route for ever and our entire system of trade is based on that route, you are right: it would be better to sail west, because there might be a western way to the Indies. Let's do it!" Getting that initial agreement is the visionary's task, and the most likely response is not "Let's do it," but "That's mad." Organizations may say they want leaders to champion new opportunities and strategies, but whenever someone proposes sailing west, there is always a crowd ready to defend their interest in sailing east.

In Shaw's play, Joan's vision threatens the two most powerful institutions in fifteenth-century Europe: the Catholic Church and the feudal aristocracy. Joan threatens the Church by claiming to be in direct contact with God, without churchmen as intermediaries. At her trial, on being asked whether her voices command her not to submit to the Church, she says, "My voices do not tell me to disobey the Church; but God must be served first." A bishop asks: "And you, and not the Church, are to be the judge?" To which she replies, scandalizing the court: "What other judgment can I judge by but my own?"[3] Simultaneously, she threatens the aristocracy by intending to speak directly with the Dauphin—the heir to the French throne—and to crown him king despite the nobles' doubts about his legitimacy. She understands people to be beholden to monarchs, not local lords. Captain Robert de Baudricourt, the first man whose buy-in she needs, thinks that's nonsense: "Don't you know that soldiers are subject to their feudal lord," he says, "and that it is nothing to them whether he is the duke of Burgundy or the king of England or the king of France?" To which Joan replies, "I do not understand that a bit. We are all subject to the King of Heaven; and He gave us our countries and our languages, and meant us to keep to them."[4]

Joan has no sense of how radical her ideas are. She thinks it obvious that God's instructions trump a bishop's instructions. She thinks it obvious that France is one nation and should be united under one king. Like Joan, the modern-day visionary tends to think that his big idea is obviously good: the clear way forward, the plan no sensible person could fail to embrace. What he doesn't see is that any idea not emanating from the existing power structure will appear to that structure dubious at best, dangerous at worst. Though they won't say it out loud as Joan's inquisitors did, the executives sitting around the conference table listening to the visionary's presentation will be thinking, "So, this upstart believes his judgment is better than ours!" And though they may not be fully aware of it, they'll be sensing the same kind of anxiety felt by the Earl of Warwick, who in private conversation with a bishop explains his dislike of Joan thus: "If this cant of serving their country once takes hold of them, goodbye to the authority of their feudal lords, and goodbye to the authority of the Church. That is, goodbye to you and me."[5] (See "On tall shoulders: Malala Yousafzai on fearful visions.")

on tall shoulders

MALALA YOUSAFZAI *on* FEARFUL VISIONS

Malala Yousafzai, a Pakistani schoolgirl shot by the Taliban and a champion of girls' education, went on to become the youngest-ever winner of the Nobel Peace Prize. She was named after Malalai of Maiwand, Afghanistan's Joan of Arc who was a teenager in 1880 during her country's struggle against British occupation. While tending the wounded on the front lines Malalai saw the Afghan flagbearer fall, whereupon "she lifted her white veil up high and marched onto the battlefield in front of the troops."[6]

In her memoir, Malala contrasts the Taliban's campaign to snuff out all sparks of autonomous thought with her schoolteacher father's encouragement of that very autonomy. "[God's] words are divine messages, which you are free and independent to interpret," he said, echoing Saint Joan's words to her interrogators.[7]

The prelates who executed Joan of Arc saw her vision of a world in which people—even young girls—can do without their guidance, and were afraid. Equally afraid, it seems, was the Taliban gunman who shot Malala in the head. Though she does not remember the event, her friends told her that his hand was shaking as he fired.

Chances are good, then, that the visionary leader will be ignored, fired, or something in between: passed over for promotion, given poor assignments, reprimanded, demoted. Should you happen to be the chief executive, naturally you'll have a better shot at getting others on board, but you'll still encounter blockers. The "bishops and lords"—your board of directors, the salesforce, powerful customers, long-time middle managers, the list goes on—all have an interest in maintaining the status quo and will be prepared to fight (or simply nod and do nothing) in order to defend it. And if, like Joan, you eschew diplomacy and make it clear you think that the bishops and lords are fools, their opposition will be all the stronger. This is not what happens in the movies, where visionary leaders sweep opposition aside with rousing speeches from horseback, but it is what happens in real life. A real-life leader, then, should prepare well before getting on that horse.

LESSONS FOR VISIONARIES

A few months after Joan of Arc announces her message from God, all her plans are fulfilled: the Dauphin gives her command of the French army and, after a string of military victories, she crowns him king, anointing him with oil at the Cathedral of Rheims in keeping with age-old tradition. A year later she is executed. Twenty-five years after that, however, her reputation is rehabilitated, and in the play's epilogue she is made a saint—as the historical Joan of Arc was, in 1920—by the same Church that condemned her. Would-be visionaries can draw three lessons from Joan's (mixed) success.

Wait for a desperate problem to emerge People will turn to a visionary only when they are in a huge predicament for which they have tried all the standard solutions and none has worked. Baudricourt acquiesces to Joan's requests and sends her to the Dauphin's court not because he finds her ideas convincing, but because he knows the dire straits the French army is in and thinks that anything, even this crazy scheme, may be worth a try. Sergeant Poulengey backs Joan, saying, "She is the last card left in our hand. Better play her than throw up the game."[8] After much hesitation, Baudricourt agrees: "This may be all rot, Polly; but the troops might swallow it ... even the Dauphin might swallow it."[9] He wouldn't have listened to such "rot" for a moment if the situation weren't desperate. Similarly, your business colleagues will never sign up to a bold new vision if they believe there are still some safe, sensible options to try. You need to wait until their back is against the wall.

Demonstrate exceptional resilience According to Gandhi, "First they ignore you, then they mock you, then they fight you, and then you win." No doubt you've heard it said that any leader who changed the world did so only after slogging obstinately through rejection after rejection, failure upon failure. "Obstinate," however, isn't quite right; great visionaries are, rather, paragons of *resilience* (one of the five leadership character traits; see Chapter 7). Resilience is a combination of perseverance and flexibility, the ability to keep going while at the same time adjusting your approach to suit each situation. In the play's first half, Joan evinces an unusual combination of dogged persistence and light-hearted adaptability: she is comradely with the soldiers, politely enthusiastic with Baudricourt, reverent with the Archbishop, open to learn from field captains, and masterful with the timid Dauphin. It's a combination that makes her unstoppable. Later, perhaps because of her success, she adopts a more purely obstinate attitude, which damages both her cause and her case.

Be willing to be judged a fool, now and later It's one of the hardest truths about bold leadership that there is no way to know, in the present, whether your bold decisions are genius or folly. History overflows with examples of leaders whom we now call inspired but who were called idiots by their contemporaries, and vice versa. The United States' purchase of Alaska from the Russian Empire in 1867, negotiated by Secretary of State William H. Seward, was dubbed at the time "Seward's Folly," but later turned out to have been a smart investment; the AOL–Time Warner merger of 2001 was hailed as brilliant when it happened, but eight years later was called the biggest mistake in corporate history. It seems we cannot tell the difference between genius and folly without benefit of history's scorecard, which means that even true geniuses are, in their day, just as likely to be mocked as admired, and that vindication for your vision may come only in the distant future, if it ever comes at all. Insist on being judged wise by everyone at all times, and your vision will remain merely a pleasant idea.

VISION, AUTHORITY, AND CHARISMA

If visionary leadership is so risky, why even make the attempt? One reason might be that you care deeply about a venture but lack the official authority to lead it. Remember the three sources of authority discussed in Chapter 6: *rational/legal*, derived from written laws and charters; *traditional*, derived from custom or established social structures; and *intrinsic*, derived from a leader's innate ability to inspire belief. A would-be leader without the first two sources has no choice but to build a platform based on the third.

Joan of Arc, utterly lacking in rational/legal and traditional authority, is an exemplar of the intrinsic kind. As Sergeant Poulengey keeps saying in Scene I, "There's something about her." Does this mean she's charismatic? Not really. Though not tongue-tied like Moses (see Chapter 1), Joan is plainspoken like him. We never see her make a speech to the troops. What we do see is her friendliness with the soldiers, her fearlessness with superiors, and her complete lack of affectation with everyone. She talks much more about what makes sense than about her divine voices. Her common sense, she says, was given her by God and is therefore more reliable than the judgment of the "fools" she sees around her. Her reliance on her own reason is threatening to the Church leaders, but her blunt self-assurance puts confidence in the hearts of the common people and soldiers. When Baudricourt rails at his steward, accusing him of being afraid of Joan, the steward replies, "No sir: we are afraid of you; but she puts courage into us."[10]

Joan's story reminds us that humble status and plain speech are no barriers to authority. Intrinsic authority depends neither on titles nor on charisma. If you're counting on intrinsic authority to get people on board with your vision, by all means study public speaking; even better, though, try to embody the three defining behaviors of a leader outlined in Chapter 1: going first, creating hope, and focusing on people. These actions are what will make others believe in you. Blustering officials don't inspire anyone, but a forthright, optimistic leader can be an inspiration to many. Here's what Bishop Cauchon says to the vindicated Joan at the play's end: "The girls in the field praise thee, for thou hast raised their eyes; and they see that there is nothing between them and heaven."[11]

REALIZING A VISION WITHOUT GETTING BURNED

With that said, I'm not surprised that many leaders choose to rely on whatever rational or traditional authority they have and leave the visions to others. Most visionaries will face some type of retribution, and most of us, understandably, are unwilling to take that risk. The risk can be reduced, however, if we absorb one more lesson—a fourth to add to the three listed earlier. Minding this lesson can increase our chances of unmixed success (see "Assessment tool: A vision's chances").

Consider a visionary leader who lived half a millennium after Joan of Arc's death. Bill Walsh was hired as head coach and general manager of the San Francisco Forty Niners in 1979. Nicknamed "The Genius" by sportscasters, he presided over one of the greatest ten-year runs in the history of the National Football League. As David Harris relates in his biography of Walsh, the Forty Niners were in a shambles when Walsh arrived—years of mismanagement had left them with a 2-14 record in the previous season—but by the time he retired in 1988, the team had won six division titles, three NFC championship titles, and three Super Bowls.[12]

Walsh was a visionary when it came to game strategy. In his early days as a high school football coach, he rejected the then standard view that football was about running and that passing made a team weak. He later took his pass-heavy formations to the pros, fundamentally changing the game. But his reputation as a strategic mastermind was, over time, overshadowed by his reputation for spotting and developing talent.

assessment tool
A VISION'S CHANCES

Use the following checklist to assess a vision's chances of success.

Rate each item on a scale of 1–5 (1 = "strongly disagree"; 5 = "strongly agree"). Total the score, and use the key underneath to interpret it.

A. The problem this vision seeks to address is truly big and urgent ___
B. People have tried the standard solutions, and none has worked ___
C. The leader is prepared to keep pursuing the vision no matter what obstacles arise ___
D. The leader is prepared to be flexible and adaptable in how the vision is achieved ___
E. The leader honestly doesn't mind being called a fool for pursuing the vision ___
F. The leader is prepared to have the vision be judged a failure ___
G. This vision promises to create success for individuals, not just an institution ___
H. The leader paints a picture of what people might do and be if they join in the vision ___

Total: ___

Key

32–40 High chance of success
24–31 Moderate chance of success
16–23 Low chance of success
8–15 No chance of success

"I've never seen anyone with an eye to match his," said John McVay, administrator of the Forty Niners.[13] With talent as with strategy, Walsh tended to reject prevailing wisdom; when it came to quarterbacks, for instance, he looked for quick feet and a dancer's agility rather than physical stature and arm strength. And once players were recruited, he had them focus entirely on becoming better football players, not on proving their toughness, which was what most of the era's coaches demanded. He was a superb teacher, and he wanted his players constantly learning and growing.

So, the fourth and final lesson for would-be visionaries is this: ***Direct your vision down and in, not just up and out***. Most leadership gurus think vision has everything to do with pointing the way to a new destination and little to do with "personnel issues."[14] Bill Walsh's success, though, shows us that the down-and-in kind of vision—about people and their potential—is just as important as the up-and-out kind. Really successful visionaries convey an idea not just of the places *we'll* go, but also of the places *you'll* go. They follow the example of some of the leaders discussed in Chapter 20: striving to see inside each team member, imagining his or her potential, and working to turn that potential into actuality. In other words, they apply vision to talent. People support this kind of leader not just because they believe in the leader's cause, but because they believe in what they will become at his or her side.

Joan of Arc instilled faith in her followers; faith, that is, in France and its glory. Once she had won her victories and crowned her king, the vision's appeal dwindled and so did her star. But a vision that increases people's faith in themselves—that offers an inspiring picture of what they might do and who they might be—such a vision, along with the leader who offers it, will never lose strength.

In James Joyce's novella *The Dead*, a moment of truth reveals a man's character, as we see next.

great author
JAMES JOYCE'S *THE DEAD*

Gabriel Conroy is a university professor with gold-rimmed glasses and glossy black hair parted in the middle. On a cold January evening, he and his wife have traveled into Dublin from the country to attend a supper dance given by his two elderly aunts.

The first half of *The Dead* takes place at the dance. We listen in on the guests as they mingle, chat, eat and drink. Among those present are Lily, the caretaker's daughter, hired for the evening to help with the coats; Miss Ivors, a schoolteacher and outspoken Irish nationalist; Mr. Browne, past his youth but still fond of the ladies and inclined to overstep the bounds of propriety with his remarks; Freddy Malins, infamous for arriving at parties, and everywhere else, drunk; and Bartell D'Arcy, a tenor with a head cold. The two hostesses, Kate and Julia Morkan, are much respected. Julia, once a stalwart of the cathedral choir, still has a strong voice and, when pressed, entertains the group with a song before supper; she meekly dismisses the praise lavished on her by Mr. Browne and Freddy, prompting the feistier Kate to deliver a tirade on how her sister "was simply thrown away in that choir."

The human foibles typical of late-night gatherings are on display throughout the party: tipsiness, rowdiness, irascibility, flirtation, boasting, flattery, and sentimentality. We see the action through Gabriel's eyes and feel his annoyance when bits of emotional shrapnel fly his way. His cool reserve and tendency to be critical of everyone, especially himself, stand in stark contrast to Freddy's spontaneous laughter and boisterous eagerness to please.

Gabriel spends much of the evening agonizing about his post-supper speech: he wants to include a quote from Browning but worries people will think he's flaunting his superior education. Of course, when it comes to that point what everyone cares about isn't Gabriel's speech but the part at the end when they get to toast their hostesses with another glass of wine and many rounds of "For they are jolly good fellows," Freddy beating time with his pudding fork. Gabriel is relieved the ordeal is over, unaware that a harder one is yet to come.

chapter 22

CHARACTER, REVEALED

The backbone of leadership character, as we saw in Chapter 17, is courage, and courage is tested whenever we face a "monster": something we've put into motion that is turning out badly and threatening our reputation. But once or twice in our lives as leaders, we'll encounter an even bigger test. We'll overhear a trusted friend or colleague talking about us as if *we* were the monster. We will hear fear, anger, or (worst of all) contempt in his or her voice. What we do next reveals our character as nothing else can.

Two leaders' stories are cases in point.

LUCIEN: A SURPRISE IN THE CHAT WINDOW

Lucien was president of McGill Builders, a midsize construction firm operating in the eastern United States. Six months ago the holding company that owned McGill had bought a similar-sized construction firm based in the west, merging the two together to create nationwide reach. McGill had doubled in size and was experiencing the usual challenges associated with mergers.

Known for his operations expertise and no-nonsense style, Lucien had been with McGill for nine years. His number of direct reports had increased with the acquisition of the new firm. Currently on his senior team of eight there were Avery, the COO; Jen, the CFO; Fred, head of Marketing; Mike, in-house counsel; and four regional vice-presidents. Fred, Mike, and two of the RVPs were long-time McGill employees, while Avery, Jen, and the other RVPs had been with the acquired company. There had been a restructuring, of course, and some redundancies. Not everyone was happy with the new organizational chart, but when grumblings reached Lucien's ears he dismissed them as a normal part of the process. He felt he could count on his experienced senior team to deal with any malcontents, especially given how supportive they all had been through the transition.

A bigger problem, he knew, was the culture clash between McGill and the newcomers. McGill had a strict policy for everything, made most decisions top down, and had a tradition of close collaboration that dated back to its days as a family-owned company (universalistic, hierarchical, and communitarian; see Chapter 16). In the acquired company, by contrast, rules and processes were interpreted freely, managers' dictates were seen as mere suggestions, and salespeople were lone rangers who expected to run their territories without interference (particularistic, egalitarian, and individualistic). Lucien saw the newcomers' culture as sloppy. The solution, he believed, was to raise standards across the board, and to that end he had brought in some Six Sigma consultants who were now working on creating consistency in the company's processes—everything from marketing to project management to requesting office supplies.

McGill had recently adopted some virtual meeting technology, which was proving useful now that the company was more widely dispersed. Lucien, ever frugal, had directed IT to purchase just a handful of licenses; on the senior team only COO Avery had one, and he was the most frequent user. Lucien had continued to run his own meetings via ordinary teleconferencing, but when his turn came to host the parent company's monthly group-wide presidents' call, he decided to take the opportunity to show off the new technology and his comfort with it. He asked his assistant to set him up with Avery's account. She got the password from Avery's assistant and gave Lucien a quick tutorial.

The presidents' meeting went smoothly. When it was over, Lucien stayed in the virtual room, playing around with the software. There was a chat window he hadn't noticed much during the session; he clicked on it now and saw a text thread between Avery and CFO Jen. It seemed to be a private chat that had occurred during a meeting Avery had hosted a week before with the Six Sigma consultants. Apparently he'd forgotten to clear the chat afterward.

Lucien scrolled down, idly reading. But when he got to this part, his heart began to race:

AVERY You going to raise that issue we discussed earlier?

JEN Nope, no point. These guys are idiots

AVERY I know. 1992 called, they want their consultants back

JEN LOL. Think we'll ever be rid of them?

AVERY Not as long as our Dear Leader has the Six Sigma bug

JEN No hope there, he's obsessive on that stuff

AVERY He's obsessive, period! Drives me nuts

JEN Me too

AVERY Just wait it out, I guess

JEN Yep. Suck it up the McGill way. Sometimes I really miss the old world

AVERY Oops, time to pay attention to Sigma bots. ttyl

The thread ended there. Hands shaking slightly, Lucien closed the chat window. He sat in silence for a minute. Then he picked up the phone and called Mike, the in-house attorney.

With Mike advising him, Lucien had IT give him access to his team members' email accounts. He read all of them going back two months and discovered, among other things, exchanges between Avery and Jen in which they shared skepticism about certain company initiatives, not to mention more snark about him; signs that Marketing Director Fred and one RVP were interviewing for other jobs; and evidence that another RVP, Sarah, had been acting as an informal "Dear Abby" to her peers, fielding their complaints about the Six Sigma initiatives and about Lucien's management style.

Every email seemed to deal a blow. The ingratitude was the worst thing: "After all I've done for these people," Lucien thought. It was disrespectful. It was subversive. He had to take action.

He put the two job hunters on performance plans, aiming to build a case for ousting them in a few months. He terminated Avery outright, citing insubordination. He didn't fire Jen, because he needed her financial expertise; nor could he afford to get rid of Sarah, aka Dear Abby. What he could and would do, though, was to put the two women in their place. With legal counsel present, he got each in turn on the phone and, in an icy rage, told them what he knew. He read them excerpts from their emails. He said he was disgusted with their behavior and was keeping them on only because HR said he must. He ranted at them for 20 minutes and ended with: "Let me be clear: You may *not* use company systems for subversive purposes."

Jen and Sarah, shaken, immediately started looking for a way out. Within six months the two of them—plus lawyer Mike—had left McGill for other jobs.

GABRIEL: LONGING TO BE MASTER

In James Joyce's novella *The Dead*, we find another leader who imagines himself master of the universe. This man, however, has character. When his moment of truth arrives, instead of succumbing to rage as Lucien did, he rises to the occasion (see "On tall shoulders: Susan Scott on fierce conversations").

on tall shoulders

SUSAN SCOTT *on* FIERCE CONVERSATIONS

"Conversations are the work of a leader and the workhorses of an organization," writes Susan Scott in *Fierce Conversations*. "Unfortunately, many conversations fail."[1] And the main reason they fail, she argues, is a reluctance to engage fully, authentically, and vulnerably with a real situation and a real person. *Fierce*—as in robust, intense, eager, unbridled—is Scott's word for the attitude she advocates.

Scott proposes seven principles for fierce conversations:

1. Master the courage to interrogate reality
2. Come out from behind yourself into the conversation and make it real
3. Be here, prepared to be nowhere else
4. Tackle your toughest challenge today
5. Obey your instincts
6. Take responsibility for your emotional wake
7. Let silence do the heavy lifting

All seven principles may be demonstrated, or not, in a brief encounter. In the final scene of James Joyce's *The Dead*, for example, we see a husband and wife engaged in a quintessentially "fierce" conversation. They both struggle but in the end succeed, mostly thanks to Principle 7.

We meet Gabriel Conroy on Epiphany night in Dublin, at his aunts' annual supper dance. Gabriel is Aunt Kate and Aunt Julia's favorite nephew: the one they rely on to carve the goose and deliver the after-supper speech, the one they count on to deal with guests who show up inebriated. He is a man of authority—and a bit of a stuffed shirt. His wife of ten-plus years, Gretta, laughs with the aunts about his fussy directives to her and the children: "You'll never guess what he makes me wear now!" she says. "Goloshes! That's the latest."[2] Gabriel seems unaware she's poking fun at him.

The story opens with Gabriel taking off his coat and making a witty (he thinks) remark to Lily, the hired help, about her "young man." Lily—whether offended by his familiarity or simply overworked, we don't know—makes a snappish reply. Gabriel senses he's made a mistake, but rather than apologize to Lily he hands her a tip and hurries, embarrassed, from the cloakroom. The scene says a lot about him as a leader: when confronted with a subordinate's agitation, his instinct is not to engage but rather to buy the person off and escape with dignity intact.

This same self-consciousness keeps Gabriel on edge throughout the festivities. In one of the dances he finds himself partnered with Miss Ivors, a fellow teacher, and she seizes the opportunity to tease him about a literary column he writes for a British newspaper. "I'm ashamed of you," she says. "To say you'd write for a rag like that. I didn't think you were a West Briton."[3] As she needles him about his holidays in France and his inability to speak Irish, he grows flustered, finally retorting that he's sick of Ireland, sick of it! Now he assumes Miss Ivors is offended, but a few minutes later she presses his hand warmly—and then, at the dance's end, serves up yet another jab. As he walks away, mind churning, he justifies his resentment:

> Of course the girl or woman, or whatever she was, was an enthusiast but there was a time for all things. Perhaps he ought not to have answered her like that. But she had no right to call him a West Briton before people, even in joke. She had tried to make him ridiculous before people, heckling him and staring at him with her rabbit's eyes.[4]

Later, still in a stew, he anticipates blundering through his supper-table speech with Miss Ivors looking up at him "with her critical quizzing eyes," happy to see him fail.

Gabriel has a tendency to over-interpret offhand comments, inflating them into malicious attempts to undermine him. Miss Ivors, he imagines, is targeting him; she has "no right" to do so. She is criticizing him ... it's not fair ... he is blameless. We saw this same prickliness in Lucien of McGill Builders, and we may see it in ourselves, too. We obsess over someone's offhand remark as if it signaled a campaign to take us down, when the real problem is simply this: No matter what our role or status, we do not have control over what other people think of us.

Throughout the evening Gabriel struggles to repress his ire at additional "undeserved" slights. But his real test of character comes after the evening is over, when he's alone with his wife in their hotel room. It is the wee hours of the morning and snow has begun to fall. Gretta has been strangely preoccupied ever since the moment when, standing in the hallway at the party's close, she heard Bartell D'Arcy hoarsely singing "The Lass of Aughrim," an old Irish tune. Gabriel is half attracted, half angered by Gretta's distant manner, and we come now to the central line of the story: "He longed to be master of her strange mood."[5]

Gabriel is a masterful man and often master of the situation, but he is not, it transpires, master of his wife's mood, still less her heart. When pressed to say what's wrong, Gretta finally bursts out crying and tells him of a boy she knew long ago in Galway, Michael Furey, who used to sing "The Lass of Aughrim." He suffered from consumption, made worse by standing at the bottom of her garden in the rain on the night he learned she was to be sent away to school. She implored him to go home, but he said he did not want to live. The story and her tears as she tells it suggest that she has never forgotten Michael Furey.

Gabriel, confronted with his wife's heartbreak and his utter impotence over her feelings, reacts at first with the same kind of resentment he felt toward Miss Ivors at the party. "A dull anger [begins] to gather again at the back of his mind"; he adopts a sarcastic tone and, based on a casual comment Gretta made earlier in the evening about wanting to see Galway again, asks her if she wishes to reunite with her old lover. Bemused by the question, she tells him Furey died at 17. "I think he died for me," she says. On hearing this, Gabriel feels suddenly humiliated:

> While he had been full of memories of their secret life together ... she had been comparing him in her mind with another. A shameful consciousness of his own person assailed him. He saw himself as a ludicrous figure, acting as a pennyboy for his aunts, a nervous well-meaning sentimentalist, orating to vulgarians ... the pitiable fatuous fellow he had caught a glimpse of in the mirror.[6]

He has reached a turning point. What will he do: Fly into a rage, accusing Gretta of emotional infidelity? Remain coolly ironic, mocking her obsession with an old boyfriend? Or claim the moral high ground, expressing disappointment in her conduct?

We may recall other leaders we've read about, leaders who discovered that someone whose thoughts they had pictured running along lines pleasing to them was actually thinking something not so pleasing. There is King Lear, enraged when his daughter's profession of love is too restrained for his liking; Creon, in *Antigone*, stunned that a subordinate not only has disobeyed one of his commands but continues to think she was right to do so; Victor Frankenstein, horrified when his newborn creature's appearance and behavior are not what he'd expected; and Joan of Arc's interrogators, shocked by her belief that she knows what God wants better than they do. And then there's Lucien, president of McGill Builders, who went on a rampage when he discovered that his employees sometimes snickered behind his back.

CHARACTER REVEALED

Our character as leaders is revealed in crises, but even more fully in those moments when we read a stray email, overhear a chance remark, or are on the receiving end of some atypical honesty and, as a result, glimpse the truth: our subordinates are out of (our) control. They are not showing us the respect we deserve. They find us unpleasant to work for. They are thinking thoughts and dreaming dreams that run counter to, or maybe just have nothing to do with, our own. They are complaining; they are gossiping; they are making jokes at our expense. In that moment of realization, how do we respond?

A leader lacking character will lose balance and topple into one or more of the eight leadership traps, whose common root, as we saw in Chapter 2, is *choosing rightness over efficacy*. But there is another root that runs still deeper: *choosing control over love*.

Lack of character comes down to lack of courage, the anchor for all other character traits. A cowardly leader is committed to self-preservation, physical and emotional, and is therefore unable to tolerate the sense of threat that arises when subordinates speak or think in ways contrary to his wishes. It is not enough that they *do* what he wants; they must also *say* and *think* what he wants, for bad words and bad thoughts (he believes) may lead to bad actions. We've all felt afraid on glimpsing the dark maelstrom that is another person's heart, and still more afraid when he or she is someone close to us, someone we trust. When Gretta says, "I think he died for me," we can relate to Gabriel's "vague terror," as if "some impalpable and vindictive being was coming against him, gathering forces against him."[7]

The question is, what do we do when seized by such terror? The leader who lacks character will quickly do something, anything, to restore the illusion (for of course it is an illusion) of control over the other's heart. The leader of character may struggle with the same temptation, but in the end will manage to hold to the mean: to courage, integrity, resilience, generosity, and concern. And the thread running through all five of these traits is *love*—not a word we customarily apply to leaders, but an apt one when we consider that it means the ability to put another's well-being before our own (see "Team tool: Moments of truth").

Gabriel Conroy, it turns out, has that ability. After his moment of humiliation, he tries to go on interrogating Gretta but finds he can't; his voice comes out "humble and indifferent." So instead he listens quietly to the rest of her tale, holding her hand and asking a question or two; and after she falls asleep, he sits for a long time watching the snow falling past the lamp-lit window. He thinks about the past. He imagines his wife as a young girl, and a boy standing in darkness under a dripping tree at the end of a garden. His imagination leads him to an understanding of Gretta's strange mood, which an hour before he had sought to master. "A strange friendly pity" fills his heart, and "generous tears" fill his eyes.

No summary can do justice to the last few paragraphs of Joyce's story. Their serene beauty calls to us to accept with love a world that we cannot control.

team tool

MOMENTS OF TRUTH

Pick a challenging situation to use as a mini case study for building you and your team's collective character as leaders. Choose a "moment of truth" that comes up often: a typical conflict with another group or a common customer complaint, for instance. (It's best not to refer to a specific situation or to name names.)

Gather your team and copy Figure 7.1 (leadership character traits) onto a flipchart or whiteboard. Review the five continuums, and then discuss the following:

1. When faced with this moment of truth, where are we often tempted to "go" on these five continuums? What does that look like?
2. What makes it difficult to hold to the mean?
3. What would *courage* look like in this situation? How about *integrity*, *resilience*, *generosity*, and *concern*? (Press for specifics.)
4. How can we, as a team, demonstrate leadership character in situations such as this?

Note that you are not required to provide the answers. The purpose of the discussion is simply to reflect, as a team, on what leadership character looks like in moments of truth.

What matters most for leaders is not our status in a hierarchy, but the impact we have, as we explore in the next part.

part VI

THE FUTURE OF LEADERSHIP

Think back to Chapter 1. There, we saw that the badge of a true leader isn't charisma, but rather three behaviors: *going first*, *creating hope*, and *focusing on people*. We also noted the three corresponding kinds of misleader: *lackeys*, who shun initiative in favor of following the party line; *tyrants*, who maintain power by creating a climate of fear; and *bureaucrats*, who treat people as mere cogs in the wheels of procedure. Since then we've explored many examples of leaders and misleaders, and we've seen how the three leadership behaviors and their opposites play out in boardrooms, on battlefields, and in the everyday interactions of leaders with their teams.

In the next chapter the three behaviors will become three levels, offering a new way to think about our aspirations as leaders; a corporate ladder of the future, if you will. And finally, using a classic work of Eastern philosophy for inspiration, we'll go one rung higher and see what a Level 4 leader is and does.

chapter 23
THREE LEVELS

Ask someone "What's your leadership level?" and you'll likely hear something like this: "I'm SVP, Product Development." "I'm a supervisor. I have a team of five." "I was recently promoted to Associate Consultant." "I manage projects; my current one has 40 people on it." In other words, you'll hear about the person's title or span of control.

The structure of modern organizations is derived from the military, with its ranks that correspond to the size of the group under one's command and its clear demarcation between officers ("management") and non-officers ("labor"). Despite the trend of the past few decades toward flat organizations, when we talk about leadership levels we still mostly take our cue from that military-corporate hierarchy. Indeed, our use of the word *flat* to describe organizations without traditional reporting structures suggests that we still equate leadership levels with those structures. We can't imagine a different way to think about leadership topography, so we call such non-traditional organizations "flat."

But they aren't flat, really; their levels just don't correspond to the tiers of a traditional hierarchy. In the worst of such organizations, level corresponds to the ability to wield power as a lackey, tyrant, or bureaucrat. In the best ones, level corresponds to the ability to make a positive impact.

INITIATORS, ENCOURAGERS, AND CULTIVATORS

There are plenty of people with no title and no direct reports who nevertheless make a big impact, and plenty of people with grand titles and many direct reports who make little to no impact (no positive one, anyway). Most would agree that the former are better leaders and deserve to have their value recognized. That's not to say that rank doesn't matter; as we saw in Chapter 6, authority backed by law or custom is a necessity for most leaders, and promotion up the ranks is one way to confer the authority a leader needs in order to drive initiatives of increasing size and complexity. Yet the fact remains that the title on a business card conveys virtually nothing about the amount and type of impact the holder is having on the world.

With two notable exceptions—see "On Tall Shoulders: Jim Collins and John Maxwell on levels of leadership"—management consultants have stuck to the traditional corporate hierarchy, based on spans of control, as their organizing framework for leadership training and development. This same hierarchy also remains rigidly in place in most companies, reinforced by organizational charts, job descriptions, grants of authority, and compensation systems.[1] True, some organizations have replaced traditional corporate titles (manager, director, vice-president, and so on) with names such as Team Leader, Accounts Maven, or Chief of Customer Delight, but even the coolest of these titles is still merely a way to indicate the type and number of people one is expected to boss.

on tall shoulders
JIM COLLINS *and* JOHN MAXWELL *on* LEVELS OF LEADERSHIP

In *Good to Great*, Jim Collins helps redefine advanced leadership with his concept of the *Level 5 leader*: a top executive who is both humble and fearless. Though personally self-effacing, the Level 5 leader has enormous drive. As an example, Collins offers Abraham Lincoln, who "never let his ego get in the way of his primary ambition for the larger cause of an enduring great nation."[2] Collins's willful yet modest Level 5 leader is not the guy (or gal) we traditionally picture in the C-suite.

Collins's five tiers, however, are largely traditional. They are (1) Highly Capable Individual, (2) Contributing Team Member, (3) Competent Manager, (4) Effective Leader, and (5) Level 5 Executive. For Collins, our impact is still tied to position in the corporate hierarchy; individual contributors are stuck at Level 1, and only executives show up at Level 5. While I don't deny that a leader's position affects the impact that he or she can have, we'd be better off if we had a way to talk about leaders' advancement without reference to spans of control.

John Maxwell, a prolific author on leadership, offers a levels framework that takes a few more steps in a new direction. His five levels are (1)

Position—people follow because they have to; (2) Permission—people follow because they want to; (3) Production—people follow because of what you've done for the organization; (4) People development—people follow because of what you've done for them personally; and (5) Pinnacle—people follow because of who you are and what you represent.[3]

But if we want to provide leaders with a new path upward, Maxwell's framework won't do. First, his levels represent the various reasons people might follow us, not the increasing scope or strength of our impact; moreover, it's not clear why reason 4 or 5 is better than reason 2 or 3. Second, his levels offer few clues as to how one might ascend them; how, for example, would one move from "people follow me because they have to" (1) to "people follow me because they want to" (2)? Third and finally, Maxwell's Level 5 is perilously close to that old cliché, "people follow charisma."

Collins and Maxwell have given the corporate ladder a shake, but they haven't toppled it. And as long as leaders' aspirations are defined by the corporate ladder and successes acknowledged only with boosts to a higher rung, our organizations will be run by good ladder-climbers rather than good leaders.

In order to shift our attention away from a leader's span of control and toward the scope of his or her impact, we need some new words for leadership levels. Here are three I suggest we try: Level 1, *Initiator*; Level 2, *Encourager*; and Level 3, *Cultivator*. Let's take a look at each level, recalling the leadership behaviors from Chapter 1 and some of the characters from our classic books (see Figure 23.1).

Level 1: Initiator Being an initiator means *going first*, which, you may remember, is the first hallmark of a true leader. An initiator doesn't follow the pack, but breaks away from the pack and says, "Follow me." Initiators will put themselves out there to achieve a goal, even if it costs them. They believe in taking action.

Brutus and Cassius, leaders of the conspiracy in Shakespeare's *Julius Caesar* (see Chapter 6), are classic initiators. They are also, of course, murderous traitors, famously condemned by Dante to the

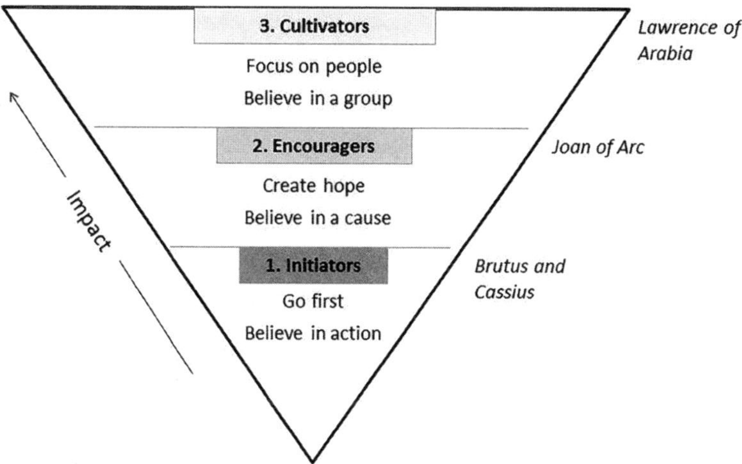

Figure 23.1 Three levels of leadership

lowest level of Hell in his *Inferno*. I do not call them role models. Nevertheless, among all the nobles who complain about "tyranny," Brutus and Cassius are the ones who step forward and do something about it. And while Cassius is driven by personal resentment, Brutus is driven by patriotic concerns: by his apprehension (warranted or not) about the destruction of the Roman Republic that may result from Caesar's takeover. He will not wait, he says in his Act II soliloquy, until the "serpent" is hatched and grown. He will kill it in the shell. Brutus takes action based on what he believes is right, not counting the personal risk. Marc Antony calls him "the noblest Roman of them all."

Level 2: Encourager Yet things can go badly for leaders who stay at Level 1. Taking principled initiative isn't enough to bring about positive change, as the aftermath of Caesar's assassination makes clear. Brutus's actions are in service of a cause, but his "motivational" speech to his co-conspirators, in which he stresses their obligation to follow through, does nothing to inspire commitment to that cause.[4] With no sense of unity or a common hope for the future, the group disintegrates; the republic is not restored.

To get to Level 2, leaders must *create hope*. They must be encouragers. Think of Joan of Arc in Shaw's *Saint Joan* (see Chapter 21). In the opening scene of the play, the steward of Vaucouleurs Castle tells Captain Baudricourt that he has tried to eject the peasant girl who's been hanging around telling the castle soldiers they must fight the English invaders, but "We cannot make her go." Baudricourt says they are a "parcel of curs" who must all be afraid of her. "No sir," says the steward, "we are afraid of you; but she puts courage into us."[5]

Baudricourt leads with sarcasm and threats; Joan leads with encouragement. Like all Level 2 leaders, her belief in her cause draws others along, making them feel stronger and more hopeful by their participation. She manages to put heart even into the pusillanimous Dauphin of France: "Oh, if I only dare!" the Dauphin says at the end of Scene II. With Joan at his side, he resolves to dare—and the next moment, confronted by an angry Lord Chamberlain (described earlier as a "monstrous arrogant wineskin of a man"), starts to back down. Joan simply puts her hand on his shoulder. Gathering all his courage, he snaps his fingers in the Chamberlain's face.

Level 3: Cultivator At the third level are cultivators: leaders who *focus on people*. Not only do they go first and create hope, they also develop a group's talent, cohesion, and culture. Joan of Arc does some of this, helping the French see themselves as one nation rather than the vassals of diverse feudal lords. Still, her attention is fixed on the mission given her by her divine "voices," and any growth in the people around her is a byproduct of that mission. She looks up and out, rarely down and in.

The quintessential example of a Level 3 leader is Lawrence of Arabia, described by Churchill as "holder of one of those master keys which unlock the doors of ... treasure-houses"[6] (see Chapter 7). Lawrence was a champion in the word's original sense: someone who sees the latent greatness in a person or people and does everything possible to unlock their potential. So dedicated was he to the unification and uplift of the Arab tribes that, two years after his swashbuckling exploits as leader of the Revolt in the Desert, he accepted a post as (again in Churchill's words) a humdrum official, charged with the wearisome diplomacy that was necessary, he knew, to fulfill at least some of his hopes for his beloved Arabia. The film that bears his name portrays Lawrence as something of a grandstander. That he may have been, but his behavior over the course of his life suggests he was also a cultivator.

To summarize: Initiators go first, and believe in taking action. Encouragers create hope, and believe in a cause. Cultivators focus on people, and believe in a group, which could be a team, an organization, or an entire nation (see "Assessment tool: The next level").

Notice that the levels are additive; a Level 2 leader goes first *and* creates hope, while a Level 3 leader does all that *and* focuses on people. Each successive level of leadership makes a broader and more lasting impact. For example, Brutus eliminated a dictator, but failed to set a new government in place. Joan of Arc expelled an invading army and united (temporarily) a nation under a king. Lawrence of Arabia unified dozens of feuding Arab tribes, helped Britain and its allies win a world war, and engaged in post-war diplomacy that gave rise to nations that endured (turbulently) for 100 years.

Notice, too, that the three misleaders stack up on the same three levels, corresponding to the scope of their pernicious impact. The lackey sits at Level 1, oozing futility. The tyrant sits at Level 2, spreading fear. And the bureaucrat—the Level 3 misleader, who treats human beings as numbers on a spreadsheet or boxes on a chart—has the worst effect of all. The bureaucrat (in the sense I mean) is no mere paper-pusher, but rather an architect of evil who takes the futility and fear produced by lackey and tyrant and constructs from them a system. The Nazi concentration camps, those horrifyingly efficient torture and killing machines experienced by Viktor Frankl (see Chapter 13) and millions more, were a prime example of the bureaucrat's dark art. It is the misleaders at Level 3 who can claim for themselves the words of Krishna in the *Bhagavad Gita*: "I am become death, the destroyer of worlds."[7]

assessment tool

THE NEXT LEVEL

While none of us resides neatly and consistently on one leadership level, it's helpful to know where we sit as a rule and what we should be focusing on in order to advance as a leader. To that end, read the four descriptions below and select the one that is most like you. Then, read the corresponding interpretation (opposite) to see which actions will help you move to the next level of leadership.

A. I do not generally think of myself as a leader. At work I am expected to contribute as an individual and to take direction from my manager or team leader. While I have no problem making decisions within the scope of my job, I leave the bigger decisions to management. I feel most comfortable when following established procedures and guidelines.

B. I like to take the initiative. No matter my official position, I am comfortable setting goals and making plans to get there. I don't wait to be told and don't have a problem going "off road" when necessary. I'm very busy and don't have much time for coaching or handholding. I'll help people if they ask, but basically I expect them to fulfill their commitments and keep up.

C. In addition to taking the initiative, I get a great deal of satisfaction from helping others learn and grow. People at work often come to me for advice, or simply for a pep talk when they're feeling down. I'm good at showing individuals why they're important and how their efforts fit into the big picture. But I am best one on one; I don't often think about growing teams or organizations.

D. In addition to taking initiative and coaching others, I care a lot about developing my entire team, function, or community. I have a vision for how this group could contribute something extraordinary to the world. Wherever I sit in an organization, I adopt an entrepreneurial view; I want to build a great enterprise—and just as important, a great culture—that lasts.

Interpretations

A. You are a *leader-to-be*. To get to the next level (initiator), practice making the first move toward a goal you believe in. Trust that people will follow.

B. You are an *initiator*. To get to the next level (encourager), hone your coaching skills. Devote part of each day to encouraging someone else's growth.

C. You are an *encourager*. To get to the next level (cultivator), imagine the future for your team, organization, or community. Work to help them realize their potential.

D. You are a *cultivator*. To get to the next level (mainspring; see Chapter 24), study the *Tao Te Ching* and reflect on how you might lead without dominating. Focus on mastering yourself rather than others.

Of course, nobody falls neatly and constantly into a single leadership category. A good leader exhibits all three behaviors to some degree, and the typical misleader is a lackey to bosses and a tyrant to subordinates. Nevertheless, these three leadership levels provide a way to begin sizing up others, and ourselves, by impact rather than by position.

Next, we see the fourth level of leadership through the eyes of an ancient Chinese philosopher.

great author
LAO TZU'S *TAO TE CHING*

The *Tao Te Ching*, one of Taoism's fundamental texts, has influenced the world's philosophical, religious, artistic, and literary thinkers since its appearance centuries ago. While its authorship and date are matters of debate, it is traditionally attributed to Lao Tzu (literally "Old Master"), a record keeper at the royal court of China during the Zhou dynasty in the sixth century BCE. There are many possible translations of the title. *Tao* means "way" or "path" and, in Taoist philosophy, implies the essential process or flow of the universe. *Te* means "virtue," "character," or "inner power." *Ching* means "great book" or "classic." So, the whole title may be translated as "The Great Book of the Way of Virtue and Power," which certainly sounds like useful reading for a leader.

But the *Tao Te Ching* is not at all the sort of leadership book that those of us steeped in the Western tradition are used to. It consists of 81 very short chapters, or verses, written in a poetic style and open to many interpretations. Taoism devotees suggest meditating on one verse at a time in order to allow the work's esoteric wisdom to reveal itself slowly and naturally. Here are a few of the central themes, with illustrative lines from Stephen Mitchell's translation:

Letting go

- Do your work, then step back/ The only path to serenity (9)
- It gives itself up continually/ That is why it endures (56)
- Let go of fixed plans and concepts/ and the world will govern itself (57)
- Trying to grasp things, you lose them (64)
- Act for the people's benefit/ Trust them; leave them alone (75)

Non-striving

- Success is as dangerous as failure/ Hope is as hollow as fear (13)
- Do you have the patience to wait/ till your mud settles and the water is clear? (15)
- Because he doesn't display himself/ people can see his light (22)
- Because he accepts himself/ the whole world accepts him (30)
- Straightforward, but supple/ Radiant, but easy on the eyes (58)

Non-opposition

- His enemies are not demons/ but human beings like himself (31)
- Give evil nothing to oppose/ and it will disappear by itself (60)
- He thinks of his enemy/ as the shadow that he himself casts (61)
- When two great forces oppose each other/ the victory will go/ to the one that knows how to yield (69)
- If you blame someone else/ there is no end to the blame (79)

Leadership

- Leading and not trying to control/ This is the supreme virtue (10)
- Mastering others is strength/ Mastering yourself is true power (33)
- True mastery can be gained/ by letting things go their own way (48)
- If you want to govern the people/ you must place yourself below them (66)
- The Tao nourishes without forcing/ By not dominating, the Master leads (81)

chapter 24

THE FOURTH LEVEL

From a present-day Western perspective, the third level of leadership may appear to be the highest rung on the ladder. But if we look eastward and back many centuries, we'll discover a book that speaks to one still higher: the *Tao Te Ching*.

The overall theme of this ancient Chinese text is difficult to state. If asked to choose a small part to represent the whole, I would choose Verse 17, which translator Stephen Mitchell renders as follows:

> When the Master governs, the people
> are hardly aware that he exists.
> Next best is a leader who is loved.
> Next, one who is feared.
> The worst is one who is despised.
>
> If you don't trust the people,
> you make them untrustworthy.
>
> The Master doesn't talk, he acts.
> When his work is done,
> the people say, "Amazing:
> We did it, all by ourselves!"[1]

WHEN THE MASTER GOVERNS

Initiators, encouragers, and cultivators—leaders on the first three levels—correspond to Lao Tzu's "next best" leader. They are loved and praised for the good work they do. Their desks are laden with cards and certificates expressing appreciation: "I wouldn't be where I am today without you." "Thank you for all your support." "Congratulations, Manager of the Year."

Perhaps you've received similar testimonials. I have, and I'm proud of them, but they are not signs of the highest level of leadership. The very best leaders don't get thank-you notes, for "When the Master governs, the people/ are hardly aware that he exists."

What name should we give these unobtrusive leaders on the fourth and highest level? In honor of Jeeves—the unflappable manservant created by P.G. Wodehouse, and a leader of whom Lao Tzu would have approved—we might call them servants. But *servant leader* is a term that in recent years has lost its strength through overuse. Socrates, the masterful teacher at the center of Plato's *The Republic*, referred to himself as a midwife: someone who knew nothing and therefore could not teach anything but, rather, drew forth the knowledge already present within his disciples. But *midwife* has obstetric associations that most leaders probably don't want to take on board. We can look to the *Tao Te Ching* for a host of other similes for the Level 4 leader, such as *water*: "The supreme good is like water, which nourishes all things without trying to" (8); or *turning point*: "We join spokes together in a wheel, but it is the center hole that makes the wagon move" (11). The Master, says Lao Tzu, is "fluid as melting ice; shapeable as a block of wood; receptive as a valley; clear as a glass of water" (15). All these terms are evocative, but again, they probably aren't going to be adopted by contemporary leaders. "I aspire to be a block of wood" is just too Zen for most of us.

A plainer name for the Level 4 leader, and the one I'm going with, is *mainspring* (see Figure 24.1). Literally, the mainspring is the chief element in a mechanism. Metaphorically, it is the most powerful agent or motive driving an endeavor. The word should take us back to Chapter 5, where with the help of Antigone and Creon we looked at what power really is: not status or position, but the ability to *get work done*. The mainspring in a clock is the piece that moves the other springs, which in turn move the hands, which in turn cause the clock to perform its function of telling the time. We don't see or hear the mainspring, but with it, the whole system does its job, and without it, the clock is just an object with numbers 1 through 12 on its face; pretty, maybe, but useless. When it comes to leadership, similarly, the mainspring is the person whose efforts are less obvious than everybody else's, but without whom everybody else's efforts come to naught (see "On tall shoulders: Peter Drucker on top management").

on tall shoulders

PETER DRUCKER on TOP MANAGEMENT

Peter Drucker's plain prose bears no resemblance to Lao Tzu's cryptic poetry. Yet, there's something about the down-to-earth wisdom of this business sage that reminds me of the sage-kings of ancient Chinese legend.

Drucker has no patience for leaders who equate their job with status. If, when asked what you do, you reply "I'm boss of this department," you're completely missing the point, he says. What you should be focusing on is your contribution to the organization's purpose. "Contribution" can mean many things, including achieving financial results, building culture, and developing people, but ultimately it must be about the customer.

Later thinkers elaborated on the "value chain" (the flow of products and services out to a buyer), but it was Drucker who came up with this stunningly simple idea: a business exists to serve customers, and how well you serve has little to do with your perch in the organizational chart.

> The man who focuses on efforts and stresses his downward authority is a subordinate no matter how exalted his title and rank. But the man who focuses on contribution and who takes responsibility for results, no matter how junior, is in the most literal sense of the phrase, "top management." He holds himself accountable for the performance of the whole.[2]

MAINSPRING LEADERS

Mainsprings come in two varieties: quiet and misfit.

Quiet mainsprings, though they are sometimes well known in their day or become well known to future ages, receive far less notice than others in their circle. They do their jobs without fanfare, perhaps even reluctantly. The Moses of Exodus (see Chapter 1) is a quiet mainspring: you may recall how he calls himself "tongue-tied" and pleads with God to choose someone else to lead the Hebrews, and how, for the first half of the book, he stays in the shadow of his brother Aaron, the skilled speaker.

Alexander Hamilton, co-author of *The Federalist* (see Chapter 10), is another example. He was a famous man, of course, but put him next to his peers—suave diplomat Benjamin Franklin, great general George Washington, brilliant theoretician James Madison—and he fades into the background.[3] More than the other American Founding Fathers, Hamilton was willing to subdue his own ideas for the sake of the common good. He didn't much like the constitution hammered out by the 1787 convention; he preferred a more centralized form of government, and late in life he groused that he had spent his entire career "propping up that useless document." Nevertheless he had joined Madison in arguing vigorously for it, believing that it was the only viable plan for the fledgling nation and that its failure would mean failure for all. Later, as the first Secretary of the Treasury and architect of the US financial system, he served as President Washington's main adviser and drafted many of his most famous speeches. Like Moses, this behind-the-scenes man told the up-front man what to say.

Then there are the misfit mainsprings: awkward, abrasive, or just plain weird. Their peculiarities cause people to regard them as idiots or sometimes even tyrants, but history vindicates them as great leaders. Take Claudius, fourth emperor of Rome, who was burdened from birth with a speech impediment and physical deformities. Novelist Robert Graves portrays him (see Chapter 6) as stuttering and limping his way through most of his life, embarrassing his family and prompting his nephew Caligula, emperor before him, to make him an unofficial court fool. But once he was on the throne (having arrived there almost by accident), he administered the empire brilliantly, fashioning a Pax Romana that lasted 150 years after his death.

Abraham Lincoln was another odd physical specimen derided by his contemporaries. He may have had Marfan's syndrome, a genetic disorder of the connective tissue that can cause, among other problems, spindly limbs, flat feet, stooped shoulders, and a bobbing head. In 1862 the *Chicago Times* called him an "irresolute, vacillating imbecile," and to the *Charleston Mercury* he was "the Orang-Outang at the White House."[4] The so-called imbecile is today universally recognized as one of the greatest US presidents.

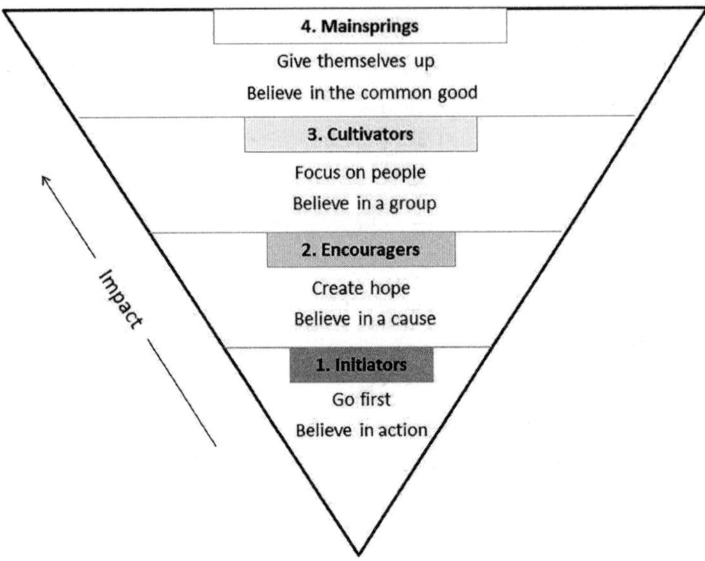

Figure 24.1 The fourth level

While mainspring leaders are often unconventional, it is not their unconventionality that makes them great. Here's what does.

First, mainsprings create institutions or cultures that last long after they're gone, shaping the world in ways that endure even when they're no longer around to shape it.

Second, mainsprings create other leaders; one can often recognize a mainspring by the promotions his or her team members receive and go on receiving years down the road.

Third, and most important, mainsprings *give themselves up*, meaning that for the sake of the common good they put aside striving for their own fame and fortune. Like T.E. Lawrence, who in order to promote Arab autonomy put a lid on his considerable skills as a military captain and became an ordinary paper-pusher, the mainspring leader is even willing to suppress his or her superior abilities and blend in, be just another team member, if that's what it takes to get the job done. As a result, mainsprings often don't get applause in their day. Good leaders hear people say "We couldn't have done it without you," but the Master (says the *Tao Te Ching*) mostly hears the sound of people rejoicing in their own success: "We did it," they exclaim, "all by ourselves!"

THE NURSE BRYAN RULE

What does all this mean for us everyday leaders, who are unlikely to be winning wars or founding nations any time soon? Based on how I've described the four leadership levels and the examples I've used, it might seem as though a Level 4 leader has to accomplish something on the world stage in order to be worthy of the name—to be like Alexander of Macedon, whose story is in Chapter 1 and who would surely not be called "the Great" had he stayed at home, riding his horse Bucephalus and studying politics and biology with his tutor Aristotle, instead of setting out to conquer the world.

To be a mainspring, however, one doesn't have to be "the Great." Just like initiators, encouragers, and cultivators, mainspring leaders can be found on platforms both large and small. Alexander was probably one, but so was Darwin Smith, the CEO and self-described eccentric we met in Chapter 12, who shunned publicity as he transformed Kimberly-Clark from a declining paper manufacturer into a thriving consumer products company. And so was Sam, the entrepreneur we met in Chapter 17, who built a small company that's still around after nearly half a century. Some mainspring leaders play stadiums while others play open mic night at the corner coffeehouse, but either way, we remember their music. Years after they're gone, they're still raising the tone (see "Reflection tool: Ten years hence").

reflection tool

TEN YEARS HENCE

No matter what your position in an organization, you have the capacity to leave a positive legacy.

1. Imagine you left your organization today.
2. Now imagine ten years have passed.
3. What do you want people to be (still) saying about you? How do you want to be (still) raising the tone and contributing value?

Peter Drucker tells the story of a hospital chief administrator, new to the job, holding his first staff meeting.[5] A difficult problem was on the table. The group debated it for some time and arrived at a solution. Assuming the matter settled, the administrator was about to move on when a participant suddenly asked, "Would this have satisfied Nurse Bryan?" The debate immediately began again and continued until a much more comprehensive solution had been constructed.

Drucker later learned the following:

> Nurse Bryan ... had been a long-serving nurse at the hospital. She was not particularly distinguished, had not in fact ever been a supervisor. But whenever a decision on a patient's care came up on her floor, Nurse Bryan would ask, "Are we doing the best we can do to help this patient?" Patients on Nurse Bryan's floor did better and recovered faster. Gradually over the years, the whole hospital had learned to adopt what came to be known as Nurse Bryan's Rule.[6]

Nurse Bryan had retired ten years before, and she was still raising standards at that hospital. She was "not particularly distinguished," and who knows how many patients had walked out of there alive because of her leadership.

postscript

LOOKING FOR OVERLAND

London, May 2010

"So, how did your philosophy degree help you write this book?"

The interviewer, who for the past 25 minutes had been asking me questions in a monotone worthy of the bored teacher in *Ferris Bueller's Day Off* ("Anyone? ... Anyone?"), suddenly raised his voice and narrowed his eyes with an air of purpose; it was obvious he saw this question as a zinger.

You couldn't blame him for trying to inject some minor excitement into the proceedings. He was the host for a business video website, and every week he faced, no doubt, a lineup of consultant-authors bent on making similar comments about similar topics with obligatory references to a Major Research Study. All the authors, topics, and studies must have merged long ago, for him, into a bagpipe drone: agility–synergy–strategy–waaaaaaah. One could understand a mischievous attempt to knock me, another expounder of bromides, off my script.

And he succeeded. I was thoroughly prepared to talk about the contents of my book. I had stats galore, anecdotes for days, and enough nuggets from our (major) research study to fill an entire issue of *HBR*. I could say why 70 percent of change initiatives fail to achieve their expected results, but I was not prepared to answer the question: "How did your philosophy degree help you write this book?" I remember chuckling nervously and launching into an explanation of how my education had helped me to devise good questions and see past superficial answers; to analyze and, um, synthesize. Mr. Interviewer let me flounder for a minute and then came to my rescue with: "I've always been told that philosophy teaches you how to *think*."

"Exactly!" I said with relief. I felt stupid for not coming out immediately with the correct response to his question; I had actually learned a long time ago that "Philosophy teaches you how to think" is the briefest and best way to justify the years I'd spent studying something of no obvious utility. Even more distressing, I knew that right then I couldn't articulate the real reason studying great books had helped me as a writer, businessperson, and leader.

Luckily for me, Mr. Interviewer was like all the best TV hosts in wanting his guest to look good. He dropped the subject and later edited my fumbles out of the final cut. Since then, I've pondered what I should have said in reply to his offbeat question. It took writing this book to figure it out.

What is the value of a liberal arts education? Recent years have seen a slew of articles, op-eds, and blog posts on the topic—a sign of higher education's eagerness to make a case for the liberal arts to students (and parents) increasingly worried that four years' expensive study won't pay off in the form of a job. In an effort to show such worries as needless, college administrators cite surveys in which employers say that abilities such as critical thinking are more important than undergraduate degrees in technical subjects.[1] They trot out statistics indicating that today's typical graduate will change jobs umpteen times and careers nearly as often. They gesture toward Apple, which likes to hire humanities majors. Bobby Fong, president of Ursinus College, sums up the argument thus: "What characterizes liberal education is the bringing together of knowing and doing in order to foster capacities that extend beyond the first job."[2]

Long-term employability is indeed a good reason for studying the liberal arts, aka philosophy, the humanities, or the great books. Those terms mean different things, of course, but the differences don't matter for my purposes here. What I'm talking about is any type of education that is intentionally *not* pre-professional; that seeks not to direct skills toward a specific job, but to open minds to the broad sweep of human knowledge and experience. And the college administrators are right: an education that isn't job specific can develop abilities tremendously useful in a protean job market, abilities such as questioning, listening, problem-solving, ethical reasoning, collaboration, cultural awareness, creativity, and learning itself. This type of education, done well, does indeed teach us (as my interviewer suggested) *how to think*. For would-be leaders facing twenty-first-century complexities, what could be more important?

But there is something more important. Knowing how to think is all to the good, but there's an even better reason for leaders to seek out a great-books education.

Consider this: Every person on earth carries burdens, past or present. These burdens might involve violence or abuse; a disability, addiction, or ill health; discrimination or bigotry; loneliness or rejection; poverty or business failure. Some people have a few small, temporary weights, while others have many big, lasting ones. Even the people with major disadvantages, however, often manage to rise above them, and when you ask these people how they did it, they will invariably mention two things: first, certain mentors who encouraged them; and second, certain books (for some people, it's movies, music, or another art form) that not only provided distraction from their debilitating circumstances, but also gave them a vision of something finer. The mentors made them believe in themselves; the books made them believe in a world better than the so-called real one.

One of the most moving scenes in literature, for me, occurs in a book by C.S. Lewis (who by now you can tell is a personal favorite of mine). Part of the Narnia Chronicles, *The Silver Chair* tells the story of Jill and Eustace, two children summoned to the magical land of Narnia and set on a quest to find the long-missing Prince Rilian, heir to the throne. Their guide for the journey is Puddleglum the Marshwiggle. Marshwiggles are gangly, web-footed humanoids characterized by their unrelenting pessimism, and although he claims to be going on the quest in order to dampen a tendency toward frivolity, Puddleglum seems a sober sort indeed. As he travels with the children through the Narnian countryside, he exhorts them continually to expect the worst.

Puddleglum's severe views are reminiscent of some leaders' devotion to the "real world." These hard-faced bosses don't believe in silly ideas such as friendship and kindness, mission and service—at least not in the workplace, which for them is about the stark realities of profit and loss. One senior manager once explained to me why he didn't bother about climate or any of that soft stuff: "Of course people have their own professional goals, but basically they come to work because we pay them," he said. "All we owe them is a paycheck, a cubicle, and a laptop."

But back to Puddleglum. Although he proclaims a dedication to the facts, his deepest commitments turn out to lie elsewhere. Three-quarters of the way through the book, he, Jill, and Eustace find their way to a vast underground land lit by oil lamps, populated by lugubrious gnomes, and ruled by an evil queen. In this Underworld, they at last discover the captive Prince Rilian, who persists under a spell that allows him to recall his true identity only at night when the queen has him strapped to a magic silver chair. During the day he supports her schemes of conquest and believes her story that at night he suffers madness and must be restrained for his own good. Puddleglum and the children cut him free of the chair, breaking the spell.

When the queen arrives and catches the four planning their escape, she feigns pleasure at Prince Rilian's "cure" and sets about lulling them into a trance. She sprinkles soporific incense on the fire and, strumming gently on a mandolin, asks them to elucidate their charming fantasies about "Overland" with its sun, grass, and sky. "What is this *sun*?" she asks. They struggle to explain and eventually tell her the sun is a bit like the lamp that hangs from the rock ceiling of the room, only much bigger and hanging from ... nothing. When Jill, half asleep, mumbles that Overland is the home of Aslan the great lion, the queen again pretends interest and asks them to explain what a *lion* is. Well, it's a bit like a cat, they say, only much bigger and stronger. "I see," says the queen, "that we should do no better with your *lion*, as you call it, than we did with your *sun*."[3]

All they're doing, she says, is looking at things in the real world and imagining them to be bigger and better; moreover, they can put nothing into the pretend world that they haven't copied from the real world, Underworld. It's a pretty make-believe, but aren't they too old for such foolish games? "Come, all of you," she says with finality. "Put away these childish tricks. I have work for you all in the real world. There is no Narnia, no Overworld, no sky, no sun, no Aslan."[4] She continues to strum the instrument, and their eyes droop shut.

It's then that Puddleglum proves his valor. Gathering the last of his strength, he strides over to the fire, stamps it out with his bare feet, and launches into this speech:

> One word, Ma'am … I won't deny any of what you said. But there's one thing more to be said, even so. Suppose we *have* only dreamed, or made up, all those things … Suppose this black pit of a kingdom of yours is the only world. Well, it strikes me as a pretty poor one. And that's a funny thing, when you come to think of it. We're just babies making up a game, if you're right. But four babies playing a game can make a play-world which licks your real world hollow. That's why I'm going to stand by the play-world. I'm on Aslan's side even if there isn't any Aslan to lead it. I'm going to live as like a Narnian as I can even if there isn't any Narnia. So, thanking you kindly for our supper, if these two gentlemen and the young lady are ready, we're leaving your court at once and setting out in the dark to spend our lives looking for Overland.[5]

"Philosophy teaches you how to think," my interviewer said. It does, and that's important. But for a leader—or anybody, really—more important than knowing how to think is knowing what to want; or, to put it another way, knowing what you'll spend your life seeking. Lackeys, tyrants, and bureaucrats, both great and petty, choose the "real world" and close their eyes to the possibility of anything better. If an employee tries to talk to them about values or mission, then like the scornful queen in *The Silver Chair*, these misleaders call it nonsense. Their big fear is that they'll be played for a fool, taken in by lamps pretending to be suns and cats pretending to be lions. "Business is about making money," they say. "Leadership means hitting the numbers. If you think otherwise, you're a child. Grow up."

My reply to them is Puddleglum's reply: "OK, suppose you're right. Suppose work is about delivering profit and nothing more. Suppose those of us who try to go first, create hope, and focus on people are just babies inventing a play-world: a world filled with pretty but fantastical ideas like generosity and concern, a world where courageous but deluded leaders chase goals that aren't businesslike. Well, that's a play-world that licks your real world hollow. I'm standing by the play-world."

And my answer, now, to that long-ago interview question would be similar: "Studying philosophy (and literature, history, politics, and psychology) helps me as a leader because it has shown me a world more real than the real one: a world worth living in and for. It makes me desire the courage of a Lawrence of Arabia or a Joan of Arc; makes me reach for the understanding of a C.G. Jung or a Ruth Benedict; makes me try, though falteringly, for the eloquence of a Lincoln or a Pericles. It lets me rise, sometimes, above the ignorance and fear that too often threaten to drag me down. It makes me want to be a better person, and want to help others want the same."

Businesses need to make money, and people need jobs. Reality makes demands that can't be ignored. But if I think about the world of the hard-faced bosses—with their "this is all we owe you" paychecks and cubicles, and their dismissal of anything that can't be captured in a spreadsheet—it looks pretty shoddy. And if I then compare that world to the one illuminated by Plato and Churchill, Shaw and Shakespeare, Austen and Lao Tzu, it looks *seriously* shoddy. Quite frankly, I'd rather be a leader in Lao Tzu's world, even if it doesn't "really" exist.

I'd rather set out in the dark, with a few good friends and a few great books, to look for Overland.

appendix

LAUNCHING A LEADERSHIP STUDY GROUP

The Greats on Leadership can serve as the roadmap for a study group. If you work in a large organization, you may want to ask your Learning and Development team to help you recruit and convene members of the group and facilitate the discussions; or you may prefer to manage the process yourself, using the guidelines and tools in this appendix.

SETTING UP THE GROUP

Follow these steps to launch your group:

1. *Recruit group members* The ideal group size is four to eight. There are advantages to having members from different functions and business units. The discussions will be easier to manage if the group is co-located, but a virtual group, meeting by teleconference, can also work well.

2. *Select group leader(s)* The group will need a discussion leader for each meeting. This could be one person or, depending on group members' comfort levels, you could rotate the responsibility. If you do decide to rotate the discussion leader role, it's still a good idea to select one person to manage the overall process.

3. *Hold a kickoff meeting* At the kickoff, have the group members introduce themselves, review the overall purpose of the group, and choose the group's focus and schedule (see Step 4). Also, make sure that everyone has a copy of *The Greats on Leadership*, and confirm the process for acquiring the classic books.

4. *Choose the group's focus and schedule* If you want to cover all 24 leadership topics addressed in *The Greats on Leadership*, use the full schedule shown in Table A.1. If you'd rather focus on a particular leadership issue, refer to Table A.2: Chapters to address specific challenges.

5. *Schedule the monthly meetings, and review the first month's assignment* Each meeting will take approximately two hours. The ideal frequency for meetings is once a month, but if people need more time to complete the assignments, once every six weeks can also work. For an outline for the meetings, see Table A.3.

6. *Check in with group members throughout the month* In between the meetings, group members will complete the readings and tools associated with that month's assigned chapter (see Monthly Assignments, below). The group leader, whether that's a permanent or rotating role, should check in regularly with group members to be sure they're on track and see what help they may need.

MONTHLY ASSIGNMENTS

During the four or six weeks prior to each meeting, group members complete the following activities individually:

In the first half of the month Read the assigned chapter of *The Greats on Leadership* and its associated classic. For suggested parts of the classic to focus on, see the synopsis at the start of the chapter.

In the second half of the month Take the tool from the chapter and apply it to your job. Note the results, what you learned, and any challenges that arose.

Table A.1 Group schedule—all chapters

MONTH	CHAPTER	TOPIC	FEATURED CLASSIC*
1	1	Leadership truths	Exodus (the Bible)
2	2	Leadership traps	*King Lear* (Shakespeare)
3	7	Character, defined	*Great Contemporaries* (Churchill)
4	11	Communication	Gettysburg Address (Lincoln); Funeral Oration (Pericles)
5	14	Personality	*Psychological Types* (Jung)
6	18	Relationships	"Boule de Suif" (Maupassant); *Richard III* (Shakespeare)
7	4	Justice	*The Republic* (Plato)
8	8	Crises	*Henry V* (Shakespeare)
9	16	Culture	*The Chrysanthemum and the Sword* (Benedict)
10	19	Accountability	*Billy Budd* (Melville)
11	5	Power	*Antigone* (Sophocles)
12	10	Dilemmas	*The Federalist* (Hamilton and Madison)
13	13	Motivation	*Man's Search for Meaning* (Frankl)
14	20	Talent	*Emma* (Austen)
15	6	Authority	*Julius Caesar* (Shakespeare)
16	9	Competition	*The Great Captains* (Dodge)
17	15	Decisions	"Lamb to the Slaughter" and other stories (Dahl)
18	21	Vision	*Saint Joan* (Shaw)
19	3	Change	*The Prince* (Machiavelli)
20	12	Character, developed	*Moralia* (Plutarch)
21	17	Character, anchored	*Frankenstein* (Shelley)
22	22	Character, revealed	*The Dead* (Joyce)
23	23	Leadership levels	Revisit: *Julius Caesar*, *Saint Joan*, *Great Contemporaries*
24	24	The fourth level	*Tao Te Ching* (Lao Tzu)

*For the longer texts, see the summary at the start of each chapter for which parts to read.

Table A.2 Chapters to address specific challenges

Chapters	Leadership challenges: Avoid leadership traps	Think and act strategically	Influence across boundaries	Coach and develop others	Drive change or innovation	Motivate a team	Build presence/ confidence
1 Leadership truths							●
2 Leadership traps	●	●					
3 Change	●	●			●		
4 Justice				●		●	
5 Power	●		●		●		
6 Authority			●				●
7 Character, defined				●			●
8 Crises	●	●			●		
9 Competition		●			●		
10 Dilemmas	●	●			●		
11 Communication			●			●	●
12 Character, developed				●			●
13 Motivation	●		●	●		●	
14 Personality				●		●	
15 Decisions	●	●					
16 Culture			●	●			
17 Character, anchored							●
18 Relationships	●	●	●				
19 Accountability					●	●	
20 Talent	●			●		●	
21 Vision			●		●	●	
22 Character, revealed							●
23–24 Leadership Levels							●

Table A.3 *Monthly meeting agenda*

TIMING	ACTIVITY
5 mins	Welcome and agenda review.
45 mins	Discuss the classic for the month. See my blog (jocelynrdavis.wordpress.com) for discussion questions, or create your own. Allow roughly 15 minutes per question.
60 mins	Share how you applied the tool. Each person takes 8–10 minutes to report on how he or she used the chapter's tool, the results, what was learned, and any challenges that arose. Group members share advice as needed.
10 mins	Plan for next month's meeting.

NOTES

PREFACE: WHAT'S IN THIS BOOK AND HOW TO USE IT

1. See Peter Stothard, "The Emperor of Self-Control," Times Higher Education website, Oct 12, 1998, https://www.timeshighereducation.com/books/the-emperor-of-self-control/161210.article; see also Carolyn Kellogg, "An American Reader: Bill Clinton," *Los Angeles Times*, Jul 4, 2009, http://latimesblogs.latimes.com/jacketcopy/2009/07/america-reads-bill-clinton.html.
2. See Alexandra Mondalek and Gus Lubin, "27 Business Leaders Name Their Favorite Books Ever," Aug 2, 2013, www.businessinsider.com.
3. Ibid.

INTRODUCTION: THE CLASSIC ART OF LEADERSHIP

1. This anecdote was told by Johnny Carson on an episode of NBC's *The Tonight Show* in the mid-1980s.
2. Information on Alexander the Great is drawn from Plutarch's *Life of Alexander* and from E.H. Gombrich, *A Little History of the World*, tr. Caroline Mustill (New Haven, CT: Yale University Press, 1985).
3. Gombrich, op. cit., p. 64.
4. For an overview of the factors that make leadership development effective or ineffective, see Thomas Diamante, "Leadership Development Programs That Work," in *The Oxford Handbook of Lifelong Learning*, ed. Manuel London (Oxford University Press, 2011), Ch. 12, pp. 164-179.
5. Brandon Hall (www.brandonhall.com), Bersin (www.bersin.com), and Deloitte (www.deloitte.com) are three good sources for research on leadership programs and their effectiveness. Brandon Hall's 2013 Leadership Development Benchmarking Survey (see findings summarized by Lorri Freifeld in "Survey: Leadership Development Programs Lack Effectiveness," *Training Magazine*, www.trainingmag.com, Sep 30, 2013) says that 75% of organizations believe their leadership programs are ineffective. Research by Bersin indicates that 80% of training content produced by large organizations is not widely used by its intended audience (see Josh Bersin, "The Black Hole of Measurement," *Chief Learning Officer*, www.clomedia.com, Feb 4, 2015). In Deloitte's 2014 Global Human Capital Trends survey, only 13% of responding companies say they do an excellent job of developing leaders at all levels (http://dupress.com/articles/hc-trends-2014-leaders-at-all-levels/). And in Deloitte's 2015 Global Human Capital Trends survey, less than 6% of survey respondents report they have "excellent" leadership programs in place to develop millennials (http://dupress.com/articles/developing-leaders-perennial-issue-human-capital-trends-2015/).
6. Steve Denning, "The Best of Peter Drucker," *Forbes*, Aug 29, 2014.
7. Peter Drucker, *The Essential Drucker* (NY: HarperCollins, 2001), Ch. 1.
8. American Management Association, "AMA Enterprise Research Lists 10 Trends Shaping Corporate Training, Development," Mar 24, 2014, www.amanet.org.
9. Francis Bacon, *Apothegms*, No. 97.
10. *Ratatouille*, Pixar Animation Studios, 2007.

1: ONE MYTH, THREE TRUTHS

1. Fox's commentary from *The Shocken Bible, Volume I: The Five Books of Moses*, tr. Everett Fox (New York: Shocken Books, 1983), p. 243.
2. The contemporary business anecdotes in this book are based on real situations or composites of real situations. The names of individuals, company names, industries, and other details have been changed to protect anonymity. Any resemblances to actual people, organizations, or events are coincidental and unintentional.
3. Regarding quotations from the featured classics: When a book has non-edition-specific verse or line references (such as the Bible and Shakespeare's plays), I've placed those references directly in the text and, if necessary, included an endnote indicating the edition. When edition-specific page references are needed, they appear in these Notes.
4. Exodus quotations are from *The Shocken Bible*, Vol. I. I have changed Moshe and Aharon (Fox's spellings) to the more familiar Moses and Aaron.
5. Susan Cain, *Quiet: The Power of Introverts in a World that Can't Stop Talking* (New York: Broadway Books, 2012), p. 60.
6. Ibid., p. 61.
7. *Norma Rae*, dir. Martin Ritt, prod. Tamara Asseyev and Alex Rose, 1979.
8. See also the works of ancient Indian royal adviser Chanakya and seventeenth-century English philosopher Thomas Hobbes.
9. John Kotter, in "Management Is (Still) Not Leadership" (HBR Blog Network, www.blogs.hbr.org, Jan 9, 2013) articulates a widely held view: management is directed toward established processes that help an organization do what it already does well, while leadership is about "taking an organization into the future ... about vision, about people buying in ... and, most of all, about producing useful change." While I agree that management is mostly about process and leadership is mostly about people, I would not go so far as Kotter in calling the two roles entirely distinct. They are, I believe, like chairs and benches: somewhat different in purpose and design, but very much members of the same family. Nor would I equate leadership with vision. Leaders sometimes pursue visions of the future, but often they simply want to mobilize their team to achieve decent results. Moreover, visions tend to fail if not supported by activities we typically associate with good managers: things like coaching, teamwork, and execution (see Chapter 21). Leaders may look to the future, but in order to get there, they must also be masters of the everyday.
10. For another look at Moses and God's relationship, see Jan Mark, *God's Story* (Cambridge, MA: Candlewick Press, 1997), a retelling of the Old Testament informed by ancient rabbinical texts. Mark's version of Genesis and Exodus emphasizes how God seeks out and forms bonds with individual humans—Abraham, Isaac, Moses, and so on—in order to further his aims for humanity. Did God, too, start out as a leader in need of a partner?

2: EIGHT TRAPS

1. C.S. Lewis, *The Screwtape Letters* (New York: Macmillan, 1959), p. 154.
2. Several websites say this piece of doggerel was originally printed in *The Boston Evening Transcript*, a daily afternoon newspaper published in Boston from 1830 to 1941. I have not been able to find any other information about its author or date.

3. Marshall Goldsmith, *Triggers: Creating Behavior That Lasts, Becoming the Person You Want to Be* (New York: Crown Business, 2015), p. 2.
4. Laurence J. Stybel and Maryanne Peabody, "Friend, Foe, Ally, Adversary ... or Something Else?" *MIT Sloan Management Review*, Vol. 46, No. 4 (Summer 2005).
5. Anatole France, "The Procurator of Judea"; tr. Frederick Chapman, in *Tellers of Tales*, ed. W. Somerset Maugham (New York: Doubleday, Doran, 1939), p. 219.
6. Ibid., p. 222.

3: CHANGE

1. Niccolo Machiavelli, *The Prince* (tr. Harvey C. Mansfield, 2nd edn., Chicago, IL: University of Chicago Press, 1998), Chapter VI, p. 23.
2. For more on change initiative failure rates, see Jocelyn R. Davis, Henry M. Frechette, and Edwin H. Boswell, *Strategic Speed: Mobilize People, Accelerate Execution* (Boston, MA: Harvard Business Press, 2010), Chapter 1.
3. The concept of the plateau as it applies to change management was developed by my colleague Dr. Maggie Walsh. She built on descriptions of product lifecycles, research in evolutionary biology, Peter Senge's work on learning organizations, and George Land's theories of growth and transformation in natural systems. For more on the plateau and the structure of change, see Kerry Johnson and Maggie Walsh, "The Challenge of Change" (The Forum Corporation whitepaper, www.forum.com, 2006); see also George Land, *Grow or Die: The Unifying Principle of Transformation* (Leadership 2000, 1997).
4. Machiavelli, op. cit., Chapter VI, p. 24.
5. Ibid., Chapter VI, p. 25.
6. Ibid., Chapter VII, p. 33.
7. Ibid., Chapter XIX, p. 74.
8. Ibid., Chapter IX, p. 41.
9. Ibid., Chapter IX, p. 41.

4: JUSTICE

1. *The Republic* quotations are from the translation by Allan Bloom, 2nd edn. (Basic Books, 1968).
2. If you plan to read the entire *Republic*, I recommend first reading Bloom's "Interpretive Essay" from the Basic Books edition, which explains the dialogue's themes in an engaging way.
3. Sean Markey, "Monkeys Show Sense of Fairness, Study Says," *National Geographic News* (www.news.nationalgeographic.com), Sep 17, 2003.
4. Robert Gandossy, "The Need for Speed," *Journal of Business Strategy*, Jan-Feb 2003.
5. Marcus Buckingham and Curt Coffman, *First, Break All the Rules* (New York: Simon & Schuster, 1999).
6. Ibid., p. 152.
7. Ibid., pp. 168–169.

5: POWER

1. *Antigone* quotations are from the translation by David Grene (University of Chicago Press, 1991).
2. Some contemporary leadership authors point to research supposedly showing that ruthless and egotistical people are more likely than the diffident and

humble to rise to the top; see, for example, Jeffrey Pfeffer's short article "Good Leaders Don't Have to Be Good" for *Time* magazine (Sept 28, 2015), in which he states that narcissism, not modesty, is the character trait that predicts selection for and survival in top leadership roles. Now, I wouldn't be surprised to find proof that ruthless drive and narcissism are correlated with high status, but the question is: Are those traits correlated with high effectiveness as a leader? Do they correlate with getting work done, achieving goals, building companies, sustaining change, and continuing to have an impact far into the future? If all you want is a big title, a big ego may work for you. If you want lasting, genuine power, you'll need quite a bit more than that.

3. A study done at the University of Southern California found that power without status can be a dangerous combination; people who were made to feel high in power but low in status were more likely to select demeaning tasks for a partner to perform. Nathanael Fast, one of the study's authors, says, "Put simply, it feels bad to be in a low-status position, and the power that goes with that role gives them a way to take action on those negative feelings." See Anne Bergman, "Power Corrupts When It Lacks Status" (USC News, Sep 21, 2011), https://news.usc.edu/32045/power-corrupts-when-it-lacks-status/.

6: AUTHORITY

1. Jennifer Reingold, "How to Fail in Business While Really, Really Trying," *Fortune*, April 7, 2014.
2. Frank Abagnale with Stan Redding, *Catch Me If You Can: The True Story of a Real Fake* (New York: Broadway Books, 2000).
3. Reingold, op. cit., p. 85.
4. Ibid., p. 87.
5. For these and other insights on Octavius's authority, see William and Barbara Rosen's introduction to the Signet Classic edition of *Julius Caesar* (New York: Penguin, 1986).
6. See Caroline Alexander, *The Bounty: The True Story of the Mutiny on the Bounty* (New York: Viking Penguin, 2003).
7. See Christopher Hibbert, *The Great Mutiny: India 1857* (New York: Viking Press, 1978).
8. Robert Graves, I, *Claudius* (New York: Vintage Books, 1934).
9. The BBC Television adaptation of I, *Claudius*, which the British Film Institute placed 12th in its list of "100 Greatest British Television Programs" and which contains some outstanding performances (most notably Derek Jacobi as Claudius), is a good substitute if you don't have time for the book.
10. Graves, op. cit., pp. 454–455.

7: CHARACTER, DEFINED

1. In his *Ethics*, Aristotle lays out this concept of the mean in detail and shows how it applies to a number of character traits (or virtues, as he calls them). I have followed his lead, since no one has yet devised a simpler or better way to understand character.
2. Winston Churchill, *Great Contemporaries*, "The Ex-Kaiser" (New York: G.P. Putnam's Sons, 1937), p. 25.
3. Ibid., p. 26.
4. Ibid., p. 27.

5. I use the term sociopath not to indicate a psychological disorder but rather as a term for leaders with particular character traits. For a clinical definition of sociopathy, often called antisocial personality disorder, see Martha Stout, *The Sociopath Next Door* (New York: Crown, 2005).
6. Churchill, op. cit., "Hitler and His Choice," p. 225.
7. Ibid., p. 228.
8. Ibid., p. 232.
9. Ibid., p. 230.
10. Stout, op. cit., p. 1.
11. Churchill, op. cit., "George Nathaniel Curzon," p. 235.
12. Ibid., p. 237.
13. Ibid., p. 237.
14. Ibid., p. 239.
15. *Lawrence of Arabia*, dir. David Lean, prod. Sam Spiegel, 1962. The film won the Academy Award for Best Picture in 1962 and appears consistently on lists of the best films ever made.
16. T.E. Lawrence, *Seven Pillars of Wisdom: A Triumph*, Introductory Chapter (New York: Doubleday), p. 24. The book was originally published in a private edition in 1926, and first published for general circulation in the United States by Doubleday, Doran in 1935.
17. Churchill, op. cit., "Lawrence of Arabia," p. 134.
18. Ibid., p. 130.
19. Ibid., p. 139.

8: CRISES

1. See, for example, Dennis N.T. Perkins, *Leading at the Edge: Leadership Lessons from the Extraordinary Saga of Shackleton's Antarctic Expedition* (New York: AMACOM, 2000).
2. For an in-depth look at leadership's role in the *Titanic* disaster, see Jocelyn R. Davis, *Leadership Failures Sink Unsinkable Ship: Business Lessons from the Titanic* (The Forum Corporation e-book, 2012, available on Amazon.com).
3. Some of Heifetz's best-known works are *Leadership without Easy Answers* (1994), *Leadership on the Line* (2002), and *The Practice of Adaptive Leadership* (2009).
4. For more on how to increase unity and agility—along with a third "people factor," clarity—see Davis, Frechette, and Boswell, op. cit.

9: COMPETITION

1. Theodore Ayrault Dodge, *The Great Captains: The Art of War in the Campaigns of Alexander, Hannibal, Caesar, Gustavus Adolphus, Frederick the Great, and Napoleon* (New York: Barnes & Noble, 1995), Lecture I, p. 1.
2. Ibid., Lecture IV, p. 108.
3. Ibid., Lecture IV, p. 112.
4. Ibid., Lecture I, p. 1.
5. Ibid., Lecture IV, p. 115.
6. Ibid., Lecture IV, p. 116.
7. Ibid., Lecture II, p. 68.
8. Ibid., Lecture IV, pp. 135–136.
9. W. Chan Kim and Renée Mauborgne, *Blue Ocean Strategy: How to Create Uncontested Market Space and Make the Competition Irrelevant* (Boston, MA:

Harvard Business School Press, 2005). At this writing, the book has sold more than 3.5 million copies.
10. Dodge, op. cit., Lecture II, p. 50.
11. Ibid., Lecture II, p. 52.
12. Ibid., Lecture II, p. 54.
13. Ibid., Lecture II, p. 55.

10: DILEMMAS

1. This passage is an excerpt from "The Call for the Federal Constitutional Convention," which was first published on February 21, 1787, and appears as Appendix I in the Random House Modern Library College Edition of *The Federalist*. See also Edward Mead Earle's Introduction to this edition, which provides useful historical context for the essays.
2. Barry Johnson, *Polarity Management: Identifying and Managing Unsolvable Problems* (Amherst, MA: HRD Press, 1996), Introduction.
3. Ibid., Ch. 2.
4. The Structure of a Dilemma diagram is based on Johnson's polarity maps; see Johnson, op. cit., Ch. 1.
5. See Johnson, op. cit., Ch. 1.

11: COMMUNICATION

1. Thucydides, *History of the Peloponnesian War* (tr. Richard Crawley, Mineola, NY: Dover, 2004), Chapter IV, p. 82.
2. Doug Stewart, "My Great-Great-Grandfather Hated the Gettysburg Address. 150 Years Later, He's Famous for It," Smithsonian.com, Nov 18, 2013.
3. See the website "Abraham Lincoln Online," www.abrahamlincolnonline.org/lincoln/sites/wills.htm.
4. Stephen Denning, *The Springboard: How Storytelling Ignites Action in Knowledge-Era Organizations* (Woburn, MA: Butterworth-Heinemann, 2001). Denning followed up with more books on storytelling techniques, including *The Secret Language of Leadership*; *Squirrel, Inc.*; and *The Leader's Guide to Storytelling*.
5. See, for example, Craig Wortmann, *What's Your Story? Using Stories to Ignite Performance and Be More Successful* (Chicago, IL: Kaplan, 2006); Daniel Pink, *Drive: The Surprising Truth about What Motivates Us* (New York: Riverhead Books, 2009); Chip and Dan Heath, *Made to Stick: Why Some Ideas Survive and Others Die* (New York: Random House, 2007).
6. Thucydides, op. cit., Chapter IV, p. 82.
7. Ibid., Chapter IV, pp. 85–86.

12: CHARACTER, DEVELOPED

1. Maria Konnikova, "The Lost Art of the Unsent Letter," *New York Times*, "The Week in Review," Mar 23, 2014.
2. Plutarch, *Moralia*, "On Education," Section iv (*The Plutarch Anthology*, e-book published by Bybliotech.org).
3. Ibid., "On Education," Section iv.
4. Ibid., "On Education," Section x.
5. Ibid., "On Restraining Anger," Section xv.
6. This is Rule 4 in the pamphlet, which was published in 1890.
7. David Brooks, *The Road to Character* (New York: Random House, 2015), pp. 263–264.

8. Plutarch, op. cit., "How a Man May Be Benefited by His Enemies," Section i.
9. Ibid., "How One May Be Aware of One's Progress in Virtue," Section x.
10. Jim Collins, *Good to Great: Why Some Companies Make the Leap and Others Don't* (New York: HarperCollins, 2001), p. 17.
11. Ibid., p. 18.
12. Ibid., p. 20.

PART IV: MINDS

1. Steven Blankaart's *Physical Dictionary* of 1694 refers to "Anatomy, which treats of the Body, and Psychology, which treats of the Soul." See *A Dictionary of Psychology*, ed. Andrew M. Colman (Oxford University Press, 2009).

13: MOTIVATION

1. Uri Gneezy and Aldo Rustichini, "A Fine Is a Price," *Journal of Legal Studies*, Vol. 29, No. 1 (Jan 2000); study summarized by Daniel Pink, op. cit., pp. 50–51.
2. Pink, op. cit.
3. Pink says the nature of the work matters, too. If your job consists of stuffing envelopes, you might be motivated by a $100 bonus for stuffing 10% more. But if you're engaged in creative, conceptual endeavors, that same bonus won't mean much, and it could even demotivate. Pink cites examples of companies selling complex business-to-business services that have done away with sales commissions and actually seen their sales rise; see "A Radical Prescription for Sales," *Harvard Business Review*, Jul-Aug 2012, pp. 76–77.
4. One of the best known is the McClelland-Atkinson model: achievement, affiliation, and power; see John W. Atkinson, *An Introduction to Motivation* (Princeton, NJ: D. Van Nostrand, 1978), and David C. McClelland, *Human Motivation* (Cambridge: Cambridge University Press, 1987).
5. Another study of intrinsic and extrinsic motivators was conducted by Amy Wrzesniewski and Barry Schwartz. In analyzing data drawn from more than 11,000 cadets at the West Point Military Academy, they not only found that internal motives (such as a desire to be trained as a leader in the Army) correlated with high performance, but also that instrumental motives (such as a desire to get a good job later in life) correlated with a decline in performance. According to their conclusions, the recipe for success in an endeavor is to have strong internal motives and no instrumental motives. See Wrzesniewski and Schwartz, "The Secret of Effective Motivation," *New York Times*, July 6, 2014.
6. See Abraham Maslow, "A Theory of Human Motivation," *Psychological Review*, Vol. 50, No. 4. The article can be accessed at http://psychclassics.yorku.ca/Maslow/motivation.htm.
7. Viktor Frankl, *Man's Search for Meaning* (Boston, MA: Beacon Press, 1959), p. 28.
8. Frederick Herzberg, "One More Time: How Do You Motivate Employees?" *Harvard Business Review*, Sep-Oct 1987, pp. 109–120.
9. Frankl, op. cit., p. 49.
10. Ibid., p. 37.
11. Ibid., p. 38. Note that this exact sentence isn't found anywhere in the Bible but is apparently inspired by Revelation 4:8-11.
12. Ibid., p. 40.
13. Ibid., p. 41.
14. Ibid., p. 83.

15. Kurt Lewin initiated research on workplace climate in 1939, and a large body of research has been built since then. See, for example, Robert Stringer, *Leadership and Organizational Climate* (Upper Saddle River, NJ: Prentice Hall, 2002); Jocelyn R. Davis, Henry M. Frechette, and Edwin H. Boswell, *Strategic Speed: Mobilize People, Accelerate Execution* (Boston, MA: Harvard Business Press, 2010); and Daniel Goleman, Richard Boyatzis, and Annie McKee, *Primal Leadership: Learning to Lead with Emotional Intelligence* (Boston, MA: Harvard Business Press, 2002).
16. Daniel Goleman, "Leadership That Gets Results," *Harvard Business Review*, Mar-Apr 2000, pp. 78-90.

14: PERSONALITY

1. *Psychological Types* quotations are from Volume 6 of the *Collected Works of C.G. Jung*, tr. H.G. Baynes, rev. R.F.C. Hull (Princeton, NJ: Princeton University Press, 1971).
2. Lillian Cunningham, "Myers-Briggs Personality Test Embraced by Employers, Not All Psychologists," *Seattle Times*, Business/Technology, Apr 13, 2013, http://seattletimes.com/html/businesstechnology/2020769531_myers-briggspersonalitytestxml.html.
3. Details on each type may be found on the website of the Myers & Briggs Foundation, licensers of the original MBTI assessment: www.myersbriggs.org.
4. Extraverted is often spelled with an "o" (extroverted). Both Jung and Myers/Briggs spell it with an "a." I have used the "a" spelling, since it is derived from *extra-*, the Latin prefix for "outward" or "outside," hence is a better expression of how an extravert addresses the world.
5. If you compare their typology to Jung's, you'll notice that Briggs and Myers add another pair of functions (judging and perceiving) to Jung's two pairs. They also make no distinction between attitudes and functions.
6. For example, www.personalitypage.com, www.16personalities.com, www.humanmetrics.com, www.personalitypathways.com, and www.personalitycafe.com.
7. David Keirsey, *Please Understand Me: Character and Temperament Types* (Prometheus Nemesis Book Company, 1984).
8. As you no doubt know, these are characters from J.K.Rowling's Harry Potter series (US publisher Scholastic), about a boy who learns at age 11 that he's a wizard and has been admitted to wizard school. A similar chart showing the Myers-Briggs types of Harry Potter characters and attributed to "simbaga.tumblr.com" first appeared on the internet in September 2013; as of this writing, it was still posted on such sites as www.readerswritersconnect.com and www.geekologie.com and could be found by typing "Harry Potter Myers Briggs chart" into a search engine. I created my version before I came across the simbaga chart, and I believe mine is a better reading of the characters, though obviously that's up for debate. I'd be delighted to hear other interpretations. As for the individual monikers and mottos in Table 14.1, some are drawn from various MBTI websites (see note above), and some are of my own invention.
9. C.S. Lewis, *The Pilgrim's Regress* (William B. Eerdmans, 1933).

15: DECISIONS

1. See en.wikipedia.org, "List of cognitive biases."
2. See, for example, Daniel Kahnemann, *Thinking Fast and Slow* (Farrar, Strauss and Giroux, 2011), Dan Ariely, *Predictably Irrational* (HarperCollins, 2008), and Richard H. Thaier and Cass R. Sunstein, *Nudge* (Caravan, 2008).
3. Roald Dahl, "Lamb to the Slaughter," in *The Collected Short Stories of Roald Dahl* (London: Michael Joseph, 1991).
4. Considered Heidegger's most important work, *Being and Time* (*Sein und Zeit*) is the foundation for twentieth-century existentialism and deconstructionist literary criticism and also a source of certain ideas, such as authenticity and moral relativism, which influenced 1960s popular culture in Europe and America. Heidegger thought philosophers from Plato onward had misinterpreted the question of *Sein*, or being itself, as a question about individual beings or entities. One way to understand the book is to see it as asking, "Why does Western philosophy assume that we relate to the world as objects to know, rather than as a subject to care about?" In these 500 pages of mind-bending philosophy, Heidegger seeks to put *Sorge*—care or concern—at the center of our concept of humanity, and humanity, in turn, at the center of our concept of being.
5. To be more precise, Heidegger believes that the view of the world engendered by breakdowns or malfunctions is a third mode of experience, sitting between the ready-to-hand and the present-at-hand; he calls it the unready-to-hand. It is not yet the wholly scientific, detached view, but it is the first step on the road toward that view.
6. See these articles by Chris Quintana in the *Santa Fe New Mexican*: "Questions Linger after Fatal Train Collision," Tuesday, April 22, 2014; "Police Say Cyclist Westbound before Train Hit Her at Zia Road," Friday, April 25, 2014; "Video Captures Bicyclist's Final Moments before Train Collision," Friday, May 2, 2014.
7. Michael A. Roberto and Gina M. Carioggia, "Mount Everest—1996," Harvard Business School Case Study, Jan 6, 2003.
8. Ibid., p. 11.
9. *Invictus*, dir. Clint Eastwood, Warner Brothers, 2009.
10. See Alex "Sandy" Pentland, "Beyond the Echo Chamber," *Harvard Business Review*, Nov 2013.
11. Roald Dahl, "Taste," in op. cit.

16: CULTURE

1. Ruth Benedict, *The Chrysanthemum and the Sword* (e-book, New York: Houghton Mifflin Harcourt, 2005), Chapter 1.
2. Ibid.,, Chapter 6.
3. Ibid., Chapter 6.
4. See Fons Trompenaars and Charles Hampden-Turner, *Riding the Waves of Culture* (London: Nicholas Brealey, 1998).
5. See, for example, Erin Meyer, "Navigating the Cultural Minefield," *Harvard Business Review*, May 2014.
6. Gert Jan Hofstede, Paul B. Pederson, and Geert Hofstede, *Exploring Culture* (Boston, MA: Intercultural Press, 2002), p. xviii.
7. Trompenaars and Hampden-Turner, op. cit., p. 33.
8. To define a culture according to three dimensions is, of course, to oversimplify. I don't doubt there are people in Japan who aren't all that community-minded

and plenty who like to challenge the hierarchy. We should nevertheless resist suggestions to come up with five, or eight, or ten dimensions as a way to deal with the nuances. Three dimensions are plenty for gaining insight into cultural differences; upping the number only adds complexity with no lessening of rigidity. The key is to use the dimensions not as labels for individuals, but as reminders to check our assumptions and look at the world from another's perspective.

9. For more on the sliding scales of culture, see Meyer, op. cit.
10. The outline of this anecdote comes from an American executive who spent a good part of her career managing the Asian divisions of a US company.

17: CHARACTER, ANCHORED

1. John Polidori subsequently also published a tale called *The Vampyre*, initially under Byron's name, in 1819.
2. Mary Shelley, *Frankenstein*, Chapter 5 (New York: New American Library, 1965), Chapter 11, pp. 98-99.
3. L. David Marquet, *Turn the Ship Around!* (New York: Penguin, 2012), Chapter 3.
4. Shelley, op. cit., Chapter 5, p. 56.
5. Ibid., Chapter 4, p. 52.
6. Ibid., Chapter 5, p. 57.
7. Ibid., Chapter 10, p. 95.
8. Ibid., Chapter 10, p. 96.
9. Nicole Winfield, "Pope Dives into Mideast Peace," Associated Press, Jun 9, 2014.
10. *The Sixth Sense*, dir. M. Night Shyamalan, prod. Kathleen Kennedy, Frank Marshall, and Barry Mendel, 1999.

18: RELATIONSHIPS

1. Stybel and Peabody, op. cit.
2. Matt Bradley and Bill Spindle, "Unlikely Allies Aid Militants in Iraq," *Wall Street Journal*, Jun 16, 2014, http://online.wsj.com/articles/unlikely-1402962546.
3. Ben Levin, "Unlikely Allies: Iraq Mess Could Prompt U.S.-Iran Effort," BBC News video posted Jun 14, 2014 (transcript provided by Newsy.com): www.ajc.com/news/news/world/unlikely-allies-iraq-mess-could-prompt-us-iran-eff/ngLWB/
4. Alex Vatanka, "Does Iran Back U.S. Military Intervention in Iraq?" cnn.com, updated Aug 12, 2014, www.cnn.com/2014/08/12/opinion/iraq-iran-us-military/.
5. Ibid.
6. The Relationship Types graphic (Figure 18.1) is my own, but the concept of the two axes and the four types is drawn from Stybel and Peabody's article, which I consider the most useful management journal article of the past 25 years. (For the book I'd nominate for the same distinction, see the notes for Chapter 10.)
7. Guy de Maupassant, "Boule de Suif," in *Guy de Maupassant: Selected Stories*, tr. Andrew R. MacAndrew (Markham, Ontario: Penguin Books Canada, 1964), p. 202.
8. My thanks go to Dr. Maggie Walsh for the term allies-in-waiting.
9. Doris Kearns Goodwin, *Team of Rivals: The Political Genius of Abraham Lincoln* (New York: Simon & Schuster, 2005), p. 369.

10. As "Boule de Suif" was for Maupassant, *Richard III* was Shakespeare's first great success. It was also the first of his plays produced in the United States, in 1750, and a century later was a favorite of President Lincoln, who had memorized Richard's opening soliloquy. Shakespeare's Richard is the physically and morally twisted man that today's scholars of English history call a Tudor fabrication; there is little evidence that the real Richard was anything like the hunchbacked murderer who plots and schemes his way through five acts. Nevertheless, Lincoln was onto something in his admiration for the play: a close study of the character of Richard yields a wealth of insight for leaders, especially about how (and how not) to operate within a shifting web of relationships.

19: ACCOUNTABILITY

1. Herman Melville, *Billy Budd, Sailor* (In *Moby-Dick, Billy Budd, and Other Writings*, New York: Literary Classics of the United States, 2000), Chapter 21, p. 879. The manuscript of Billy Budd was discovered 28 years after Melville's death in 1891. His wife had begun to edit it before putting it away in a drawer; her superimposed notes along with Melville's faded handwriting and copious revisions made the novella difficult to reconstruct. There have been three published versions of the text: one from 1924 and 1928, the second from 1948, and the third—the Hayford-Sealts text, today considered authoritative—from 1962. The version I quote here is the latter.
2. An Australian business leader who spent many years running consulting firms in India provided me with the basis for this story.
3. Frankl, op. cit., p. 132.
4. Melville, op. cit., Chapter 11, p. 855.
5. Ibid., Chapter 19, p. 878.
6. Ibid., Chapter 21, p. 884.
7. For more on how justice meted out with so-called objectivity is often perceived as injustice, see Chapter 4.
8. See Dennis F. Thompson, "Responsibility for Failures of Government: The Problem of Many Hands," *American Review of Public Administration*, online first Mar 9, 2014, http://arp.sagepub.com/content/early/2014/03/05/0275074014524013.
9. Melville, op. cit., Chapter 21, p. 887.
10. See Roger Connors, Tom Smith, and Craig Hickman, *The Oz Principle* (Englewood Cliffs, NJ: Prentice Hall, 1994); see also Connors and Smith, "How to Create a Culture of Accountability," www.asme.org, Mar 2011.
11. Melville, op. cit., Chapter 21, p. 889.
12. W. Edwards Deming, *Out of the Crisis* (MIT Press, 1986), Preface.
13. See Michel Baudin, "Deming's Point 8 of 14 – Drive Out Fear," Michel Baudin's blog, Oct 27, 2012, www.michelbaudin.com.
14. Deming, op. cit., p. 18.

20: TALENT

1. James Edward Austen-Leigh, *A Memoir of Jane Austen*, first published in 1869 (Oxford University Press, 1967), p. 157.
2. Linda A. Hill, *Becoming a Manager* (New York: Penguin, 1992), p. 22.
3. Ibid., p. 21.
4. Ibid., p. 150.

5. Ibid., p. 148.
6. Jane Austen, *Emma* (*The Complete Novels of Jane Austen*, Vol. Two, New York: Vintage Books, 1976), Chapter 3, p. 17.
7. Ibid., Chapter 8, p. 46.
8. See Buckingham and Coffman, op. cit. For more on Gallup's research on the link between strengths-based feedback and employee performance, see Jim Asplund and Nikki Blacksmith, "The Secret of Higher Performance," *Gallup Business Journal*, May 3, 2011, www.gallup.com/businessjournal/147383/secret-higher-performance.aspx.
9. Austen, op. cit., Chapter 43, p. 280.
10. Ibid., Chapter 49, p. 324.

21: VISION

1. George Bernard Shaw, *Saint Joan* (Rockville, MD: Wildside Press), Scene I, p. 3.
2. Machiavelli, op. cit., Chapter VI, p. 23.
3. Shaw, op. cit., Scene VI, p. 106.
4. Ibid., Scene I, p. 14.
5. Ibid., Scene III, p. 51.
6. Malala Yousafzai with Christina Lamb, *I Am Malala* (New York: Little, Brown, 2013), Chapter 1.
7. Ibid., Chapter 10.
8. Shaw, op. cit., Scene I, p. 11.
9. Ibid., Scene I, p. 16.
10. Ibid., Scene I, p. 4.
11. Ibid., Epilogue, p. 140.
12. See David Harris, *The Genius: How Bill Walsh Reinvented Football and Created an NFL Dynasty* (New York: Random House, 2008).
13. Ibid., p. 70.
14. As you may recall, "personnel issues" is the phrase used by the sales managers in Linda Hill's research study (see Chapter 20) to refer dismissively to talent management.

22: CHARACTER REVEALED

1. Susan Scott, *Fierce Conversations: Achieving Success at Work and in Life, One Conversation at a Time* (New York: Berkley, 2002), p. xix.
2. James Joyce, "The Dead," in *Dubliners* (New York: Modern Library, 1969), p. 180.
3. Ibid., p. 189.
4. Ibid., p. 190.
5. Ibid., p. 217.
6. Ibid., pp. 219–220.
7. Ibid., p. 220.

23: THREE LEVELS

1. At this writing, a new term for "flat" organizations is becoming popular: holacracy. Tony Hsieh, chief executive of Zappos, drew attention when he announced in late 2013 that the company would adopt holacracy, which is defined by the website www.holacracy.org as: "a new way of running an organization that removes power from a management hierarchy and distributes it across clear roles." Holacratic organizations seem to want to do away entirely with leadership levels, a goal I see

as neither realistic nor beneficial; nevertheless, I welcome the idea as one that might prepare the ground for some rethinking of the whole issue.
2. Collins, op. cit., p. 22.
3. John Maxwell, *The 5 Levels of Leadership* (New York: Center Street, 2011).
4. Compare Brutus's speech to the conspirators (*Julius Caesar*, Act II, Scene i) with King Henry's "Saint Crispin's Day" speech to the troops at Agincourt ("we few, we happy few, we band of brothers"; *Henry* V, Act IV, iii), and you'll see the difference between an initiator and an encourager.
5. Shaw, op. cit., Scene I, p. 4.
6. Churchill, op. cit., "Lawrence of Arabia," p. 139.
7. Bhagavad Gita, Chapter XI, Verse 32. This line was famously quoted—some scholars say misquoted—by Robert Oppenheimer in an interview about the Trinity nuclear explosion (the first full test of the atomic bomb).

24: THE FOURTH LEVEL

1. Lao Tzu, *Tao Te Ching*, tr. Stephen Mitchell (New York: CUNY, 1995; http://acc6.its.brooklyn.cuny.edu/~phalsall/texts/taote-v3.html), Verse 17. The *Tao Te Ching* has been translated into Western languages more than 250 times, giving rise to debate about the merits of various versions. Mitchell's translation has been criticized by some scholars as insufficiently literal and praised by others for its beauty and accessibility to present-day readers. A number of other translations are easily found on the internet by searching on "Tao Te Ching."
2. Drucker, op. cit., Chapter 14.
3. Alexander Hamilton seems to be making a comeback. As I write this, people are protesting the US Treasury Department's plans to take his face off the $10 bill and replace him with a woman of historical significance. Op-eds are telling the treasury to leave Hamilton alone; online petitions are circulating. He is also, surprisingly enough, the title character in the #1 musical on Broadway. The achievements of this quiet mainspring and student of the classics are well summarized by *Bloomberg View* columnist Justin Fox: "Hamilton ... set the U.S. on a path to becoming a world economic power with the insights he gleaned from a few books." ("Dump Jackson, But Don't Throw Alexander Hamilton Off the $10 Bill," reprinted in *Santa Fe New Mexican*, June 22, 2015.)
4. Fred Hiatt, "Press Wars Are Nothing New in U.S.," reprinted from *The Washington Post* by *Santa Fe New Mexican*, Jan 2, 2015.
5. Drucker, op. cit., Chapter 14.
6. Ibid.

POSTSCRIPT: LOOKING FOR OVERLAND

1. See, for example, the Association of American Colleges and Universities public opinion survey, "It Takes More Than a Major: Employer Priorities for College Learning and Student Success," Apr 2013 (access the full report at www.aacu.org/leap/public-opinion-research). Also see the video "Hiring Liberal Arts Majors," *Chief Learning Officer*, Jun 10, 2014 (www.clomedia.com/media/videos/play/202).
2. Bobby Fong, "Liberal Arts Are as Vital as Ever," *Philadelphia Inquirer*, Feb 2, 2014.
3. C.S. Lewis, *The Silver Chair* (Harmondsworth: Penguin, 1953), Chapter 12, p. 155.
4. Ibid., Chapter 12, p. 155.
5. Ibid., Chapter 12, pp. 156–157.

INDEX

ACKNOWLEDGMENTS

Let me begin by thanking Nicholas Brealey and Sally Lansdell for their encouragement and guidance in bringing *The Greats on Leadership* to publication.

Now let me thank the book's three main sources of inspiration. The first is St. John's College, a liberal arts college with two campuses: one in Annapolis, Maryland, and one in Santa Fe, New Mexico. St. John's is one of the originators of the much-imitated "great books" curriculum, an interdisciplinary approach to learning based on the study and discussion of classic works in the humanities and sciences. As the spouse of a faculty member, I've had a chance to observe the approach and to admire its results. St. John's is one of the few places remaining today where one can get an education that is—again, in Plutarch's words—not the filling of a pail, but the lighting of a fire.

The second is The Forum Corporation, a Boston-based leadership and sales training company founded by John Humphrey and Richard Whiteley. As a longtime employee there I had many wonderful managers who, in different ways and with different styles, showed me what good leadership looks like: Mona Cohen, Kathy O'Regan, Mimi Bennett, Kerry Johnson, Joe Wheeler, Ted Higgins, Galina Jeffrey, Ron Koprowski, and Ed Boswell. I also had many colleagues who demonstrated that leadership has little to do with a title and everything to do with the positive impact one makes; some who spring to mind are Andre Alphonso, Tom Atkinson, Jeff Baker, Steve Barry, Aly Brandt, Ellen Foley, Elizabeth Griep, Kate Haney, Kevin Higgins, Dottie McKissick, Will Milano, Rosie Mucklo, Stacy Neff, Vivien Price, and Amy Tananbaum. My special thanks go to Maggie Walsh, whose thinking on leadership suffuses these pages, and to Sylvia Celentano—Manager of the Year in Perpetuity—who has shown me that leadership, excellence, and laughter are inseparable.

Third and finally, there's my husband, Matt, and daughter, Emily. Emily wrote first drafts of many of the classic book summaries and, along with her father, provided valuable suggestions for the books discussed herein. But more than that, Matt and Emily inspire me with their love of the classics. Like John Ruskin, they know there are two sorts of books: "the books of the hour, and the books of all time." With their ongoing achievements and their ability to raise the tone of any endeavor, they are living proof of the latter's power.